Sunset

Landscaping

ILLUSTRATED

By the Editors of Sunset Books and Sunset Magazine

The essence of outdoor living is captured in this handsome combination of pool, patio, steps, walls, and plantings. Landscape architects: Eriksson, Peters, Thoms & Associates.

Sunset Publishing Corporation • Menlo Park, California

Sunset on landscaping

To create a beautiful, useful, and enduring landscape is a deeply satisfying accomplishment. But where do you begin? How do you actually *do* it? That's where *Sunset's Landscaping Illustrated* comes in: it explains both the art and the science of landscaping.

Step by step, this book tells you how to plan, design, and install your home landscape. Its five chapters give you more than 50 color photos of successful landscapes, guidelines for planning and design, ideas for garden structures, choices of plants to use in your garden, and how-to instructions for installing your landscape.

The photos will spark your imagination, the information on planning and design will unlock the mystery of this process, the illustrations of structures and the many plant charts will help you make choices, and the illustrated step-by-step sequences will guide you when it comes to putting everything together.

Landscaping Illustrated is part of a comprehensive team of *Sunset* garden and outdoor building and remodeling books. We suggest you also consider *Introduction to Basic Gardening; Basic Masonry Illustrated; Ideas for Building Barbecues; How to Build Decks; How to Plan & Build Fences & Gates; Garden & Patio Building Book; Hot Tubs, Spas & Home Saunas; Lawns & Ground Covers; How to Build Patio Roofs; Ideas for Patios & Decks; Ideas for Swimming Pools; How to Build Walks, Walls & Patio Floors.* Any or all of these will be valuable supplements to your garden and building library and, ultimately, to your home.

We'd like to thank the following professionals who lent their expertise to the preparation of the manuscript: Fred C. Boutin, Horticulturist, Tuolumne, California. ● Robert Chittock, Landscape Architect, Seattle, Washington. ● Max Z. Conrad, Professor of Landscape Architecture, Baton Rouge, Louisiana. ● Alan D. Cook, Senior Horticulturist of Dawes Arboretum, Newark, Ohio. ● Robert W. Dyas, Professor of Landscape Architecture, Ames, Iowa. ● Fred Galle, Retired Director of Callaway Gardens, Hamilton, Georgia. ● Richard E. Gardner, Landscape Architect, Des Moines, Iowa. ● Hugh Hedger, Horticultural Instructor, Oklahoma City, Oklahoma. ● Warren Jones, Professor of Landscape Architecture, Tucson, Arizona. ● Gene Joyner, Urban Horticulturist, West Palm Beach, Florida ● Patrick and Randalle Moore, Landscape Architects, Alexandria, Louisiana. ● Robert and Susan Ross, Landscape Architects, Alexandria, Virginia. ● Robert Savage, Horticulturist, New Windsor, New York. ● Joseph Witt, Curator of Washington Park Arboretum, Seattle, Washington.

We'd also like to thank Karen Boswell, who scouted for gardens to photograph, and the many homeowners who then allowed us to photograph their gardens.

Finally, our thanks to Fran Feldman and C. Tate Snyder, our copy editors; they made sure we said what we meant, said it clearly, and said it succinctly.

Book Editors:
John K. McClements
Scott Fitzgerrell

Contributing Editors:
Philip Edinger
Susan E. Schlangen
Cynthia Overbeck Bix
Pamela Evans
Alvin Horton

Design:
Joe di Chiarro

Illustrations:
Rik Olson

Photo Stylist:
JoAnn Masaoka

Photography by **Tom Wyatt**

Additional photography: Roger DeWeese: 11 top; 23 top. Derek Fell: 83 bottom left & right; 90 left; 94 right. Pamela J. Harper: 82 left; 94 left. Jack McDowell: 3 right.

Cover: Part of a comprehensive landscape remodeling project, this nicely articulated set of raised beds and steps forms the transition between a new patio, set at house level, and an expanse of lawn. Another view of this landscape appears on page 11. Landscape architect: Robert Babcock & Associates. Photograph by Tom Wyatt. Cover design by Naganuma Design & Direction.

Simple patio links house and garden in an overall scheme that improves the utility of both. Ornamental pear tree and pots of geraniums and lobelia add attractive accents. Landscape architect: Michael Westgard.

Editor, Sunset Books: Elizabeth L. Hogan

Eighth printing March 1991

Contents

Landscaping in the grand manner can often be seen when fine old estates such as this one are opened to the public. Here, pool plantings of cattails and water lilies soften the crisp formality of clipped hedges and elegant brickwork.

Skillful stonework creates a retaining wall, a stream, a pair of waterfalls, and a koi pond. Design: Bob Rubel.

A GALLERY OF GARDENS

Most of us learn by example, and that's the reason this book begins with photographs. Nothing will get your landscaping ideas going faster than a trip—real or vicarious—through a series of beautiful gardens. Whatever the size of your home or the scale of your landscaping project, we think you'll find something in virtually every one of the more than 50 photos that follow to fuel the engines of imagination.

This garden gallery has seven divisions. "First impressions" (pages 6–9) deals with front yards and entries, important areas where you particularly want to put your best foot forward—perhaps even set the style for the rest of your landscape. "Gardens for outdoor living" (pages 10–15) follows with ideas for everything from full-scale entertainment areas to gardens with the accent on privacy and serenity.

"Design problem: Limited space" (pages 16–19) is a section that confronts a common situation and shows you how to get the most out of a small yard. The next two sections also deal with special design problems: landscaping property boundaries (pages 20–21) and landscaping hillside lots (pages 22–25).

The two final sections, designated "Garden style," feature country gardens (pages 26–27) and gardens organized around specific themes (pages 28–31).

Before any worthwhile project is begun, there is first a dream. This chapter will start you dreaming and set you on your way to a wonderful garden reality.

Groups of graceful melaleuca trees punctuate the terra cotta tile of a west-facing patio, shading the house from the afternoon sun. The patio is set low in the surrounding lawn, which forms a soft, rounded edge where it meets the tile. Beds of impatiens and pots of Madagascar periwinkle add color accents. Landscape architect: Don Craig.

First impressions

Transformation
A glance at the "before" photo above shows what magic good landscaping can achieve (right). Where once all was desolation, now a variety of plant textures and colors—impatiens, agapanthus, pittosporum, polypodium, and raphiolepis—borders a sinuous brick entry path. Sheltering melaleucas provide a verdant canopy, complementing the pathway plantings beneath. Design: Greg Grisamore of Roger's Gardens.

Waterway
Spill fountain and a pool full of water hyacinths make an attractive accent for those who walk along this cheerful sideyard entry (view is from the house doorway). Further along the path leading to the street, a "living" fence is planted in panels of impatiens, ferns, and ivy. Podocarpus trees stand sentinel at intervals along the walkway. Design: Lew Whitney of Roger's Gardens.

Diversion

Before and after views show how a change of direction at the front entry worked wonders for a bedraggled front yard. Since this is the sunniest side of the house, an entry incorporating a private patio was designed to take advantage of the previously unused space. Now the front yard is the focus of outdoor living for the proud owners, who did most of the work themselves—and it's a pleasant experience for anyone approaching the house. Landscape architect: Thomas L. Berger.

Home turf

Concrete turf blocks and used-brick dividers lend distinction to this motor-court entry (two inconspicuous garages accommodate three cars). It's a green alternative to what might have been only a bleak expanse of paving. Architect: Bert W. Tarayao. Landscape architect: Richard E. Harrington.

...First impressions

Creative conservation

A lion's head saved from the wrecker's ball and converted into a fountain provides the focal point in this tranquil, owner-built entry composition. The encircling wall of broken concrete (salvaged when the driveway was torn up) gives a sense of enclosure. A fine crape myrtle provides shade, while lushly growing campanula covers both ground and wall. Landscape architects: Eriksson, Peters, Thoms & Associates.

In a quiet courtyard

Mexican pavers and a gentle murmur of falling water set the mood in this courtyard entry. Purple brunfelsia flowers stand out against the dominant greens, browns, and whites. Beyond the fountain, bougainvillea softens a high privacy wall. Landscape architects: Jeffrey W. Stone and Lois Sherr.

On display

When the outdoor living area is in front, it must always be on view as part of the home's entry. This remodeling project attractively unites an existing pool and entry by means of brick—used for paving, steps, and raised beds. Native oaks mingle with Japanese maples, pelargoniums, petunias, fortnight lilies, agapanthus, and tree ferns. A firepit and deck (see also page 10) extend the area's usefulness. Landscape architect: Paul McMullen.

Double duty

Here, entry and outdoor living area are one, so the pool deck is an entry walk, the entry walk a space for relaxing and entertaining. The pool's stepped edge gives it the character of a decorative garden pool. Large planter boxes provide planting accents. Architect: Richard Stark. Landscape architects: Stone & Fischer.

Gardens for outdoor living

A fresh new face
This replanted garden and patio area wears a new look, thanks to striking pots and borders of marigolds, marguerites and alyssum. A fine old Russian olive tree, surrounded by low-growing bearberry, commands center stage in the patio. Design: R. David Adams.

Bridging the gap
New deck steps right over a dry creek to connect the house with a new brick patio (for another view, see page 9). Part of the deck wraps around a sunken firepit, where it becomes a seat in this more intimate area. Bordering plants include fortnight lilies, ivy, ferns, umbrella plant, and geraniums. Landscape architect: Paul McMullen.

Learning to cope

This yard provided both a challenge and an opportunity. Largely desolate, the area received a complete overhaul —only a low, railroad-tie retaining wall defining a natural drainage channel was saved. This swampy area was simply filled with river rock. The rest of the design uses sweeping lawns to set off beds and planting groups that include daylilies, liquidambar, umbrella plant, daisies, and agapanthus. Landscape architect: Roger DeWeese Incorporated & Associates.

Stepping out

This view of the cover house shows how a new seeded-aggregate concrete patio mediates the change in level from house to lawn. The patio incorporates a series of built-in planters and steps (see also the cover view) that effect a graceful transition; the planters also contain ranks of locust trees that shade the south-facing patio. In the distance, a lovely border of perennials marks the lawn's edge. Landscape architect: Robert Babcock & Associates.

...Gardens for outdoor living

From scratch

The lush suburban oasis below rose from a flat tract of undeveloped land (right). Earth from the pool excavation was mounded at the rear of the property, creating a raised site for the planting screen, koi pond, deck, and spa (see also page 32). The seating area and firepit at left mark the original grade. Landscape architect: Michael Kobayashi/MHK Group. Additional design: American Landscape, Inc.

An art of contrasts

The bold symmetry of this contemporary house is echoed in the shape of its pool and spa. In contrast, the subtle landscaping uses freeform beds of trailing gazanias and a picturesque grouping of boulders to soften the edges of the formal design. Architects: Buff & Hensman.

Lights up
This garden lighting design extends outdoor living well into the evening. A pair of dimmer-controlled underwater pool lights, with a twinkling border of bud lights to mark the step, gives gentle, overall illumination. Low-voltage lights accent pyracanthas that climb brick pillars supporting the low wall and glass windscreen. Podocarpus trees in the large bed at rear have their own lights. Landscape architects: Stone & Fischer.

Masonry magic
Flashed brick and glazed, patterned tile create a trim, formal look in this entertainment area. The low walls around the spa and firepit do double duty as retaining walls and seats. The openwork iron fence makes a secure border without obstructing the view. Landscape architect: John Hourian.

...Gardens for outdoor living

Oriental overtones

In an original approach to the outdoor room idea, this small gazebo cantilevers over a rock-edged swimming pool. The open-sided redwood structure, styled to resemble a traditional Japanese teahouse, blends easily with the redwood deck beyond and with the pines native to the area. Architect: William Churchill. Landscape design: Edwin Simon.

A sense of seclusion

In this multilevel design, the back yard was graded lower than the rest of the property as a means of enhancing the height of the surrounding plantings and the sense of enclosure. This creates visual interest and shuts off the view from several tall buildings nearby. Beyond the waterfall, sliding latticework screens enclose a still more private area that harbors a spa and small deck. Landscape architects: Bill Talley and Dave Roberts.

Playtime

This private redwood grove makes an ideal setting for children to romp in. Red-wood bark surfaces the play area and is a natural complement to the trees.
A concrete path frames the lawn and play area, doubling as a bike path and mow strip. The final stage of this project calls for a swimming pool in the lawn area.
Landscape architect: Taro Yamagami.

An elegant new look

Remodeling made quite a difference at this house. The old pool house and shade structure (above) were removed to make way for two elegant pavilions with a connecting overhead (right); the old terrace and pool deck were resurfaced with brick and seeded-aggregate concrete; and the old pool was given a dramatic coat of dark plaster.
Landscape architects: Fry + Stone Associates.

Design problem: Limited space

Sanctum in the city

This small, narrow yard, pleasantly secluded from the urban hubbub, is a gardener's delight. Ferns, rhododendrons, azaleas, violets, impatiens, and pieris abound in containers and carefully maintained raised beds. Both photos show how the jog in the path keeps the eye from immediately taking in the property boundaries. An added touch: in this zero-lot-line area, the owner elected to give the neighbors a view of his garden (right), rather than fence them out with a high divider that would be unsightly to both. Landscape architect: Kenneth Pedersen.

Small jewel

This garden is only 20 feet wide, yet it's visually spacious. Angled multilevel decks do the trick, causing the eye to rove over the design and creating a series of intimate spaces and stopping points about the yard. A mature Brazilian pepper tree provides a focal point—and a handy anchorage for the hammock. A fine collection of cycads grows in the foreground. Landscape architect: Todd Fry.

Getting it right

Newly remodeled yard (right) features a brick patio as before (above)—but there's no comparison. The new deck and shade structure extend the living space, enhancing both house and yard. Landscape architects: Fry + Stone Associates.

...Limited space

An intimate retreat
Sensitive landscaping transforms this narrow city lot into a lush garden setting with the accent on privacy. Steppingstones lead from the house to a hidden patio beyond. Oriental touches include stone monuments, bamboo, and Japanese maple. Other plants include baby's tears, nandina, gold dust plant, camellia, tree ferns, and pittosporum. Design: Marc Miyasato.

On the rocks
This extremely narrow yard dictated a landscaping design that would be easy to maintain—and attractive to view from inside the glass-walled house. The completed project, a stone garden with plantings of pittosporum, nandina, daylily, sago palm, fescue, and sedge, makes a handsome foreground to the expansive sea view. Round concrete steppingstones provide easy access to the area. Architect: Gordon Glass. Landscape design: Lew Whitney of Roger's Gardens.

All decked out

Decks that serve as walkways unite this small-space scheme. One deck crosses over an arm of the small swimming pool, then zigzags its way around a generous spa to meet another deck that traverses the property, linking the spa with a gazebo tucked away in the greenery at left. The vine-covered trellis provides privacy and shade and is lighted at night. Landscape architect: Woodward Dike.

Still center of the turning world

This lush, pocket-size garden centers on a still pool surrounded by radial paving and curved seating walls; it provides a serene spot for unwinding at day's end. Everything was done by the owner, working in stages over a number of years. Landscape architects: Eriksson, Peters, Thoms & Associates.

Design problem: Landscaping the edges

Overlook
The potentially dangerous edge of this drop-away lot is handled with skill. A short block wall—added several feet in front of the hill-holding retaining wall —ensures safety without sacrificing the view. Lush plantings fill the space between the walls. The result: an attractive planting bed, a wonderful view, and plenty of security. Design: Greg Grisamore of Roger's Gardens.

Windows on the world
Sometimes a short, dense hedge is all you need for security against a steep drop-off. In this garden, a sturdy wisteria-draped trellis rises from the boxwood to frame and edit the view, turning it into a series of "pictures." Landscape architect: William Louis Kapranos.

Strolling
This lovely pathway leads viewers along a graceful, natural curve past lush plantings of marigolds and marguerites that soften and disguise the boundary running between two houses. To the left, specimens of saxifrage, Japanese lace leaf maple, and two kinds of heather invite particular attention. Design: R. David Adams.

A little mystery
Where does the property end? This intriguing pathway hints at hidden spaces just around the corner but actually goes nowhere. The property ends at an adobe wall just a few feet beyond the stone lantern. The path and its attendant plantings are part of a scheme to mask the boundaries while hinting at greater spaces beyond. Landscape architects: Stone & Fischer.

Cornered
In this small yard, the large spa was sited as far as possible from the house, maximizing the size of the patio. Plantings in the raised bed create a soft, ambiguous edge to the property. Stone used throughout unifies the area visually. Landscape architects: The Peridian Group.

Design problem: Hillsides

Taking the high ground

Railroad ties secured by galvanized pipes march uphill, providing access to a steep lot. The slope is planted with white trailing ice plant—a low-maintenance ground cover that prevents erosion. Railroad-tie planters hold peach and pear trees and a colorful bank of lantana. Landscape architects: Fry + Stone Associates.

Faithful retainers

This beautiful group of plantings—osteospermum, pine, aloe, agave, yucca, daylily, nasturtium, eucalyptus, dracaena, pittosporum, and gamolepis—is so lovely to look at that it's easy to forget these plants work hard at holding a steep hill. Landscape architects: Lang & Wood, with Roger's Gardens.

Easy stages

The attractive downslope entry at right features a series of short stairways separated by broad landings. The design breaks up what was a single fatiguing flight (below) into an easily negotiated stroll enlivened by pots of marigolds and alyssum set against a background of bamboo, agapanthus, pittosporum, and Japanese maple. Landscape architect: Roger DeWeese Incorporated & Associates.

Leafy ramparts

This hill is quite steep, but the artful design of its terraces disguises the fact. Only the undulating stone-veneer retaining wall, with its bed of phlox and violets, is designed to be seen; the upper terraces are well hidden. At the top, a tall hedge of clipped pittosporum firmly bars the view from a street just above, and diffuses its sounds as well. Landscape architect: Casey Kawamoto.

...Hillsides

Hideaway
The oak-lined site of this pool, deck, and spa gives plenty of privacy, making all
the effort and engineering worthwhile. The pool is set into a terrace cut into a
steep slope; the deck is built out over the slope, extending the usable space. A
retaining wall behind the pool (not seen in this view) keeps the hill above at bay.

Master planning

This is a two-stage design for a hillside lot: in the foreground, a concrete entry court, ornamental pool, and fountain; in the background, a new deck that traverses a steep slope and gives access to a new swimming-pool area located upslope to the right. The patient owners waited 15 years between the two stages of the project. Landscape architect: Robert Chittock.

Scaling the heights

The owners of this steep site wanted to make the most of it. The result: a pool and spa backed by tile-trimmed retaining walls, and—42 feet higher—a deck with a wonderful view. A set of simple wooden stairs leads past a noble pair of Monterey pines to give access to the area above. Landscape architect: Don Craig.

Garden style: The country garden

Poetry in stone

The old-world charm of the cottage garden is well-suited to this rustic, yet elegant house. Casual gravel paths encircle abundant beds of tulbaghia, all within an enclosing ashlar wall that's in perfect harmony with both house and garden.

Beside the still waters

A large shallow pond, filled with water lilies, becomes the focal point of this flower-lover's delight. Coprosma, impatiens, iris, agapanthus, pansies, and lamb's ears surround the stone-edged pool. Carefully placed Chinese containers full of chrysanthemums add a formal touch that snaps the whole composition into focus. Design: Miriam Petrovo-Miloradovitch.

Pattern maker

This charming country garden takes a casual approach to the knot or *parterre* style (see page 37). The garden is divided into two enclosures. Above, herringbone brick paths set off boxwood-lined beds of petunias and sweet alyssum. At right, a second area uses basketweave brick as a background for similar, larger beds. Both enclosures feature surrounding beds of roses and iris. Rustic picket fences with rose-covered arbors protect the garden. Design: Alan Reed.

Garden style: Designs with a theme

The dominant element
This garden provides a lavish example of a simple tenet: use a strong central element to give order and focus to a design. Here, the star-shaped pool that frames the fountain dictates the shape of the lawn, flower beds, and paving. Landscape architect: Emmet L. Wemple & Associates.

The flowering border—I
Desiring a soft screen to hide a plain but serviceable fence, the designer chose a bright border of cosmos, marigolds, lobelia, and dusty miller. The seeded-aggregate patio, part of an earlier land-scaping project, is set well above, for maximum view. Landscape architect: Michael Westgard. Patio design: R. David Adams.

The flowering border—II

Here the English flowering border is seen in something like its native setting —a fine old Tudor-style house. Lush beds of dahlias, cosmos, lobelia and dwarf marguerites soften the foundations of a formal patio and staircases. Design: R. David Adams.

The formal style

Often thought of as suitable only for large estates, the formal style is actually well-adapted to small spaces, which can be maintained without undue effort. This intimate patio features a pergola, small pool and fountain, nicely detailed seeded-aggregate paving, and crisp lattice fencing. The manicured plantings include holly trees, pittosporum, ivy, rhododendrons, statice, impatiens, begonias, marguerites, and dianthus. Landscape architect: Robert Chittock.

...Designs with a theme

Sentimental favorites

For many, a garden will always mean roses, an ancient shrub that's been cultivated for hundreds of years. Here, a generous circular rosebed allows ready viewing of the flowers. The arbor beyond, currently under gentle assault by a climbing rose, will eventually be covered with blooms.

A natural look

Stone, plants, and water make a pleasing composition with a hint of wildness in it. These plantings include cedrus, dwarf nandina, Japanese maple, and pittosporum. Design: Edwin Simon.

A touch of the tropics
The Tasmanian and Australian tree ferns lining a lava pathway give an unmistakably tropical feeling to this garden. A thick carpet of ivy lies beneath the shade-loving ferns; overhead, trumpet vines cascade from a heavy trellis. Landscape architects: Jeffrey W. Stone and Lois Sherr.

Desert dwellers
Cactuses and succulents, with their distinctive forms and textures, create unique accents in a garden. Sun loving and drought resistant, they need little care when planted in the proper situation. This grouping includes yucca, echinocactus, cereus, and opuntia.

GUIDELINES FOR PLANNING & DESIGN

You'll seldom find an opportunity to be so creative, or to enjoy such practical, long-term benefits from your creativity, as when you plan and design a new landscape or remodel your old one. A vital, functioning landscape transcends mere decoration to become a unique expression of your personality and life style.

Your first steps require that you narrow down just what you and your family need from a landscape, and that you accurately record what you have to work with. Then you'll want to decide which garden style best suits your tastes and your site. Use the guidelines in this chapter to keep from overlooking any of the numerous factors to consider in the design process; use the sketching techniques described to get a realistic sense of what can work for your particular property.

Special features in this chapter offer you hints on how to use color in landscape design, how to landscape the same site in different ways, and how to solve various remodeling challenges. Though many beautiful gardens are designed by professionals, you can achieve an esthetically successful landscape on your own by referring to "Basic landscaping principles" (page 38) throughout your planning. And if you *should* find yourself out of your depth in terms of time, money, or skills, you can always turn to "Helpful resources" (page 45) for assistance.

Like a man-made oasis, this refreshing composition includes watery comforts for people, fish, and plants. Landscape architect: Michael Kobayashi/MHK Group. Additional design: American Landscape, Inc.

First step: Determining your needs

Before you evaluate your site and its surroundings, let alone draw a plan or pick up a shovel, try to be perfectly clear about what you want your landscape to give you, and what you're prepared to give it. Now is the time to plan your *ideal* home environment. Be generous with yourself; make a list of the features and materials that you prefer. You can figure costs later and compromise where necessary. A careful consideration of both your life style and your resources, at this early stage of planning, will richly reward you later on.

Public or private landscape?

One of your basic decisions will be how much of your house and landscape to open to public view. You can landscape either for privacy or for display — or for some of each.

Do you have a house whose beauty should be shared with neighbors and passers-by? Do you want to minimize barriers between your property and that of your neighbors? Or will your home and garden be your refuge, presenting to the outside world only an agreeable screen? Maybe you'll decide on a public area just large enough to blend with others along the street, while reserving most of the landscape for your private use and enjoyment.

Landscaping for your special needs

Evaluating your special needs will help you to answer the question of how much of your space should be reserved for private use. It will also be a giant first step toward producing your new landscape design (see pages 39–42). If you're remodeling your landscape, you are probably already aware of some of these needs.

Entertaining. Both the style and the scale of entertaining you do are important considerations. Do you need a large patio or deck with outdoor cooking facilities? Can you serve a dinner for four in the same area without your guests feeling lost in an over-large space? Will you need off-street parking?

Recreation. What outdoor activities do you and your family enjoy? Sports such as horseshoes, badminton, croquet, and swimming require different amounts of space and special facilities. Perhaps you'll want to allow room for a children's play area. Hobbies sometimes call for an enclosed or semi-enclosed structure, such as a studio for painting or sculpting, or a lath house or greenhouse for growing ornamentals like bonsai or orchids. You may want to set aside some space for such activities.

Relaxation. What types of sedentary relaxation do you and your family enjoy in the home landscape? For example, do you need a shady place for reading? Do you want a hammock in a quiet spot — or a hot tub?

Gardening. A garden not only beautifies the landscape, it can also provide your home with cut flowers, vegetables, fruit, nuts, and berries. Do you like the idea of having edibles and cutting-flowers double as ornaments in your landscape, or will you want them concealed in a special area? How much space do you want for gardening? Remember to limit your plans to the space you can realistically cultivate.

Work, storage, and service. Don't overlook the purely practical! Make a careful inventory of utilitarian needs that demand space in the landscape. You might need areas for refuse cans, clotheslines, air conditioning and heat pumps, and for dry storage of firewood, garden tools, equipment, and fertilizer; you might also need space for other kinds of work that you prefer to do outdoors or in a special structure. For example, would you like a shop area for woodworking, welding, or other activities whose noise and fumes make them unsuitable for the house or outdoor living areas? A boat or recreational vehicle, too, may need housing and servicing space, as well as an access route to the street.

Your landscape & your resources

Time, effort, and money are equally important factors to consider in successful landscape planning. What is your budget for creating or remodeling your landscape? How much time and effort are you willing to give to that work?

If you can't have your ideal landscape right away, you needn't settle for an inexpensive, uninspiring compromise. Instead, consider landscaping in stages: plan your ideal landscape, and decide which features to install now and which to add later. Expensive features such as a pool or spa can always be substituted in the future for less expensive elements, such as a lawn, that can be enjoyed now. (Remember, though, that if you install a pool later, you'll need to tear up at least a portion of your landscape.)

Developing your environment by stages *can* be more satisfying than doing it all at once, and actually living in the landscape may help you to refine your plan as you go along. You may find that you can't keep up both that large lawn *and* the vegetable garden you wanted, given your life style. Or you may discover a need you either hadn't thought of or hadn't had previously — such as a play area for children or a larger entertaining area.

Perhaps the truly critical question to ask yourself at this earliest stage is how much time, effort, and money — realistically — you'll be able to devote to the maintenance of your landscape over the years. Remember that in the long run a modest, low-maintenance landscape will serve you better than a neglected, high-maintenance one.

Start with your base map

The first step in turning your ideas and ideals into practical reality is to take a long, careful look at what you have to start with—your given factors. Even if you're remodeling a landscape you've lived with for years, this close examination — or "re-viewing" — is essential. You may make startling discoveries about what you thought was the familiar, if you try to record the necessary information objectively, accurately, and completely.

Use your accumulated observations about your site and its setting to create a base map such as the one shown below. Keep in mind that accuracy, clarity, and completeness are your objectives. Be as precise as possible; guesstimates or outright errors at this stage can cause you disappointment later — when, for exam-ple, you lose a tender shrub to a cold spot or find that your new sun deck is in deep shade when you most want to use it. Even worse, imagine damaging a utility line due to a careless notation of its depth!

To draw your base map (and later, your final plan), you'll need 24- by 36-inch graph paper (¼-inch scale, unless the size of your property requires ⅛-inch scale), an art gum eraser, a straightedge, several soft- or medium-lead pencils, a circle template, and a pad of tracing paper. Optional are sketching paper, a drafting board, drafting tape, a compass, an architect's scale (very useful!), a T-square, an eraser shield, and one or more drafting triangles. For measurements in the landscape itself, you'll need a 50- or 100-foot tape measure; shorter tape measures are exasperating to use and can lead to inaccurate measurements.

You can draw your base map directly on graph paper or on tracing paper placed over graph paper. If you plan to have a blueprinting company make copies of your base map, though, it will have to be drawn on tracing paper; a blueprint machine will not accept regular graph paper.

Starting with the dimensions of your property and proceeding through all the information listed here, you will gradually be covering a good deal of your graph paper (or tracing paper) with written and sketched details, so make each entry as neat and concise as possible. You'll be glad later on, when you lay your final plan over the base map and want to extract its information easily.

(Continued on next page)

A SAMPLE BASE MAP

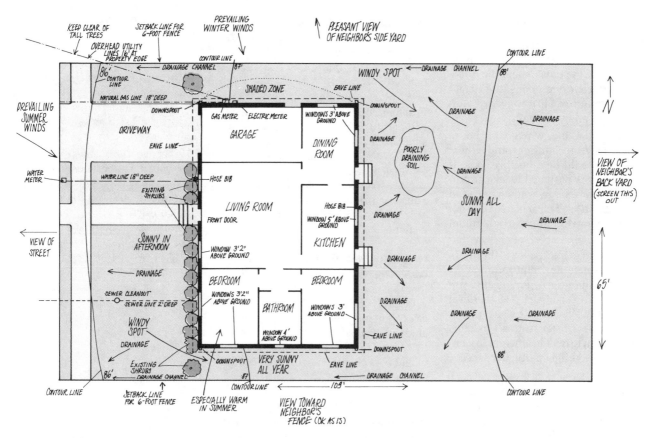

A preliminary step in any landscaping project is to make a base map—a scale drawing showing the important features and characteristics of the property. The base map above includes the exact location and orientation of every major plant and structural feature. Sun and wind patterns, views, slope and drainage characteristics, and other essential data are all noted. This drawing becomes the foundation on which the final landscape plan is built.

...Start with your base map

You can save yourself hours of painstaking measuring and data-gathering at this point by obtaining much of your information — from dimensions and orientation to relevant structural details and gradient — from the deed map, the house plans, and the contour map. If you don't have these resources, check at your city hall, county offices, title company, bank, or mortgage company.

The following specific information should appear in one form or another on your base map.

Boundary lines and dimensions. Outline your property accurately and to scale, and mark its dimensions on the base map. It's wise to follow the practice of landscape architects and have your property surveyed and boundary lines verified. Otherwise, your neighbor may someday have the right to insist that you tear down a fence or move a flower bed.

The house. Show your house precisely and to scale within the property. Note all doors to the outside and the direction that each one opens, the height above ground of all lower-story windows, and all overhangs.

Consider, too, where your house overheats from sunlight and where sunlight would be a heating boon. If your house is designed to take advantage of solar energy, you may need to note areas to keep clear of trees and tall shrubbery or structures, for maximum sunlight.

Also take time to look at the house itself. Evaluate its architectural style; even if it fits no category neatly, you can probably establish its relative level of formality. What are its visual pluses and minuses? Later you will use this information to decide whether to camouflage or highlight particular aspects.

Exposure. First draw a north arrow; then note on your base map the shaded and sunlit areas of your present landscape. Also note the microclimates — hot and cold spots and windy areas — that you'll want to take into account in designing your new landscape.

Note any spots where cold air set-tles and frost is heavy. Remember that cold air flows downhill like water, "puddles" in basins, and can also be dammed by walls or solid fences. Indicate the direction of the prevailing wind, and any spots that are especially windy and may require protection of some sort.

Utilities and easements. Show on your map the locations of meters and hose bibs, and the depths and locations of all underground lines, including the sewage line or septic tank. If you are contemplating having tall trees or structures, show the locations and heights of all overhead lines.

Does your deed map show easements, as for a trunk sewer, or underground telephone or electrical lines that service neighbors? If so, note them accurately on your base map and check legal restrictions limiting development of those areas.

Downspouts and drain systems. Mark the locations of all downspouts and of the catch basins and drainage tiles (see pages 132–133), if any, that they drain into.

Problem soil. Is the soil in any spot compacted, shallow, or root-matted? If so, you may want to note these problems on your base map. Are there pH or nutrient deficiencies? To find out, you can have your soil tested at a laboratory or use a soil-testing kit, available at many nurseries and garden centers.

Gradient. Draw contour lines on your base map, noting high and low points (here's where the official contour map is helpful). If drainage crosses boundaries, you may need to indicate the gradient of adjacent properties as well, to ensure that neither you nor your neighbor is channeling runoff onto the other's property.

Drainage. Surface drainage, of course, corresponds to gradient. Where does water from paved surfaces drain? Note whether drainage is impeded at any point so that soil remains soggy, and whether runoff is rapid enough to cause erosion.

Codes and covenants. At this point, check at municipal or county offices to see if local zoning codes or subdivision covenants restrict the location, height, or type of plantings or structures. Be certain of the precise location of setbacks (property boundaries where construction is prohibited) and right-of-ways. Note any restrictions on your base map.

Existing plantings. Particularly if you're remodeling an old landscape, you should note any existing plantings, from trees to bulbs, that might be desirable to retain or that would require a major effort to remove.

Views. Show all views, attractive or unattractive, from every side of your property. At later planning stages, you'll want to keep attractive views open, maybe even accentuate them, and screen unattractive ones. Note vantage points where relevant — for example, "Good view of bay from upstairs."

The environs. In addition to the site-specific information listed above, you'll want to step back a bit further and consider some larger factors before you can assume your base map is complete.

What are the visual characteristics of your neighborhood? Are there prevailing landscape and architectural styles? You might want to think twice before conflicting with a shared style — after all, no property is an island.

Finally, consider (and note on your base map) the relation of the street and its traffic to your house.

Choosing your garden style

Formal or informal?—that's one of the first decisions you must make in choosing a garden style.

Formal landscapes are symmetrical, with straight lines, geometric patterns, and perfect balance; they often include sheared hedges, topiaries, and a fountain, pool, or sculpture. If your house has a formal facade — with a centered entryway and windows balanced symmetrically on either side of it — and your site is level or symmetrically terraced, you may opt for a formal landscape style, but keep in mind that most formal styles require heavy maintenance.

Informal styles, on the other hand, are often lower maintenance, tending toward curves, asymmetry, and apparent randomness (though they, too, follow the basic landscaping principles outlined on page 38). Either formal or informal landscape styles will complement formal architecture and flat terrain, but informal architecture and irregular terrain generally call for informal landscape styles.

Illustrated below are some of the garden styles you have to choose from. Endless variations are possible; for example, by merely changing the plant selection, the contemporary American style could easily become a tropical paradise. Note that the knot and Spanish garden illustrations are formal, while the others are informal in varying degrees, from the asymmetry of the oriental to the profusion of the cottage.

A SAMPLING OF STYLES

Knot. Small, flat, rectangular plots are well-suited to the formality of the medieval knot garden style. Above, clipped hedges of true dwarf boxwood enclose sage and other herbs, with English lavender for soft color. Gravel walkways and a central sundial continue the geometry that brings order and tranquility to this tiny urban haven.

Oriental. Restraint and simplicity achieve the serene effect shown above. This naturalistic arrangement uses rocks and gravel with a few plants of varying size and texture —Japanese maple, lily turf, aucuba. Note the split-bamboo fencing that forms a fine-textured boundary. Gentle mounds and a garden pool would suit a larger area.

Wild. You can suggest woodland, meadow, rocky alpine slope, or desert simply by choosing appropriate plants. This woodland setting is created by scattering Japanese spurge, sweet violets, and ferns around a large rock and beneath dogwood and a clump of birches. The larger the area, the more varieties can be added.

Cottage. For centuries the English have excelled at packing an astonishing variety of annuals and perennials into a small space with great effect. Here, welcoming bachelor's buttons, larkspur, iris, dianthus, and dusty miller are unified by color and set off against the deep green of a curving yew hedge.

Spanish. The interior courtyard of this Spanish-style house features a central fountain, adobe walls and retainers, and wrought-iron grillwork. Careful plantings of olive and dwarf citrus trees create a cool, formal oasis. Bougainvillea on a south-facing wall and symmetrical planters of geraniums lend brilliance to the scene.

Contemporary American. This popular style can include multilevel decks, raised beds, planters, overheads, paved areas, swimming pools, and night spotlighting. Plants are usually informal and low maintenance. Above, typically uncluttered, architectural lines are softened by nandina, wisteria, and containers of annuals.

Basic landscaping principles

Whatever landscape style you choose, observing the four basic landscaping principles will ensure that your garden is a pleasure to behold. Through years of study and experience, landscaping professionals have absorbed these guidelines so completely that they never lose sight of them throughout the design process. It's likely that you can't match a professional's study and experience, so it's a good idea to return to this section repeatedly as your plan develops; and when your design is complete, check back to make sure you haven't forgotten or altered your original intentions amid the flurry of other planning considerations. These guidelines are your best guarantee of quality and durable design for your enjoyment in the years to come.

Unity. A unified landscape is all of one piece, rather than disjointed groupings and scatterings of features. No one element stands out; instead, all the parts — plants, gradient, and structures — work together harmoniously. Strong, observable lines and the repetition of geometric shapes contribute significantly to the unity of your landscape, as does simplicity — for example, using just a few harmonious colors and a limited number of plant varieties. Be prepared to give up the idea of having every one of your favorite plants around you, and avoid designing too many distinct units that will have to be tied together. In fact, as you work on each landscaping area, you may find it best to design a unified background first — a lawn or patio, perhaps. Think of this background as a neutral element, a "blank canvas" on which you'll assemble your landscaping units to provide balance, proportion, and variety. Just remember that the more units you have, the harder it will be to achieve unity.

Balance. To balance a landscape is to use mass, color, or form to create equal visual weight on either side of a center of interest. In a formal landscape, balance may mean simply creating one side as a mirror image of the other. In informal styles, balance is just as important, but more subtle: a large tree to the left of an entryway can be balanced by a grouping of smaller trees on the right. Likewise, you can balance a concentration of color in a small flower bed on one side of a patio with a much larger and more diffuse mass of greenery on the other side. Studied asymmetry can be pleasing, too, but take care — too much of a good thing can become an irritating lopsidedness!

Proportion. In a well-designed landscape, the various structural and plant elements are in scale with one another. Start with your house; it will largely determine proportion in your landscape. When choosing trees and shrubs, keep their ultimate sizes and shapes in mind. Though a tree when young may suit your front yard, it could overwhelm your house as it matures. If you find it difficult to imagine a sapling's final size and shape, look at several mature specimens. This knowledge is essential to good planning.

Variety. Break up a monotonous landscape by selecting plants in a variety of shapes, shades, and textures; or add interest by juxtaposing different materials. Imagine the pleasant surprise afforded by spotting a copper beech among greenery, a sculpture around a bend in a path, or a break in a screening hedge that reveals a view of distant hills. A perfect balance between the principles of unity and variety is difficult to achieve, but well worth the effort.

The unplanned landscape: The yard shown above suffers from a lack of planning. Cars and people are forced to share the same entry. The unkempt hodgepodge of plantings may be the result of neglect, a series of owners, or just poor judgment. The key elements of unity, balance, and proportion are missing — probably because they were never considered.

The planned landscape: This drawing shows a remodel of the same landscape. The meager entry path has been widened, and unity of line and material ties the driveway and a new side yard path and mowing strip together. A raised bed now sets off the front windows. New plantings are balanced and in good proportion — both to each other and to the house.

Designing your landscape

Once you've determined what you want from your landscape and what you have to work with, the most creative part lies before you: the design itself. At this point you begin to put ideas for your new landscape onto paper.

Already you may have made occasional sketches; now sketching becomes the focus of the design process. Maybe you'll make some quick sketches on small, handy pads as ideas occur to you. However, your most productive sketching will be done on sheets of tracing paper laid over your base map, to remind you constantly of basic site features and conditions.

For hours, or off and on for days and weeks — as long as you need — you'll sketch and doodle, with little concern for neatness, precision, or fine detail. As you sketch, you'll begin to work out use areas and circulation patterns, and to make general decisions about what kinds of plants and structures you'll need and where to place them. Simultaneously, you'll be using the information under "Groundwork" (pages 41–42) to determine the needs of the land itself in relation to the other factors in your landscape. At some point or gradually during this enjoyable stage of designing, your final design will crystallize, bringing with it a sense of real achievement.

Defining use areas

Begin by reviewing your landscaping needs (page 34). What areas do you want to assign to entertaining, recreation, relaxation, gardening, and work, storage, and service? Make a list to keep before you as you lay sheets of tracing paper over your base map and begin to experiment. A typical list of use areas might include front and back lawns, children's play area, patio, deck, spa, lath house, and vegetable garden, plus service yard and tool shed.

Decide whether areas can serve multiple functions — for example, whether a portion of the back lawn might also be the children's play area, and whether a roofed and enclosed part of the lath house might serve as the tool shed.

Making balloon sketches. Sketch "balloons" — rough circles or ovals — on your tracing paper to represent the location and approximate size of each use area. As you make sketch after sketch, concentrate on logical placement and juxtaposition of areas. Does the vegetable garden receive full sun? Is the children's play area in full view of your main living areas? Is the spa easily accessible from the master bedroom and from the deck? Do you really want the patio where you've sketched it, next to the service yard?

Figuring circulation patterns. How direct and logical are foot-traffic connections between use areas? Is too much traffic channeled through areas meant for relaxation? Visualize not only your own movements but also those of guests, gardeners, letter carriers, and impulsive children. Consider whether the lawn mower and garden cart can be moved from tool shed to lawn without disturbing plantings — or someone's repose.

Testing ideas. As you make sketches, don't limit yourself to the abstract information of the base map, but experiment directly on the landscape. Pace off areas or use stakes or chairs to help visualize spaces and distances; walk through contemplated traffic paths. You might even want to climb a stepladder to study the view from a proposed deck.

Bounce your ideas off others who know the site, then modify your sketches as needed. Develop alternative plans in case some new factor arises to make you reconsider the balance of the whole design.

Designing with structural elements

In Chapter 3 (pages 48–79) you'll find a wealth of ideas and information to help you select among materials and designs for fences, overheads, gazebos, and other landscape structures. At this stage you need only determine what basic *types* of structures will serve you best, and where to situate them.

One productive approach is to ask yourself what problems a structure might solve. Even though each structural element will have a primary use, you can extend that use or devise multiple uses, as the following examples illustrate.

Surfacing elements. If you want to create a permanent, flat surface for an outdoor living area, to cover wet ground or shallow, rocky soil, to utilize a steep slope without altering its gradient, to create a variety of levels in a flat area, or to satisfy several of these needs, consider building a single-level or multilevel deck.

Paved surfaces, too, can serve multiple functions, given a little imagination. For example, could your concrete driveway not only guide the car into the garage but also carry runoff in the opposite direction — to the storm drain?

Retaining structures. Erosion of a slope can be checked, and the area opened up for living and gardening, if you use retaining walls.

Think about constructing them so that they are topped by raised beds; such a design can allow for rapid soil drainage and better growth of vegetables or flowers. Go a step further: add wide caps to your raised beds to provide seating as well. Retaining walls can also take the shape of garden steps for easy traffic flow between different levels of your landscape.

Circulation elements. A walkway may be intended primarily to pave the way from the house to the gazebo. But at the same time, it can accentuate graceful contours in the landscape, or serve as an attractive divider between garden areas — for example, by separating flower border from lawn with a sinuous line.

In less-trafficked parts of your garden, a path of redwood rounds, irregular flagstones, or railroad ties can go beyond the pedestrian provision of solid, dry footing; they can do as much as any element to define your style.

(Continued on next page)

...Designing your landscape

Enclosing and sheltering structures. A fence or a wall can provide not just privacy and wind protection but also support for a flowering vine in a drab, flat boundary area of your garden—or a strong visual link between the house and a detached deck. A white picket fence could be the perfect complement to your cottage-style front garden, allowing passers-by to enjoy the sight but barring foot traffic through the flower beds.

A high, steel-mesh fence covered by evergreen vines not only offers security and privacy, but in windy areas is a better screen than a wall or solid fence, which can create heavy turbulence.

A screened garden room could provide a comfortable shield from sun, insects, and the neighbors' view from a high apartment building overlooking your garden. Similarly, an overhead could both shade you and create privacy while performing as a flattering architectural extension of your house.

Recreational structures. If you're planning a swimming pool, perhaps it could do double duty as a reflecting pool. Imagine it situated on the axis between a living area and a double row of trees or a sheared hedge framing a sculpture or graceful gazebo. If you plan to have a hot tub, could you use decking, lattice and vines, planters, and a grouping of outdoor furniture to make it the focal point of an intimate garden-within-a-garden?

Designing with plants

In Chapter 4 (pages 80–127) a broad selection of plants awaits you—plants of diverse sizes and habits, suitable for widely varying growing conditions and landscaping uses. Both the encyclopedic descriptions and the specialized charts will guide you in choosing specific plants for your purposes. But for now, choose general types only — "evergreen screen," "flowering shrub," "patio tree," "annuals in containers," and so forth —to fulfill the needs of particular use areas. Label those types in your sketches as your final plan begins to take shape.

For most people, plants *are* the landscape, or the essence of it: the living, constantly unfolding element of most immediate beauty. But plants can be as useful as they are beautiful. Your concern now is designing with plants, not choosing them or considering their cultural needs. Concentrate on their esthetic and utilitarian functions in the larger picture. Weigh the following points and review the principles on page 38 before you pick the types of plants that will populate your landscape.

Practical plants. Consider the numerous practical uses of plants in the landscape. Trees and shrubs can be made to function as fences or walls to shield you and your house from onlookers and from the elements. Many low plants are suitable for covering bare ground, inhibiting weeds, retarding erosion, and even lowering the temperature of a very sunny area. We've all relied on plants to provide food, seasoning, and inexpensive table decor. And not least among practical plant functions is the tried-and-true jungle gym a small, sturdy tree can provide for active children.

Plants as structural elements. In a successful landscape design, plants function as an integral part of the design, not as frills. A low hedge can define an area of the landscape far more gracefully than a wall of the same dimensions, and a tall hedge provides a more pleasing backdrop for a flower border than would a fence, while affording just as much privacy. In a garden corner, a brilliant flowering shrub or an intriguingly gnarled small tree might be a more appropriate accent than a sculpture. A variety of vertical, spreading, and roundish plant forms is as pleasant to the eye as is a carefully planned variety of structural forms in architecture.

Plants for texture. Every kind of plant has a distinctive texture, or visual surface, created by the size and shape of its leaves and the way it holds them to catch and reflect sunlight. Textures may be airy or dense, smooth or rough, fine or coarse. Two kinds of plants may have similar leaves but hold them so differently that their textures are quite dissimilar.

In designing your landscape, choose plants that have a variety of textures, but don't overdo it; maintain a continuity. As a general rule, graduate textures, rather than shifting abruptly. You'll find that small areas seem larger if they're designed with fine-textured plants, whereas coarse textures can make large areas seem smaller.

Fast- and slow-growing plants. When you actually plant your new landscape, you'll naturally be eager for certain plants to mature, especially if they are to cover or soften the lines of structures, retard erosion, or cover bare ground. Specify "fast-growing vine" on your sketches; later on you can look for help in Chapter 4 to select just which fast-growing vine that will be.

You may also want some slow-growing plants to fill special needs. For a formal hedge, topiary, or planting beneath low windows, slow-growing shrubs are preferable, since they are far easier to maintain than are fast-growing ones. A rank vine needing frequent pruning and thinning would be as unwelcome an addition to a pergola as a fast-growing, large tree would be to a patio.

Landscape professionals sometimes plant fast-growing vines or ground cover in the same area where they plant slower-growing trees and shrubs, so the slower-growing plants will have an attractive background against which they can mature. As the "permanent" plants become established, the background plantings are cut back, or even removed.

You can do the same in your own garden by planting such fast-growers as gazania, nierembergia, lantana, or osteospermum; these make attractive background plantings and add the bonus of seasonal color.

Deciduous and evergreen plants. To create an especially beautiful and functional environment, capitalize on the fact that some plants shed their

A word about color...

Like the interior of a house, a garden needs harmony to be attractive, and an important component of garden harmony is the judicious use of color. Just as the colors of a beautiful room stand in a coordinated relationship to one another, so do they also in a lovely garden. Keep color in mind, then, as you design both the structural and plant elements of your landscape. And don't forget to take your house into account; since it's the most prominent feature of your landscape, its color or colors should harmonize with those of the other landscape elements.

Structural elements such as brick, tile, stone, and wood all have distinctive, generally earthy colors. Though the colors of masonry materials are generally permanent, wood colors are not. Redwood and cedar, for example, may be highly colored when new, but they will weather to softer, quite different hues after a year or so, changing your color scheme as they do. Keep in mind that paints and stains are available for all structural materials, including masonry.

In general, plantings should combine harmonious colors representing a continuous segment of the color wheel: red, red violet, and violet, for example. The smaller the landscape, the narrower the segment should be. Use complementary colors — those opposite one another on the color wheel — sparingly, for accents.

You can create striking contrasts by the occasional use of light and dark opposites — for example, light yellow marigolds with dark blue lobelia. To draw the eye to a focal point in the garden, dark or brilliant colors are appropriate. Always use restraint—a lovely garden is restful to the eye, rather than a source of constant visual stimulation. A range of muted colors provides the most restful effect.

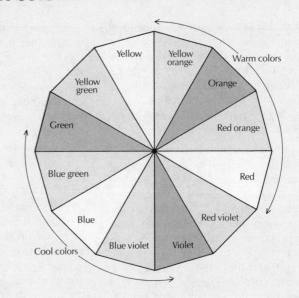

To brighten large areas, use the warm colors of the red-orange-yellow range. Because they make a distant planting seem closer, warm colors are also helpful at the rear of long, narrow areas.

The cool colors of the green-blue-violet range, on the other hand, can make a shallow space appear deeper. The cool hues are easily lost in shaded areas, but will show to greater effect when massed.

Plant colors span a wide spectrum, and not only within the realm of flowers. All foliage is not simply "green"; the range of shades is actually quite large.

---

leaves annually, while others keep them. For screens, most ground covers, and plants used architecturally (such as sheared hedges), you'll probably want evergreens. Touches or masses of green lend life and substance to the winter landscape.

But one of the special joys of a garden can be its dynamic link with the changing seasons. Brilliant autumn foliage, new green spring foliage, and bright berries or fruit are seasonal accents as welcome as blossoms. And what could be more functional than a deciduous tree that envelops a house and patio in cool shade in summer, then sheds its leaves to admit warmth and light in winter?

Plants in containers. Their value can't be overstated. Containers can bring flowers, vegetables, shrubs, even trees to decks high above ground level, or to pavement, doorstep, or tabletop. Hanging planters can raise the visual level of a garden, lending softness and color to eaves and overheads.

You can exchange planters of flowers that are passing their peak of bloom for others that are just approaching theirs. Containers also allow tender plants to winter over in a sheltered spot or on a sun porch (trays with casters make light of the moving problem).

In formal landscapes, colorful planters accentuate the symmetrical placement and shaping of the permanent plants. Used formally or informally, containers invariably isolate and point up the beauty of the plants within them by acting as showcases.

Groundwork

Designing your landscape isn't only a matter of planning use areas and making decisions about structures and plantings. An integral part of this process is constant observance of the "lay of the land" and making decisions about its grading, drainage, and irrigation needs, as part of the whole landscape picture.

Grading. Whenever you can fit your use areas into the existing topography with little or no disturbance, you'll save time, effort, and expense. You're lucky, however, if the gradient of your landscape presents no problems and allows for a use plan that suits you. More often, existing topography has inherent problems, or you will decide

...Designing your landscape

to alter it in order to make your ideal design work. Then you must *grade* the land: reshape it by removing soil (cutting), by bringing in or relocating soil (filling), or both. Chapter 5 will give you the how-to's of grading when you reach the point of action (see pages 130–131).

Why grade, specifically? Aside from the vital need to ensure good surface drainage, grading is often required for other practical reasons—and some purely esthetic ones. Maybe an uneven area destined to become lawn or patio needs smoothing out. Perhaps you've opted for an oriental garden style that calls for the creation of interesting contours. Flat, open landscapes frequently cry out for added vertical dimension: sculpting a berm near a patio will create privacy while it improves the esthetics of your yard. Or your property may lie on a slope so steep that without skillful grading and terracing it would remain unstable and useless to you as a garden space.

Who should do the job? If the grading is simple and you have the time and inclination to do it, you can save money and have the satisfaction of having literally shaped the land you'll live with for years to come. But many special situations require that you obtain professional help or, at least, advice.

If an area around existing trees is to be graded, call in a tree expert who understands how to grade without jeopardizing the trees' health. If steep or unstable slopes require terracing, call in a landscape architect or civil engineer: someone who can foresee all the implications and who is familiar with legal requirements. In short, rely on the expertise of professionals for major grading, including grading of *any* unstable area.

Drainage. At the same time that you're observing gradient or planning to alter it, you'll also be studying drainage on your site. Wherever drainage is a problem, note on your base map and final sketches the area and the solution, if you can determine it. For information on specific methods for improving drainage, see pages 132–133.

If your landscape is nearly flat, be sure that it has adequate surface drainage: a minimum slope of nearly three inches per ten feet of unpaved ground. A steeper gradient is better for slow-draining, heavy soils. Also be sure, of course, that runoff is directed away from adjacent property and toward a storm sewer. Runoff from roofs and paved surfaces, which is rapid, sometimes requires special solutions such as catch basins or drain tiles (see pages 132–133).

Steep slopes absorb far less rainwater than do flat areas and may drain fast enough to cause erosion problems. To retard erosion, such slopes need terracing and, sometimes, special structures. Appropriate ground covers and other plantings can also be used to slow runoff; the chart on page 93 lists attractive plants that cope well with unfavorable hillside conditions.

Subsurface drainage, or percolation, is the downward penetration of soil by water; it's slow in clay soils, compacted surface soils, soils with mixed layers and interfaces, and soils overlying hardpan. Poor subsurface drainage is also a problem where the water table is close to the surface. Sumps and drain tiles offer solutions in such cases.

On steep clay slopes most water runs off; nevertheless, retained water can cause mud slides. Get professional help to plan and install a drainage system for any steep clay hillsides you may have.

Irrigation. Chapter 5 offers guidance in selecting and installing the watering system or systems exactly suited to your landscape's needs (see pages 170–171). In the planning stages, simply make sure that your final plan shows not only existing hose bibs but also where bibs will be needed to service your new areas. If you revise your final plan or draw up a new planting plan, remember to change the locations of hose bibs, if necessary.

Bear in mind when designing your watering system that planted areas beneath overhangs, dense foliage, and greedy trees need special or extra irrigation.

Drawing up your final plan

Now that you know exactly what your use areas will be, what general types of structures and plants will fulfill the needs of those areas, and what alterations of gradient are called for, you're ready to draw up your final plan.

To be sure that the present and future sites will bear an accurate working relation to one another, draw your final plan on tracing paper placed directly over your base map. Label structures and plants as shown on the sample final plan on the facing page, trying to keep in mind what your plan will look like in three dimensions and in color. Make your plan as neat and concise as possible, and be sure your sketches and notations are bold enough to be read easily. (If you need copies of your final plan, a blueprinting company can make them quickly and inexpensively.)

If your final plan is too cluttered to read easily, if it calls for complicated structures such as decks or overheads, or if contractors are going to rely on your plan for information on construction or planting, you'll probably need some more specialized drawings: a construction plan for each complex structure, a planting plan, and/or an irrigation plan. If this is the case, you may want to give your base map and final plan to a landscape architect or drafting professional to make those specialized versions.

The final plan

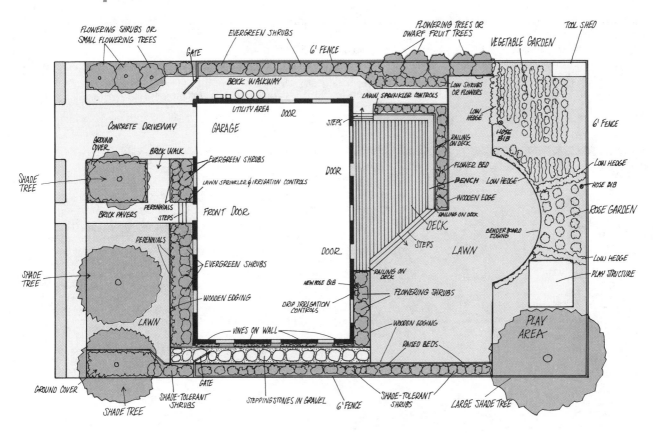

FLOWERING SHRUBS OR SMALL FLOWERING TREES
GATE
EVERGREEN SHRUBS
6' FENCE
FLOWERING TREES OR DWARF FRUIT TREES
VEGETABLE GARDEN
TOOL SHED
BRICK WALKWAY
LAWN SPRINKLER CONTROLS
LOW SHRUBS OR FLOWERS
LOW HEDGE
UTILITY AREA
DOOR
STEPS
6' FENCE
CONCRETE DRIVEWAY
GARAGE
HOSE BIB
RAILING ON DECK
LOW HEDGE
GROUND COVER
BRICK WALK
EVERGREEN SHRUBS
DOOR
FLOWER BED
HOSE BIB
SHADE TREE
LAWN SPRINKLER & IRRIGATION CONTROLS
BENCH
LOW HEDGE
BRICK PAVERS
PERENNIALS
FRONT DOOR
WOODEN EDGE
ROSE GARDEN
STEPS
RAILING ON DECK
PERENNIALS
DECK
LAWN
STEPS
LOW HEDGE
SHADE TREE
EVERGREEN SHRUBS
DOOR
BENDER BOARD EDGING
PLAY STRUCTURE
RAILING ON DECK
WOODEN EDGING
NEW HOSE BIB
FLOWERING SHRUBS
LAWN
DRIP IRRIGATION CONTROLS
PLAY AREA
VINES ON WALL
WOODEN EDGING
GROUND COVER
GATE
RAISED BEDS
SHADE TREE
SHADE-TOLERANT SHRUBS
STEPPING STONES IN GRAVEL
6' FENCE
SHADE-TOLERANT SHRUBS
LARGE SHADE TREE

These plan and perspective drawings show how the sample base map on page 35 might be developed into an effective landscape suitable for a couple with small children. The design dresses up the property, provides separate outdoor areas for children and adults, and can be completed in stages by the owners at a modest cost.

New brick pavings provide access both to the front door and to the back yard; less costly concrete stepping-stones are used in the south-facing side yard. In the back yard, a deck connects the home's rear doors and provides a well-defined area for entertaining. Vegetable and rose gardens are situated at the rear of the yard, along with a play lot for the children.

Low hedges, beds and borders, and flowering trees and shrubs add pattern and color to the landscape. In summer, deciduous shade trees cool the play area and the sunny west side of the house. Hose bibs, sprinklers, and drip irrigators are planned for easy installation during construction. Design consultant: Paul McMullen.

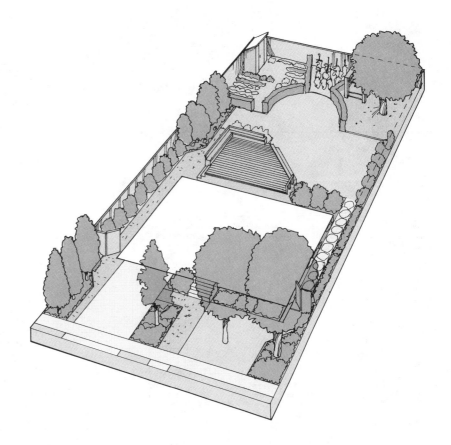

Three variations on a theme

Like the plan on page 43, each of the drawings below represents a possible development of the sample base map shown on page 35. But here, the hypothetical clients have no young children and plan to do a lot of entertaining. Landscape architect Paul McMullen provided the following three solutions to the problem of creating a unified, attractive, and functional landscape design that could be easily and economically installed and maintained by the clients themselves.

In keeping with the life style of the clients, the outdoor living areas needed to be suitable for both social gatherings and private relaxation.

Plan one features a grid of paving (exposed-aggregate concrete in this case, though other materials would serve) that eases the distinctions between driveway, entry walk, and side yard path, and so helps to unify the spaces within the property. In back, a firepit forms a strong central focus for a radial patio; a more private sitting area is tucked into a secluded corner. Lawns are small for easy maintenance, and most shrubs and flowers are confined to the property boundaries, providing privacy and keeping inner areas open. Deciduous trees shade the south side.

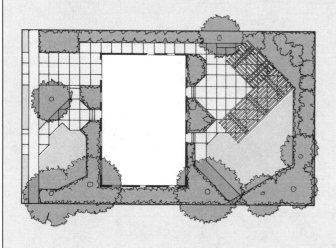

Plan two uses the same unifying paving grid, but introduces strong diagonal elements. Chief among these is a large overhead that provides a practical and decorative focus for the patio. The diagonal lines are carried through in the planting beds, where they add pattern interest within the overall scheme. Again, lawn area is minimized, shrubs and flowers are concentrated at property boundaries, and large trees are used for shade. (A perspective view of this design is shown on page 49.)

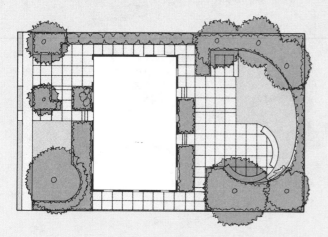

Plan three uses a nearly unbroken paving grid front to rear, but brings the grid to a halt at a large semicircular seating alcove with a curving built-in bench. A smaller seating alcove, rectangular this time, provides visual counterpoint on the opposite side of the patio. The curved line is used several times to frame planting beds and lawn areas, the largest of which flows in a smooth, all-embracing ellipse at the rear of the yard. In this design, the sunny, south-facing side yard is paved—perfect for an intimate container garden or nursery. Once again, lawns are small, and flowers, shrubs, and trees ring the property.

Helpful resources

In the process of shaping your final design, you'll want to consider certain external factors. Do you want to call in professional help to refine your plans or carry out your design? To whom should you turn for information about legal matters? How will you finance your project? You'll find that many resources are available to you when you know where to look.

Landscaping professionals

Even if you plan to do most of the design and installation work yourself, you may want to call in landscaping professionals for specific tasks. For example, you may want a professional to evaluate or polish your final plans, or to design a particular structure. Or you may feel confident about your plans, but need help in carrying them out. Whatever your needs, there are professionals available to help you at every stage of the landscaping process.

Whenever you consult a professional, you'll get the best results by being precise about the service you want. Have some idea of your budget, both for professional consultations and for the entire project. Keep in mind that professional help need not be extremely costly, especially if you hire a professional on a limited or short-term basis.

Whatever type of professional you approach, look for evidence that he or she listens carefully to your ideas and respects your needs. It's always a good idea to ask for references so you can see some of the person's work and talk to former clients. It's also wise to get more than one estimate.

When you hire someone to install your landscape, be sure you have a clear contract for specified services, including a guarantee that your design will be followed and that work will be completed by a certain date — if possible, with a per-day penalty clause. (Check with your homeowners' insurance agent to find out who is liable in case of injury or property damage.) Expect to pay a deposit, but before making the final payment, be sure all work has been completed to your satisfaction.

Finding the right help for the work to be done can save you money and the possibility of having to do the job over again. The following are available for you to choose from.

Landscape architects. Landscape architects hold one or more degrees in their field and are trained (and, in many states, licensed) to design both commercial and residential landscapes. Many are willing to give a simple consultation, either in their office or at your home, for a modest fee. They alone are licensed to prepare designs for a fee, which may be an hourly rate, a flat sum, or a percentage of construction costs.

Landscape designers. Usually landscape designers limit themselves to residential landscape design. They are unlicensed and meet no specific educational requirements, though many are extremely skilled and experienced. In some states they are barred from certain kinds of structural designing.

Landscape contractors. These professionals are trained (and, in some states, licensed) to install landscapes: plantings, pavings, structures, and irrigation systems. Some also offer design services, which may be included in the total price of materials and installation. They can also interpret and implement the plans of a landscape architect.

For specialized construction such as installing a swimming pool, pouring a concrete patio, or building a fence, specialty contractors are available.

Nursery personnel. Retail nurseries are, of course, in business to sell plants, but some encourage business by offering design services. Often, there is no charge for this work if you buy their plants. In addition, some nurseries have highly skilled personnel who are available for outside consultations, or who are able to recommend good local professionals.

Gardeners. Requiring no special training, professional gardeners may do everything from planting and highly skilled maintenance to simply mowing and raking; fees vary accordingly. In some states, they are prohibited from installing landscapes unless their fees fall below a certain limit.

Legal considerations

Your city or county building department personnel can help you determine which codes and ordinances will affect your landscaping plans, and what permits and inspections are required. If your plans call for a deviation from regulations, you will probably need to apply for a variance; submitting a detailed plan is often required.

Financing

If you think you'll need financing for landscape construction and/or planting, you should have a detailed plan and an itemized cost estimate before you begin shopping around for a loan. To put together an estimate, you'll need to price materials and obtain bids from professionals. Ask consultants for quotes on hourly rates and on approximate hours involved. Be exact in describing the details of your plan. (A description such as "a 20-foot fence" will no longer suffice.) Remember that the materials you choose and the construction method used can affect estimates quite a bit.

With your plan and itemized cost estimate in hand, you're ready to apply for financing. You'll probably find that loans for construction are more readily available than loans for planting. However, if you're just buying your property and can arrange to include landscaping costs in the first mortgage, you can cover all types of costs, and at the lowest possible interest rates. If you're a long-time homeowner, you may be able to secure a home equity loan to cover landscaping costs.

If you're remodeling your landscape...

Remodeling your landscape may mean erasing all features and starting afresh, or simply cutting back and thinning out growth, or following some middle path. Beyond a simple face-lift, whatever kind of remodeling you do calls for the same preliminary step-by-step analysis and planning you'd use in creating a home landscape where there had been none. Remodeling, however, offers some unique advantages and opportunities.

A fresh start

Maybe you've bought property whose landscaping neither suits your taste nor meets your needs. Or maybe you're just tired of your old landscape and want both a new overall look and different specific features. In any case, after removing the old landscape you'll be in the same position as the homeowner who has bought or built an unlandscaped house. If you've lived with the old landscape for a while, though, you have the important advantage of being familiar with the site; you're aware of its limitations, assets, and potential.

Make the most of a fresh start by boldly altering the basic character of the landscape. You might introduce a different garden style; reshape contours; create different use areas and reroute foot traffic; and/or make major structural changes, such as adding a high, cantilevered deck to give new perspectives and privacy. If the soil in an area is useless for planting, you might cover it with a deck or raised bed. Or perhaps you'll decide to convert an existing deck or patio to a year-round living space by erecting an overhead and glassing in the space. Your imagination and budget set the limits to the approach you'll take.

A face-lift

Has your yard, landscaped years ago, deteriorated into a jungle? A simple face-lift may be able to turn the calendar back to the days when the landscape was functional and appealing.

Thinning and cutting back old plantings may open up new vistas, make sunbathing and gardening possible where moss was growing, and reveal the handsome forms of mature trees and shrubs. Structural elements may require no more than simple repair and sprucing up. Unlike the homeowner who starts from scratch, you can enjoy all the advantages of a mature landscape instantly, and at little expense.

A revision

Most likely you'll opt for neither of the extremes described above, but will decide to keep part of your old landscape and modify the rest. Perhaps your pruning and thinning for a possible face-lift revealed diseased trees or shrubs or decaying, unappealing features that call instead for a true revision. Or maybe your needs have changed since you created the original landscape: the children's play area stands unused and should be replaced—perhaps by a swimming pool and enclosed patio. If you've bought property whose landscape more or less suits you, you may still want to update it and adapt it precisely to your taste. For any number of reasons you may want to make slight to radical changes.

Homeowners who have successfully revised their landscapes offer this advice: If a magnificent tree domi-

A FRESH START

Before: The plain concrete walk connecting the porch and sidewalk was narrow and dull, the steps made for an abrupt change in level, the plantings lacked imagination, and the whole scheme afforded neither privacy nor design interest. Clearly, a radical improvement was needed, requiring a radical approach: everything had to go.

After: A complete redesign adds both beauty and privacy. A broad stone walk sweeps up to the entrance, two sets of shallow steps provide smoother gradations of level, and large-scale plantings in new beds screen the house. On the porch, new pillars support a heavy trellis that will shade the doorway, once vines have grown enough to span the timbers.

nates the rear garden, plan the garden around it; but be ruthless in removing features that, even though individually attractive, would make a hodgepodge of your new landscape or limit the scope of your planning. Be sure to consider how each change will affect the overall impression.

A note on recycling

No matter how minimal your remodeling scheme, always think about how you might recycle discarded features advantageously. Concrete fragments could be used to build a stonelike wall or stairway in a cottage garden. Bricks from a dismantled patio could pave that much-needed guest parking area. The flowering vine on the arbor scheduled for demolition could be cut back and retrained onto a trellis to soften that large expanse of stucco on the façade of the house. The group of camellias now exposed to full sun by the removal of a sickly oak might better embellish that empty spot on the shady east side of the house. This kind of creative recycling can save you a lot of time and money that will be better spent on quality materials for another remodeling feature.

A FACE-LIFT

Before: The yard was neglected and overgrown. Large shrubs and trees blocked views from the windows and shut out the sun. Still, there was much to be saved if the plants could be made to work for the house, rather than against it. This landscape needed careful editing, rather than extensive remodeling.

After: The large trees and shrubs look fresh and healthy again, thanks to judicious pruning and thinning. One tree has been removed, allowing the sun to shine in—and the owners to see out. A new flowering border brightens the front garden, and adds variety and color to the house. The house now welcomes visitors.

A REVISION

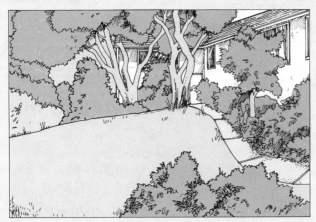

Before: The steep lawn was useless for recreation, and the overgrown shrubs to the rear had become sparse and woody; the large trees, however, were real assets. The shrubs along the house were also overgrown, and their placement lacked balance, unity, and proportion—three principles of good design that should be enlisted when revising any landscape.

After: The yard is now the focus of outdoor living. The slope was graded to form terraces for a swimming pool and wood deck. New plantings replace the old, and mature trees were pruned and thinned to form a lacy backdrop. Concrete used for coping around the pool and for the retaining wall unifies a composition that revises both the function and appearance of the yard.

SELECTING THE STRUCTURAL ELEMENTS

Now that your plan is beginning to take shape, you're ready to focus on the structural elements of landscaping—the myriad things you can build in your garden. Use this chapter to facilitate the selection process. Each two-page spread is devoted to a single subject: on the left-hand page is a discussion designed to help you make choices, acquaint you with benefits, and warn you of pitfalls; the right-hand page features a montage of full-color illustrations showing the diversity of effects a particular structural element can create in your garden.

The chapter covers a full range of subjects. It begins with pavings, walks, steps, edgings, and raised beds (pages 50–59). Different kinds of barriers—retaining walls, freestanding garden walls, and fences and gates—are discussed in the next section, followed by a spread on decks and another on screens and overheads (pages 60–69). The final pages of the chapter are devoted to garden amenities: outdoor rooms, garden pools, hot tubs and spas, swimming pools, and garden lighting (pages 70–79).

Use this information to help fine-tune your plan, adapting the visual material to your own needs and heeding the written suggestions. As you read, refer to the photographs in chapter one (pages 4–31) for more ideas; also look at the how-to sequences in chapter five (pages 128–174) for an idea of what's involved once it's time to build.

Coordinated structural elements including paving, walks, edgings, fences, and an overhead shade structure work in harmony in this landscaping design. (See page 44 for a discussion of this project.) Landscape architect: Paul McMullen

Choosing a patio paving

Nothing can enlarge your home more quickly and simply than a paved patio. The area becomes another room that extends living space beyond your walls.

When you're choosing the material for the paving, think simple. Avoid using too many textures and colors in one space. Whether your house is formal or rustic, adjacent pavings should harmonize.

Your choice may also be limited by what's available locally. Most paving materials are heavy, and costs mount quickly as distance from the source of supply increases.

Decide early whether to do your own paving or have it done. Some materials are easy to install; others aren't. Installation directions for some of the more popular pavings are on pages 140–145.

Be sure to plan for adequate drainage. Any time you pave an area you interfere with the natural percolation of water into the ground. You'll need to pitch the paving surface slightly, directing runoff toward natural drainage or installed drains (see pages 132–133).

Use the following description of the various paving materials together with the illustrations on the facing page to help you choose from the many available options.

Poured concrete. This versatile material can be poured in any shape, can cover broad expanses, and can be finished in a smooth, rough, or pebbled texture. Used with imagination, concrete can be elegant and refined, but its ultimate appearance depends largely on the quality of its design and installation.

The durability of properly installed concrete is unquestioned. Site preparation (grading the earth and building forms) can be time-consuming, but the actual pouring and finishing often go quickly. You may be able to prepare the site yourself, then let professionals take over. A professional can also stamp and tint concrete to resemble stone, tile, or brick. The patterns simulate either butted joints or open ones which can be grouted to look like unit masonry.

Concrete pavers. Standard concrete pavers are square, round, or rectangular, and colored grey, pale green, or brick pink. Exposed-aggregate surfaces are often available. Pavers are easy to use, suitable for projects done in stages, and relatively inexpensive. You can lay them in mortar over concrete or on a sand bed. Standard pavers offer many pattern possibilities; interlocking pavers have unique patterns, require no mortar, and are self-aligning.

Brick. Brick works well in both formal and rustic settings. It's easy to work with, just rough enough for good traction, and comes in a variety of colors, textures, and sizes. Most brick, though, is relatively expensive.

You can mortar bricks over concrete or set them on sand beds, either butted or with mortared joints. Use one of the patterns, or bonds, shown below, or combine two or more for design interest. The small unit sizes make for easy handling, and you can work in stages.

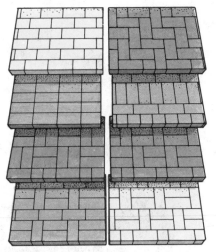

Brick bond patterns are nearly limitless; these are but a few.

Stone. Stone pavings offer the warmth of a thoroughly natural material, and most are very durable. Disadvantages include their high cost, the weight of the material, and a surface that may be slick when wet.

Flagstone and slate are both sedimentary rocks that split naturally into irregular-shaped flat slabs ideal for paving. Thick stones can be laid in sand on stable soil. You can fit them together in an irregular pattern, usually with minimal cutting, or you can purchase stones cut in uniform shapes for a more formal appearance.

Tile. Exterior tile, either terra cotta or the more durable high-fired type, combines earthy good looks with elegance. These unglazed tiles, in the colors of the clays from which they were made, range from about ⅜ inch to 1 inch thick and are usually square or rectangular.

Tile is as easy to lay as brick, and can be set either in sand or in mortar over concrete. Tile is more difficult to cut than brick, though, so it's best to design your paving to accommodate full-size units. Tile is expensive; it's also slippery when wet unless the surface is especially rough.

Wood. Decay-resistant wood such as cedar, cypress, and redwood, and specially treated wood such as railroad ties, pilings, and pressure-treated lumber can be used alone or with other paving materials for a natural look. Blocks, rounds, ties, and boards can be arranged in patterns. All can be set in earth, sand, or gravel.

Charm, moderate cost, and easy installation are assets, but all wood pavings will eventually decompose.

Loose pavings. With few exceptions, pavings of rock and gravel are less suited to outdoor living areas than they are to pathways or areas where they can function as a type of ground covering. Low cost and easy installation are strong points.

Gravel surfaces need raking because the stones tend to "travel" when walked on; this can be minimized by using a compacted base of crushed rock beneath the gravel.

Stamped and grouted concrete

Mortared brick

Brick in sand

Loose gravel

Tile mortared over concrete

Interlocking concrete pavers

Concrete pavers

Exposed-aggregate concrete

Mortared stone

Planning garden walkways

Ideally, a good pathway should combine the virtues of beauty and function, taking you from one point to another in a graceful, natural way on the surface most appropriate to the situation. Achieving this finely tuned combination in a garden walkway takes planning, which begins with careful consideration of route, scale and proportion, and, finally, materials.

Route. Some of the most successful walks are never laid out on paper. Instead, they're traced directly on the ground by footsteps — footsteps that take natural, unforced paths to desired goals. You, too, can achieve this same effect in your garden. Simply wander over your property and note the most natural and beautiful routes between the use areas you defined in your initial planning (see page 39).

You'll find that although the shortest distance between two points is, of course, a straight line, garden walks work best when they ignore this idea to some degree — at least where pure utility is not the overriding concern. Whether made up of meandering curves or straight sections of paving, walks are most interesting when they provide a sequence of experiences along the way.

You may, for example, plan your walk to alternately reveal and conceal features such as special plantings, garden sculpture, an interesting view — even the house itself, if your property is large enough. On a smaller lot, you can expand visual space by concealing the pathway's end, or by the use of "forced perspective," where the width of the path is gradually diminished to make it appear longer.

Though it may sound odd, it's not natural to walk for any distance in an exactly straight line. For proof of this axiom you need only look at large open spaces such as parks, and note the well-worn paths that flow in long, shallow curves through the grass.

For the person laying out a garden pathway, this has three messages. First, it explains the subconscious discomfort with straight, narrow paths; second, if you want a natural look, it suggests designing a pathway that proceeds in a naturally meandering fashion; and last, it explains why a straight walk of good proportion will produce a formal, "designed" look. See the drawings below for two examples.

Curving paths follow natural routes and complement an informal garden.

Straight walks lend an appropriate angular quality to a formal garden.

Scale and proportion. Much of walkway design is just common sense. The path to a frequently used point—your front door, for instance — should accommodate a number of people at once; allow comfortable, safe, and easy access; and appear important enough to suggest that it's the primary entry, thus ensuring that visitors don't become confused and arrive at your back door by mistake.

Other walkways should be developed with a similar sensitivity to use.

Casual paths through a flower garden can be narrow and winding; but if a pathway must accommodate heavy equipment, it should be made wider, without abrupt changes of direction, to allow easy maneuvering.

Remember that it's easy to fashion a walkway that's too narrow; it's rare, in the home landscape, to design one that's too wide. Major pathways should be at least 4 to 5 feet wide; more casual walks, on the other hand, can be as narrow as 2 feet, but 3 feet is a better minimum.

Materials. Keep appropriateness uppermost in mind when you select the material for a walkway. Major access walks should be made of brick, concrete, unglazed tile, or stone slabs —materials that allow easy traffic flow and provide an even, nonslick surface. On the other hand, a rustic path of wood rounds may be just the thing for a romantic country garden. It's best to avoid using glazed tile or uneven stone for walks.

Appropriateness involves more than safety, however. Though the practical advantages and disadvantages of the various paving materials (see page 50) still apply when they're used for walks, each has its unique character and has come to be associated with certain types of houses. The illustrations on the facing page will give you an idea of how some of the most popular materials look when used for garden walks.

Random stone with topsoil joints

Concrete steppingstones

Wood rounds

Gravel or crushed rock

Wood blocks in benderboard grid

Patterned railroad ties

Concrete slabs

Bricks in sand

Designing garden steps

The role of steps in garden landscapes goes beyond their obvious practical purpose: steps can be gracious garden accents that set the mood for an entire landscaping scheme. So when you're planning steps, you'll want to consider both function and appearance.

Scale is another important consideration. Principal entries require steps that both invite people in and allow several to arrive at once. Service yard steps, on the other hand, need to be scaled down to fit their more limited use.

Think also about materials — brick, stone, wood, tile, and concrete are all possibilities (see the illustrations on the facing page). You'll want to choose materials that harmonize with adjacent pavings and structures. Consider combining materials to effect a transition between unlike surfaces. For example, you can link a brick patio to a concrete walk with steps made of concrete treads and brick risers.

Regardless of the material you use, be sure to put safety first. Step surfaces should provide safe footing in wet weather.

To plan your steps, you must consider the relationship between the proportions of the steps and the dimensions of the slope the steps will climb. Work out your plan in detail on graph paper. Try different combinations of risers and treads, widths, and configurations to achieve the necessary change of level.

If your steps will touch a public access area, such as a sidewalk, or will be connected to a building, you may need to show your drawing to your building department and obtain a permit.

Understanding step proportions. The flat surface of a step is called the tread; the vertical surface is the riser. Ideally, the depth of the tread plus twice the riser height should equal 25 to 27 inches. For both safety and ease of walking, the ideal dimensions are a 6-inch riser with a 15-inch tread.

As the chart above shows, riser and tread dimensions can vary, but the riser-tread relationship remains the same. Risers should be no lower than 4

inches and no higher than 8 inches. Treads should never be smaller than 11 inches. And all the risers and treads in any one flight of steps should be uniform in size.

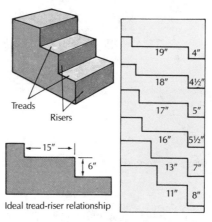
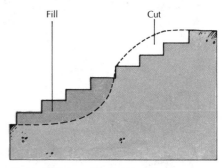

Ideal tread-riser relationship

Tread-to-riser ratio remains constant, even as dimensions vary.

Measuring the slope. To measure the change in level (also called the "rise") of the slope, set up a measuring device like that shown below. The distance from A to B is the rise. The distance from A to C is the "run" or minimum horizontal distance your steps will cover.

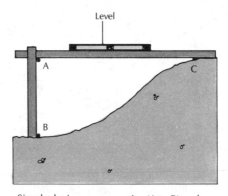

Simple device measures rise (A to B) and run (A to C) of slope.

Calculating step dimensions. To calculate how many steps of a particular dimension will fit into the run, divide the total rise of the slope by the desired riser height of the steps. Now find the corresponding tread size on the proportion chart. To determine whether the steps will fit into the run, multiply the tread size by the number of steps. The result should be approximately

equal to the run from A to C. Adjust the number of steps and the riser and tread dimensions to best fit your slope.

Your garden layout and the purpose for the steps will influence your decision about width. Simple utility steps can be as narrow as 2 feet, but 4 feet is the usual recommended width for outdoor steps. To allow two people to walk side by side, steps should be at least 5 feet wide.

Fitting the terrain. Rarely will the steps fit exactly into a slope as it is. Plan to cut and fill the slope, as shown, to accommodate the steps. If you fill any areas, you'll need to firmly tamp the soil or other fill material to prevent the steps from settling.

Cut and fill slope, if needed, to fit steps to terrain.

If your slope is too steep even for steps with 8-inch risers, remember that steps need not run straight up and down. Some of the most attractive and easily traversed steps curve or zigzag their way up a slope. These create a longer walking distance between levels, but make the slope gentler.

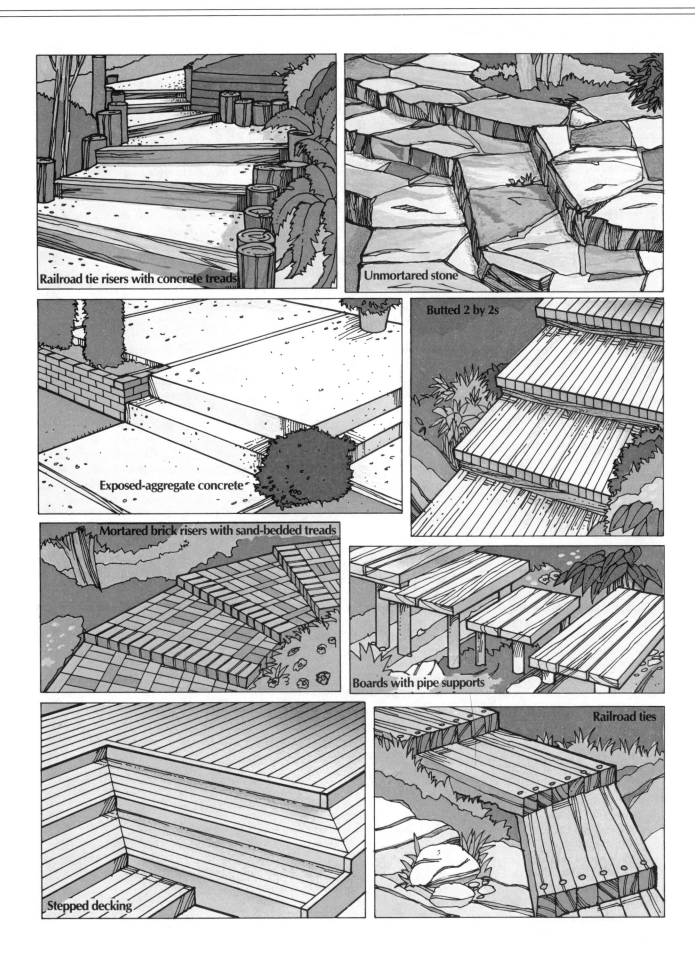

Railroad tie risers with concrete treads

Unmortared stone

Exposed-aggregate concrete

Butted 2 by 2s

Mortared brick risers with sand-bedded treads

Boards with pipe supports

Stepped decking

Railroad ties

Accenting with edgings

Edgings that border lawns, pavings, and planting areas are roughly analogous to picture frames. Though neither is strictly necessary, they both serve some useful functions: they separate differing elements, give a finished look to the areas they surround, and offer decorative accents that don't distract from the main focal point.

As you plan your landscaping scheme, think about how and where you want to use edgings. Edgings can be both practical and esthetic, as shown in the drawings on the facing page. How you'll use edgings will largely determine their material and construction. (Instructions for installing edgings are on pages 136–137.)

Functions

Sometimes, edgings perform strictly necessary functions, such as setting off a lawn from an adjacent paved area or holding paving units in place. Other times, edgings are used for their decorative effect alone. Often, in fact, edgings will fill both of these roles in admirable fashion.

Practical edgings. Some garden edgings are installed for purely practical purposes. This includes the mowing strip that separates the lawn from adjoining surfaces. This strip neatly contains the turf and also provides a surface for mower wheels so the blades can easily trim the edge of the grass. Mowing strips can be made of masonry blocks or poured concrete. Wood is the least used material for mowing strips because it can be easily damaged by the mower.

Often, edgings are required to hold pavings — particularly those made of unit masonry—in place. Edgings lining gravel or pebbly walkways prevent the stones from traveling.

Decorative edgings. A garden edging may exist solely for decoration. Though a poured concrete patio can function just as well unadorned, it will look much sharper and dressier if you give it a neat border of bricks. Even a brick terrace can be enhanced in appearance if it's edged with a band of the same material laid in a different pattern. A patio or terrace composed of masonry units, such as concrete pavers, with dividers spaced every few feet practically requires an edging made of the same material as the dividers to achieve a finished appearance.

Edgings can be used to visually link elements in the landscape. One way to do this is to use a single material to edge areas of several different materials. Edging a lawn, an exposed-aggregate patio, and a gravel path with brick, for example, will tend to unify the overall design. Or the edging can actually connect parts of a garden: a brick-edged patio may taper off to a brick path that leads to another area, again edged with brick.

Though most edgings are set flush with the surfaces they adjoin, you can, for example, cast a concrete strip as a curb or set masonry blocks on end so they project above ground level. A raised edging high enough to retain soil behind it becomes a raised bed. For information on designing a raised bed, see pages 58–59.

Materials

Most garden edgings are made of brick or other masonry blocks, wood, poured concrete, or stone. All these materials give clean, sharp edges. Lines need not be straight: concrete can be poured to follow the snakiest of curves, and bricks, short lengths of wood set vertically, and benderboard also adapt to sinuous lines.

Brick. The easiest edgings to build are brick-in-soil edgings. Be sure to check soil conditions first, though; the soil must be very firm so the bricks will be held securely in place.

Depending on the look you want, you can set the bricks horizontally, vertically, or even at an angle. Putting them at an angle yields a sawtooth effect that may be just what you need to decorate a particular area.

Wood. If you want to use wood for edgings, it's essential to choose a wood that is highly resistant to rot and termites — for example, pressure-treated lumber or the heartwood of cedar, redwood, or cypress. These woods will give you many years of trouble-free service. Benderboard, when applied in layers, works well for curves.

And don't forget large timbers and railroad ties. Both produce unusual and attractive edging designs, as shown on the facing page.

Poured concrete. You can use poured concrete to construct "invisible" edgings underground, or use it for edgings that will be at ground level (see the facing page for an illustration of a ground-level poured concrete edging).

An invisible edging is actually a hidden, underground concrete footing that retains both the paving units and their setting bed. Paving units, such as bricks, are placed in the wet concrete to conceal the footing. Invisible concrete edgings are strong and particularly effective with brick-in-sand pavings; they're also adaptable to other paving units, as well.

Poured concrete edgings that are at ground level can be left unadorned; or you can give them an exposed-aggregate finish. Another option is to have a professional stamp and color them in a manner that complements the area the edgings surround.

Uncut stone. A rustic or woodsy landscape may provide a good setting for edgings of uncut stone. Carefully laid, such a material can appear both natural and neat. The trick is to set stones so their textures, colors, and shapes harmonize and look as though they were part of the original landscape.

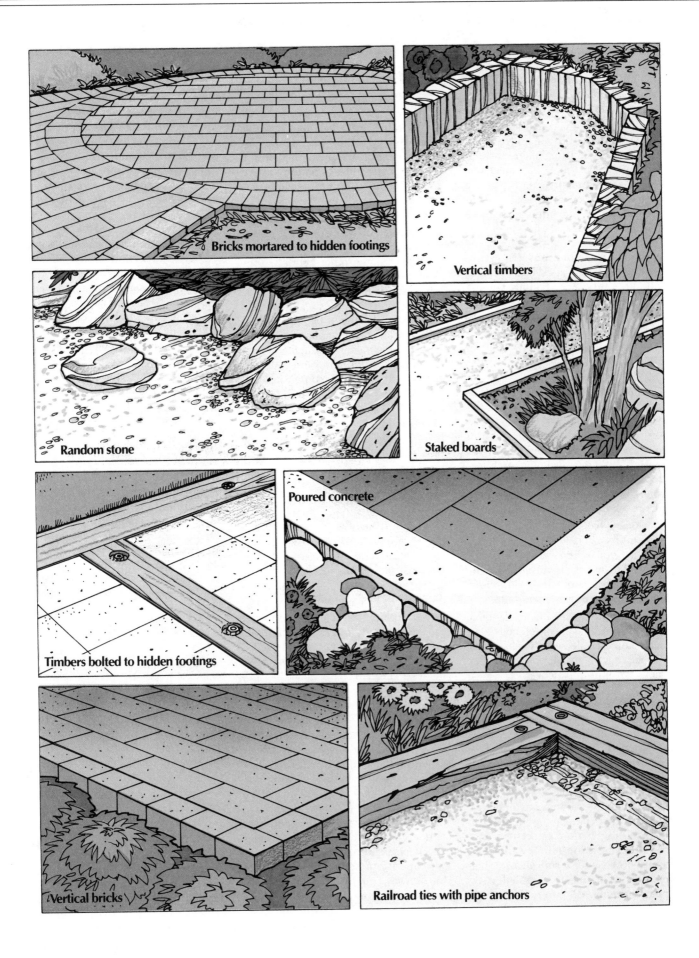

Bricks mortared to hidden footings

Vertical timbers

Random stone

Staked boards

Timbers bolted to hidden footings

Poured concrete

Vertical bricks

Railroad ties with pipe anchors

Dressing up your garden with raised beds

Raised beds combine decorative interest and purely practical function in a single package. Moreover, raised beds are usually easy to build and, depending on their size, moderate in cost.

Some raised beds exist solely for design reasons; others are installed primarily to facilitate some form of gardening. Most meet both needs. A glance at the drawings on the facing page will give you an idea of the diversity of function and appearance that's possible with raised beds.

Architectural functions. On gently sloping hillsides, raised beds can provide level areas for planting; when a lot is pancake flat, they create needed visual relief and elevate special plantings into positions of prominence. On unadorned patios, raised beds can be used to produce decorative effects and to separate spaces.

Placed against a retaining wall or high fence, a raised bed reduces the wall's visual impact by softening the abrupt change between horizontal land and vertical barrier. Raised beds that adjoin a house extend its architectural lines into the garden, providing a zone of transition and a place where plants can frame and soften the house.

Raised beds can be used to create and emphasize patterns in your landscape. Even when their walls are reduced to low curbs, raised beds will preserve the lines of a design in spite of what plants — or gardeners — do.

When provided with broad tops at a convenient height, raised beds also make comfortable seats. Higher beds can serve as both supports and seat backs for built-in benches.

Gardening functions. For the gardener, raised beds offer control over soil composition and drainage. Where soil is poor (or nonexistent, as in a rocky area) and drainage inadequate, raised beds make it easy to create areas of fertile, well-drained soil — often at a considerable savings in time and money when compared with the cost of installing a drainage system and then trucking in topsoil. Or you can fill a raised bed with a soil mixture that meets special needs; coupled with precise drainage control, this enables

you to grow rhododendrons, azaleas, and other plants that are fussy about their root environment.

Another advantage to raised beds is that they elevate plants to a convenient working level where they're easier to tend — and to enjoy. You'll appreciate this relationship if you're planning a garden that invites or requires active involvement, such as a vegetable garden or a garden for cut flowers.

Raised beds are also a boon in low-maintenance schemes. They keep plants organized and confine soil, dead leaves, and other debris within their borders, thereby reducing the work involved in cleaning up the yard. Many attractive landscape designs use raised beds separated by expanses of nicely detailed paving as a means of reducing maintenance. Such a design can enhance your home and your garden — and give you the time you need to enjoy both.

Construction. Raised beds are usually easy to build. The vertical supporting face acts like a small retaining wall, with one significant difference: a raised bed rarely has to withstand the soil pressure that's exerted on most retaining walls. So even though structural soundness is important, it's almost always less complicated and costly to achieve. See pages 146–147 for construction details.

It's very important to plan for drainage. If the bottom of the planting bed is open, water will drain out directly into the ground. But if the bed is closed at the bottom, you'll have to design weep holes on the sides a few inches up from the base. Space them 2 to 3 feet apart.

Materials. Any of the materials suitable for retaining walls (see pages 60–61) can be used for raised beds. Just as with other garden structures, coordinating these materials with others already in place — or contemplated in your landscaping plan — will produce the most pleasing result. If you plan to build a raised bed higher than 3 feet, check local codes for regulations.

Wood is especially versatile, as the drawings on the facing page show. Railroad ties and other large timbers,

though somewhat awkward to handle, make attractive, rustic walls for raised beds. In a naturalistic landscape, you may want to consider using staked logs. Unadorned wood planks and stakes complement nearly any landscape design and are easily adapted to various shapes and sizes. Whatever design you choose, always remember to use pressure-treated lumber or the decay-resistant heartwood of cedar, redwood, or cypress.

Raised beds made of unit masonry are strong and enduring, and can be constructed in many different shapes and styles. A planting bed made of brick can lend elegance and distinction to a formal garden scheme. Even a plain concrete block wall can be dressed up with a veneer of stone or brick for a more finished look. Poured concrete or broken pieces of old concrete from former sidewalks or other pavings also work well for raised beds.

Beds for established trees. When you want to lower the soil level of your yard and at the same time preserve a mature tree, you can surround the tree with a raised bed. The bed will keep the soil around the tree at the proper level and prevent the tree's roots from being exposed. The size of the bed will depend on the size of the tree. Directions for constructing such a raised bed are on page 147.

Broken concrete

Brick

Railroad ties or timbers

Post and board

Stone veneer on concrete blocks

Vertical lumber

Staked logs

Boards with pipe stakes

Choosing a retaining wall

If your lot is on a hillside or has sloping areas, you may need to include a retaining wall in your landscaping plan. Because a retaining wall must be designed to withstand the push of soil without slipping, you'll want to pay careful attention to its siting, design, and material—and you may need professional help in the form of soils and structural engineering.

No slope is reliably static. Once the earth absorbs a certain amount of water (the amount varies with soil type), it begins to want to move downhill; at worst, the earth becomes a suspension of soil particles in water and flows freely.

A retaining wall acts like a dam, and the pressure exerted on it can be enormous. Expansive clay soil, once saturated, can produce literally tons of pressure on the back of a retaining wall. If you live in an area subject to seismic activity, the wall must withstand shock loads as well.

For these reasons, designing and building a retaining wall may be best left to a professional. Most localities require a permit for a retaining wall; many also specify that walls more than a few feet high be designed and supervised by a licensed engineer. It's a good idea to consult your building department, even for a low retaining wall; it's essential if you're planning a wall more than 3 feet high, if you have expansive soil, or if you live in a seismic zone.

In the discussion that follows, you'll find guidelines for choosing a site, design, and material for your retaining wall. Building tips are on pages 138–139.

Site planning

In general, it's best to site your retaining wall so it results in the least possible disruption of the natural slope.

The drawing above shows three typical locations. Notice that in each case the retaining wall rests on cut or undisturbed ground, never on fill. Where possible, it's a good idea to use several low terrace walls, as shown in the third method, rather than one high wall. Low walls are easier and less expensive to build; also, the lighter strain on the smaller walls means that engineering is less critical.

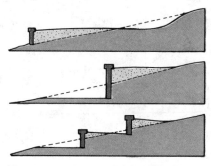

Three ways to site a retaining wall: top, slope is cut away and earth moved downhill; middle, earth is cut away and moved above wall; bottom, total wall height is divided between two terraces.

Planning for drainage is essential. Usually, you'll need a gravel backfill to collect the water that dams up behind the wall. Water in the gravel bed can be drained off through weep holes in the base of the wall, or through a drainpipe that channels the water into a storm sewer or other disposal area.

Materials

When you're choosing a material for your retaining wall, consider more than personal preference: you'll have to select a material compatible with the engineering requirements of the job. Here again, a professional can provide reliable data on the performance of all the common materials. You can use any of the following—with certain limitations—to build a secure retaining wall. Refer to the illustrations on the facing page as you read.

Wood. This is a popular choice for two good reasons: it's attractive, from the rough-sawn, rustic appearance of railroad ties and unsurfaced timber to the trim, smooth look of dimension lumber; and it's easy to work with.

Be sure to use a decay-resistant wood such as redwood, cedar, or cypress, or pressure-treated lumber designed for direct contact with the earth. Wood retaining walls tend to be more limited in potential size than their masonry kin. The higher the wood wall, the more care you'll have to devote to structural integrity.

Uncut stone. For low walls, you can lay uncut stones without mortar or footings — their irregular shapes will help lock them together. For higher walls, both cut and uncut stones require concrete footings and mortared joints for stability.

Broken concrete. Irregularly shaped chunks of broken concrete—pieces of former sidewalks or concrete slabs— are surprisingly attractive and natural looking when laid rough side up in walls. The broken edges and relatively consistent thickness of the concrete give the appearance of sedimentary stone. Broken concrete is easy to lay dry; for greater stability in higher walls, you'll need a concrete foundation, and the pieces should be mortared together.

Masonry blocks. Rectangular manufactured building blocks such as concrete and adobe are suitable for retaining walls, especially when reinforced with steel. Brick, because of the small size of each unit and consequent great number of mortar joints, is sound only for retaining walls up to about 2 feet high. Steel reinforcing will extend this limit somewhat.

Poured concrete. Where engineering is critical, the monolithic strength of poured concrete may be the only solution. Figuring precise dimensions and the amount of steel reinforcing needed can guarantee the required strength.

The finished wall surface need not be flat and uninspiring: lining the interior surfaces of the forms with rough-sawn lumber, for example, will produce an attractive surface texture. An exposed-aggregate finish can also add interest to a concrete wall.

Board-textured poured concrete

Dry-laid stone

Timber cribbing

Vertical timbers

Broken concrete

Post and board

Brick veneer on concrete blocks

Selecting a garden wall

Planning a garden wall begins with a definition of its purpose. Walls provide privacy and security, edit views, screen out wind and noise, and hold the earth at bay. (These last types, called retaining walls, are described on page 60.) Fences also perform many of these functions, but walls do them with an unmatched sense of permanence — some of the oldest structures in the world are walls.

Once you're clear about a wall's function, you can determine its location, height, width, and visual permeability. You'll also need to decide on materials, keeping in mind that coordination with existing materials and with the style of your home and its landscape is usually best.

An essential planning step, particularly if you contemplate building a wall higher than 3 feet or one that will be near your property line, is to check local building codes for height and setback restrictions and for specific regulations governing construction.

Among the typical materials for garden walls are the various kinds of masonry blocks, uncut stone, and poured concrete. Examples of walls made of these materials appear on the facing page. On pages 151–156 you'll find instructions for building masonry walls. Look them over; they may have an influence on the wall you choose.

Regardless of the type of wall you settle on, it will most likely need a solid concrete footing like the ones shown below — typically twice as wide as the wall itself (remember this when adding a wall to your plot plan).

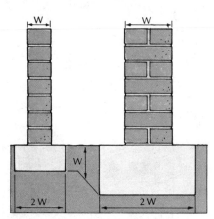

Typical foundation dimensions are proportional to width (W) of wall.

Masonry block. If you're building the wall yourself, the easiest material to use is masonry block: brick, concrete block, or adobe. Each comes in uniform rectangular units that make planning and building relatively simple. Because walls of these materials are assembled piece by piece, you can build your project in stages.

Each material is available in a variety of dimensions, textures, and colors. Many have modular proportions (each dimension is a simple multiple or division of the others) that simplify design and construction. Design options are built into each material. In addition, you can choose a decorative pattern for laying the courses, incorporate a solid or openwork face, vary the thickness, and employ combinations of materials. Often, a more expensive material, such as brick or stone, can be used as a veneer over a less costly one (see the drawing below).

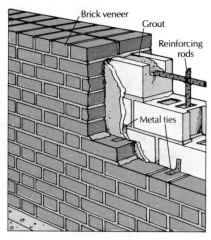

An easily reinforced core of concrete block makes a sturdy, economical base for a veneer of more costly brick.

Uncut stone. In the hands of a sensitive stonemason, stone forms walls that are without peer for harmonizing with the landscape. The centuries-old New England countryside stone walls (ironically called stone fences) emerge so naturally from the landscape that they hardly seem to have been constructed.

You can lay stone walls dry or with mortar. Flat stones are best for dry walls; rounded ones usually require a stabilizing bond of mortar. In general,

it's difficult and time-consuming to build a wall out of stones because of their irregular shapes and sizes.

Building-supply yards may offer a variety of stones, sometimes shaped for easier handling. If a particular stone is prominent in your region, you'll achieve the most natural-looking result if you use that kind of stone for your wall.

Poured concrete. A wall of poured concrete offers many design possibilities because surface texture and shape are established by the wooden forms you make (see the drawing below). Most of the work goes into constructing and stabilizing these forms; the actual pour is accomplished quickly. You should probably call in a contractor for any poured concrete wall more than 4 feet high.

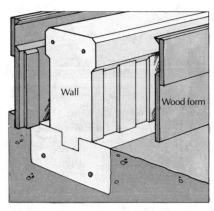

Poured concrete wall takes on pattern of forms in which it's poured.

Because a poured concrete wall is structurally one unit, it is unexcelled for strength. Most poured concrete walls incorporate steel reinforcing. Depending on how this reinforcing is engineered, the same basic structure can be scaled to designs ranging from low seating walls to walls of imposing dimensions.

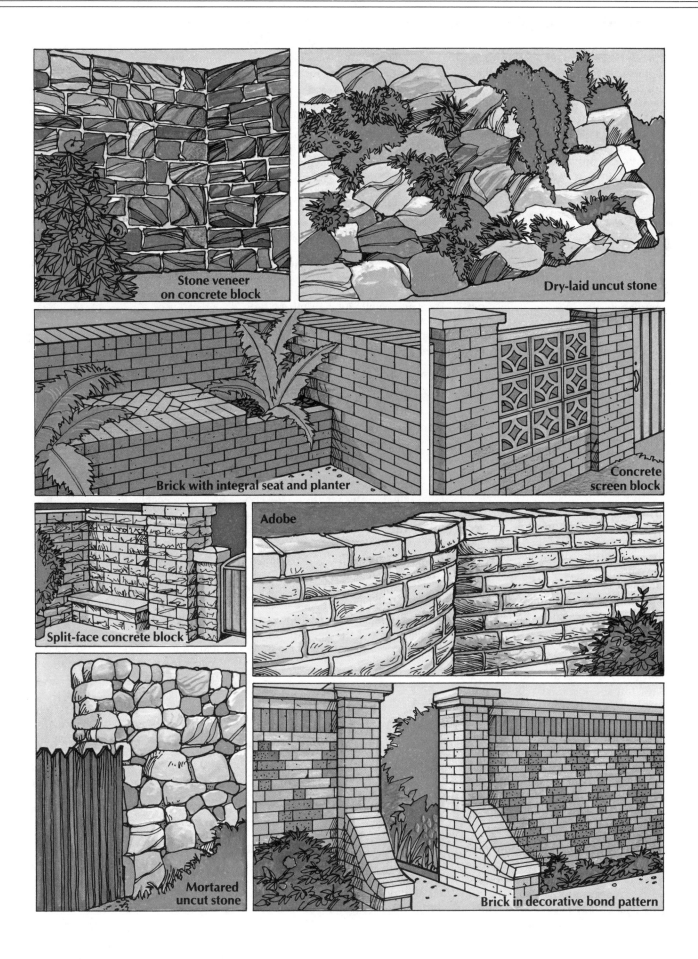

**Stone veneer
on concrete block**

Dry-laid uncut stone

Brick with integral seat and planter

**Concrete
screen block**

Split-face concrete block

Adobe

**Mortared
uncut stone**

Brick in decorative bond pattern

Planning for fences & gates

There's more to fencing than simply delineating your property's boundary lines. Fences can also separate different use areas in your garden, provide privacy, shield you from the elements, and ensure safety from hazards in or near your yard. The gates you add not only provide access but can also serve as decorative accents.

Fences

A wood fence is a good project to design and build yourself, especially if you have some basic carpentry skills. The key to success is careful planning. Instructions for building fences and gates begin on page 162.

Local restrictions. Most communities have regulations restricting fence height. In many places the maximum allowable height is 42 inches for front yard fences and 6 feet for back yard fences. Sometimes, high fences are allowed if they have a very open design. And if you have a swimming pool, you may be required to fence it in for safety.

Siting the fence. Make certain you have the property line clearly established if your fence will be on or near the boundary line between your property and your neighbor's. If you're not sure, call in a surveyor.

Normally, a boundary fence is commonly owned and maintained by both neighbors. Make every effort to come to a friendly agreement with your neighbor on the location, design, and construction of the fence. If necessary, put the fence entirely on your land, a few inches inside your boundary.

Finally, consider the land itself. Few lots are perfectly smooth, flat, and tree of obstructions. If your fence line runs up a hill, you can build the fence to follow the contour of the land, or you can use stepped panels to maintain pleasing horizontal lines.

Design. Though the design possibilities are many (as illustrated on the facing page), fences fall into either of two types: solid or open. The one you choose may depend on the function of your fence — one for privacy would usually be solid, for example— or, if either would do, simply individual taste.

In any case, be sure to coordinate fence style with the style and materials of your house. A picket fence that would be incongruous with a contemporary stone and glass house will look right at home with colonial brick or New England clapboard structures. A louver or board fence can complement a variety of house styles.

Materials. Most wood fences have three main parts: vertical posts, horizontal rails or stringers, and siding. Posts are usually 4 by 4 timbers; rails are usually 2 by 4s. Siding can be anything from rough grapestakes to ready-cut pickets, finished boards to plywood panels.

Timbers for posts should be made of pressure-treated or decay-resistant wood to keep them from rotting in the ground. Redwood and cedar heartwood are naturally insect and decay resistant. If possible, use treated wood for the entire fence. "Living" fences are made of two layers of chain-link fencing enclosing planting mix and moss; plants set in this mix soon grow to cover the fencing.

Paints and stains. If you're using redwood, you can let it weather naturally. For fir or pine, painting or staining is recommended. Paint or stain rails and siding (especially where they will touch or overlap other parts of the fence) before you attach them to posts.

Gates

An entry or garden gate, working in harmony with a fence or wall, can make an opening statement about your home: a low picket or airy lath gate invites people in with a friendly look; a high, solid gate seemingly shields a private world within.

Design. You may want to build the gate in a style and material that match the fence. Or you can choose a contrasting material or design, such as a wood or wrought-iron gate in a brick wall.

In choosing a design, think about function as well as appearance. After all, no matter what a gate looks like, it has to *work*, and it must keep working in spite of considerable wear and tear. When you design a gate, it's a good idea to show your sketch to someone at a lumberyard who knows carpentry so you can find out whether your plan is feasible.

Size. The width of your gate may be dictated by an existing fence or wall opening. But if you're building both a gate and a fence or wall, you can adapt the measurements to your particular needs.

The minimum width for a gate is usually 3 feet, but an extra foot creates a more gracious feeling. If you anticipate moving gardening or other equipment through the gate, make the opening even wider. You might consider a two-part gate for an extrawide space, or even a gate on rollers for a driveway.

Materials. Choose high-quality materials that will withstand weather and years of constant use. A basic gate consists of a rectangular frame of 2 by 4s with a diagonal 2 by 4 brace running from the bottom corner of the hinge side to the top corner of the latch side, preventing the gate from sagging. Siding fastened to the frame completes the gate.

Be sure the lumber you buy isn't warped. It doesn't take much of a curve to throw a whole gate frame out of alignment. Also check to see if the lumber is seasoned. If it's green, lay it flat and let it dry for at least a month.

Choose both hinges and latches for strength. It's better to select a hinge or latch that's too hefty than one not strong enough. Plan to attach both hinges and latches with long galvanized screws that won't pull out, and be sure to use galvanized hardware.

Board and batten

Picket

Grapestake

Split rail

Alternating board

Louver

Clapboard

Oriental

"Living"

Board and lattice

Adding a deck to your landscape

Just a glance at the examples on the facing page will reveal one good reason for the appeal of a wood deck—its versatility. A garden deck can satisfy a myriad of needs, from providing a cozy corner for reading and relaxation to extending the living and entertaining area of your home to the outdoors. And it's the use of wood that makes it possible. No other building material can be used so easily and in so many different ways to create outdoor living surfaces.

A wood deck is always constructed above the ground—anywhere from a few inches to many feet. You can design it freestanding or plan to attach it directly to your house. You'll find instructions for building a simple wood deck on pages 157–159.

The many uses of decks

What a wood deck can do for your garden is limited only by your imagination. In general terms, though, decks function in three basic ways.

As space enlargers. A wood deck attached to the house will extend the indoor living area to the outdoors in one smooth flow. Detached from the house, a deck can hover over or nestle into the landscape, and provide a secondary site from which to enjoy the out-of-doors. If you're planning or already have a swimming pool, hot tub, or outdoor room, an adjoining deck can enhance its appearance and extend its usefulness.

As space reclaimers. Consider a hilly or uneven site, the narrow or odd-shaped space between house and fence, and the irregular spaces within a grove of trees — these are but a few examples of wasted or useless outdoor space that a deck may be able to reclaim. A friendly wood deck, with perhaps some screening for shade, privacy, or wind control (see pages 68–69), can transform such areas into attractive, useful focal points.

As problem solvers. Faced with an unattractive entryway consisting of a small concrete porch and narrow steps, or an old, cracked concrete patio

or pathway, you may choose to knock them out and start anew, at considerable cost and effort. On the other hand, a quicker, more gracious, and more economical remedy is to simply deck over the offending features.

Decks are also often used as pathways and steps. The post and beam support structure makes it possible to avoid heavy excavation by "floating" paths and steps over poorly drained, rocky, or uneven terrain.

If you live in a harsh climate where winter weather would be unkind to a wood deck, you can construct a portable modular deck that can be safely stored indoors during winter months. This is also an attractive alternative for home renters: when moving time comes, the deck can go along.

Deck design & materials

A wood deck, whether ground hugging or raised, consists of a foundation of concrete footings and piers that support a substructure of posts, beams, and joists (see the illustration below); decking is laid over the joists to form the flooring.

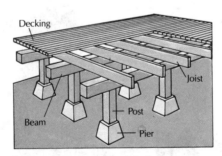

Schematic view of typical deck construction shows how piers, posts, beams, and joists support decking.

Though the support structure must be fairly rectilinear, the ultimate shape of the deck is determined by the decking, and here imagination is about the only limit. You can also lay the decking in a pattern for further design interest.

Once you've embarked on a deck-building project, you'll find it easy to incorporate any of a range of additional features. These include built-in seats and benches; integral planters

and raised beds; and attached screens and overheads.

One advantage of a deck as a do-it-yourself project is that the engineering has probably already been done for you. Standard span tables are widely available to aid you in your design; these tables list safe working spans by dimension for each of the common lumber species. The *Sunset* book *How to Plan & Build Decks* is one source for these tables; it also contains fully detailed design and building instructions for a wide range of decks.

You'll find that a low deck is the simplest one to build. Generally, decks that are cantilevered out from the upper story of a house or over water or a promontory should be designed by a qualified structural engineer and installed by a professional. Decks on steep hillsides or unstable soil, or decks more than a story high should receive the same professional attention.

For any deck, be sure to check with your building department for code regulations; you will probably need to obtain a building permit before you begin construction.

Use only decay-resistant redwood, cypress, or cedar heartwood, or pressure-treated lumber. Regardless of the wood you use, weathering will eventually take its toll on the deck's appearance. Coating your deck periodically with a water-repellent wood preservative will prevent water absorption and so reduce the swelling and contracting that lead to cracking, splintering, and warping.

Ground-level deck with tub and integral raised bed

Pathway decks

Attached deck

Multilevel radial deck with tub

Garden deck with built-in seating

Freestanding deck

Cantilevered deck

Sheltering with screens & overheads

Screens and overheads can provide privacy and shelter, expand outdoor living spaces, and help connect those spaces to the other elements of the home and garden landscape. Moreover, they lend themselves to a multitude of styles and designs — some of the many possibilities are illustrated on the facing page.

Screens and overheads go hand-in-hand with other structural elements, such as patios, decks, swimming pools, tubs, and spas. You can plan for a screen or overhead when you're designing your landscaping scheme, or add one to an existing garden. The purpose your screen or overhead will serve largely determines where you place it and how you build it.

Screens

You can use almost any type of fence structure as a screen. But generally, screens are lighter in both appearance and weight than fences. Depending upon its size, scale, and location, a screen may require a building permit; when in doubt, always check with your building department. Most screens are designed to be permeable to some degree; this permits light and air to filter through.

A basic screen begins with the same horizontal and vertical framing used for a fence, but from there the design options multiply. The framing may hold panels of wood lath or louvers, acrylic, glass, or fiberglass; or it may support screening made of canvas, reed, bamboo, or even decorative rope work. The choice is yours, though you'll need to take into account the purpose of the screen.

Advantages. Imaginatively designed and thoughtfully placed, screens can successfully solve many outdoor-living problems.

Screens can create outdoor rooms by defining and separating different activity areas. Screens also can ensure privacy, provide protection from wind and sun, and create an illusion of quiet by visually blocking out sources of noise. An unattractive part of your yard, such as a service or storage area, can be successfully hidden by a screen. The screen itself can often become a decorative element in the landscape by serving as a backdrop or support for plants or art work.

Materials. Select the material for your screen according to your purpose: wood lath or reed screening to filter sun and wind; glass or acrylic for wind protection without loss of view; adjustable louvers or simple canvas shades for a flexible approach to climate control. For screens that will serve as supports for plants, choose lattice panels or trellises.

As with a fence, you'll want to use decay-resistant wood such as cedar, cypress, redwood, or pressure-treated lumber, especially for posts and other elements of the screen that will come in contact with the earth. Sometimes, a less durable material, such as reed screening, can be installed in a sturdy, permanent frame that allows you to change the screen panels as they wear out, maintaining a fresh look.

Overheads

When planning an overhead, you have many options, but your final design should be determined by the function you want the overhead to serve. Instructions for building a basic overhead—either freestanding or attached to your house—begin on page 160. For a complete description of overheads, see the *Sunset* book *How to Build Patio Roofs.*

Advantages. An overhead structure that's well designed and carefully sited can add immeasurably to your pleasure outside. Use an overhead for privacy, for shade where and when you want it, and for protection from wind and rain. An overhead can also become a design element in your landscape by enclosing an otherwise indeterminate space. You can also design an overhead to support a vine, thereby creating an arbor as shown in one of the drawings on the facing page.

Design and construction. An overhead can have an open design that filters sun, wind, and view, or it may have a solid roof for rain and wind protection or for greater privacy. The same frame can be roofed with a variety of materials: wood lath or lumber, reed mats, acrylic or glass panels, canvas, or shade cloth. Be sure that the roofing you choose will create the environment you want.

The entire structure may be freestanding — over all or part of a detached patio, for example—or it can be attached to your house (the easier type to build). A simple rectangular design will provide a basic structure which can then be embellished as you wish.

With few exceptions, support for an overhead comes from a simple post and beam frame that can be easily built by a do-it-yourselfer. As with most outdoor structures, this frame should be built from sturdy, decay-resistant wood such as cedar, cypress, redwood, or pressure-treated lumber

Framing connections, which often determine the overall style of the overhead, can be made most easily by means of the many prefabricated metal connectors so widely available. For a traditional appearance, you can use more elaborate timber joinery.

Remember that if the roof is solid, it must be slightly pitched to allow water to run off. To permit easy clearance and avoid producing a closed-in feeling, make the overhead at least 8 feet high.

Before beginning any construction, be sure to have your plans approved by your building department; the overhead must conform with local regulations on size, location, design, and construction.

Lath screen and overhead

Reed screens

Glass or acrylic overhead

Sliding canvas overhead with roller shades

Arbor

Glass or acrylic wind screens

Stretched canvas overhead

Adjustable louvered overhead and screen

Planning for an outdoor room

The term "outdoor room" defies definition, simply because such structures are very diverse, as the drawings on the facing page show. A common idea unites them, however: they all add to the usefulness of your dwelling and may perform functions not possible within it.

Gazebos and garden pavilions stand apart from the house and may have open or closed roofs and full or partial walls. Enclosed patios are generally extensions of the house itself, and can be fully or partially enclosed. Greenhouses and bathroom-equipped pool pavilions almost qualify as separate houses of a sort; garden work centers, on the other hand, may not contain definable "rooms" at all.

Design considerations. Though it's generally best to coordinate the style and materials of an outdoor room with those of your house, there are situations where you can make an individual and quite different design statement with a detached structure that serves as a decorative focal point in your garden. For example, traditional gazebos, essentially Victorian in character, complement a variety of landscapes.

Providing comfort in an outdoor room may call into play structural elements discussed elsewhere in this chapter. Access will likely involve walks and perhaps steps; the paving or decking must be appropriate for the room's use; sun or wind may have to be controlled by screens or overheads.

Depending on the scope of the project (and your skill), an outdoor room may require professional assistance. You should always have local building officials check your plans to be sure they conform to code requirements. You'll probably need a building permit as well.

Gazebos and pavilions. These are the most flexible outdoor rooms: their structure can be substantial or quite light (lattice and lath are popular materials), and their style can vary from strikingly modern to thoroughly traditional. Their function is to provide at least some shelter while offering contact with the outdoors.

Usually, you'll want an unobstructed paved or decked floor, suitable for everything from solitary reading and letterwriting to a vigorous game of ping-pong. It's also possible to build in such amenities as sinks, barbecues, and spas.

A pool pavilion or house can be simply a place to change in privacy and hang up wet towels and bathing suits. Or it can be a shade more elaborate and include a shower and lavatory. Of course, some pool pavilions are a lot more elaborate and are designed as warm-weather retreats complete with sauna, living and sleeping areas, and storage space.

Whatever its use, a gazebo or pavilion should be carefully sited, since it will inevitably draw the eye. Design it for comfort and provide an easy and inviting pathway to it.

Enclosed patios. If you're planning just a simple patio, consider enclosing all or part of it. Compared with the cost of a conventional room addition, an enclosed patio can be very economical and serve almost the same function. And if the patio already exists, you're way ahead of the game.

Patios on the sunny side of the house usually require an overhead of some sort — sometimes just a lath or lattice screen, sometimes a weatherproof roof. If the roof is weatherproof, adding fixed or movable walls converts the patio into a full-fledged room.

The example on the facing page shows bifold glass doors enclosing a roofed corner of a large patio. Such a design has year-round functions, providing shelter from wind and rain and from extremes of temperature. It also extends outdoor living well into the evening, and buffers the house from heat and cold. Indeed, if its solar orientation is favorable, you may find that the enclosed patio brings with it a noticeable energy benefit.

Greenhouses and garden work centers. Though both have gardening functions, these two variations on the outdoor room are fundamentally different. A greenhouse is a room with a garden inside; a garden work center is a "room" inside a garden. Both provide shelves and storage for planting materials and a place for the gardener to work.

Greenhouses are specialized structures. If you're planning to include one in your landscape, here are some points to note. Both freestanding and attached (lean-to) greenhouses are widely available in kit form; you can also purchase plans and build one yourself. Either route is preferable to simply striking off on your own, since designing a greenhouse in which plants will thrive requires technical knowledge.

At this stage, you'll also want to consider siting. The amount of sunlight the greenhouse will receive in the different seasons of the year may be critical. If you want to include running water, electricity, and heat inside the greenhouse, you'll need to plan for plumbing and electrical connections. For a complete discussion of greenhouses, see the Sunset book *Greenhouse Gardening*.

A garden work center can be quite simple, perhaps just a collection of potting benches, shelves, and storage bins under a shade structure (see the facing page). The design can range from purely functional to quite fanciful, depending on the location of the structure in your landscape.

Whether you're adding a full-function greenhouse or just the simplest of garden work centers, try to site it so it will be easy to transfer gardening supplies from car or truck to the structure.

Attached greenhouse

Contemporary gazebo

Garden pavilion

Enclosed patio room

Traditional gazebo

Pool pavilion with dressing rooms

Garden work center

Adding a garden pool

Including a pool or fountain in a garden is a practice almost as old as gardening itself. Early depictions of gardens from ancient civilizations show pools, fountains, and rivulets in spaces shared by plants and people.

Always consider a garden pool as part of your total landscape. The following discussion will help you plan its location, style, and construction. Directions for building two types of garden pools appear on pages 168–169. Keep in mind that harmony and appropriateness are the keys to the difference between a landscaping jewel and an awkward eyesore.

Pool siting & design

You'll need to consider site, size, shape, and style in planning for a garden pool.

Pool location. Finding the right location for a pool is not always simple. Consider whether you want it front and center, hidden away in an alcove, or adjacent to the house so it can be viewed from within. Remember that drainage considerations may restrict your choice of location.

If you want fish and plants in your pool, you'll need to plan for sun. Water lilies, for example, require a minimum of 4 to 6 hours of sun a day; more is desirable. On the other hand, too much sun can lead to algae problems.

Pool style. Pools can be grouped into three broad styles: informal, formal, and natural. Informal pools include those made from "found" objects such as barrels and tanks, and custom-built geometric or abstract shapes.

Formal pools look best when set in formally landscaped areas. Shapes tend to be symmetrical and classically derived. Fountains and sculpture are characteristic accessories; brick, stone, and smooth concrete are typical materials.

Natural pools usually have no square corners, perpendicular walls, or manmade edges—or at least appear that way. Achieving this look can be quite a challenge. The use of native stone, soil, and plants, as in carefully designed oriental pools, can reinforce the impression that the pool has always been there. A freeform concrete shell is the typical base.

Plants. Garden pools open up a new gardening world — that of water plants. Three kinds of water plants thrive in pools: those with roots in soil, such as water lilies; floating plants, such as water hyacinth, with roots that dangle in the water; and oxygenating plants, which are completely submerged. Within the pool, movable boxes make it easy to control soil depth.

Fish. Fish species popular in garden pools include ordinary goldfish and their fancy Japanese relatives, koi. Mosquito fish, named for their favorite food, are worth including in most pools. You'll need to plan for fish at the beginning. Koi, for example, require a pool at least 18 inches deep and 10 feet across. Though goldfish will tolerate shallower, smaller pools, there's danger from predators in shallow pools.

Water plants or a circulating pump—or both—will ensure proper oxygenation of the water, and snails help keep algae at bay. Fish will winter over if the pool doesn't freeze solid.

Plumbing. A small, shallow pool can be filled by a hose and emptied by siphoning or bailing. As size and depth increase, however, so does the need for plumbing.

The most basic plumbing feature is a drain. Plan on connecting it to a channel of drain tiles or to your house drainage system. An overflow pipe in the pool can prevent flooding. Around the pool, a gravel-filled trench helps carry away surface water, and a raised lip keeps runoff out of the pool.

A simple submersible, recirculating pump is a worthwhile addition. Concealed underwater, a pump can power a filter system, aerate the water, or supply a stream, fall, or fountain. You'll need to have plug-in access to a 120-volt circuit for such a pump.

Pool ecology. Perfectly clear water in a garden pool is unnatural. On the other hand, a pool choked with algae is hardly desirable. A natural balance is the goal. In a well-balanced pool, fish take in oxygen and expel carbon dioxide; plants use the carbon dioxide and release oxygen.

There are no rules that will apply to all pools for achieving this balance. In general, oxygenating plants are healthful for fish and compete with algae for sunlight. Snails eat algae, but too many may attack your plants. A pump and filter can help keep water clean and oxygenated, but many pools can achieve a good balance without them.

Materials

Brick, block, and poured concrete are the traditional pool builder's materials. At the design stage, keep in mind some general points.

Brick and block. Bricks make a lovely material for pool copings, but require careful waterproofing when used for walls. Concrete blocks are somewhat easier to use, since their larger size and hollow cores make for fewer mortar joints and easier reinforcing.

Poured concrete. Where possible, opt for a concrete shell; you can always dress it up with stone, tile, or brick trim. Poured concrete is the most plastic and impermeable material available for pools, and what it lacks in looks can often be disguised. A stiff concrete mix can be placed in freeform excavations with wall angles exceeding 45°. Vertical walls require carpentered forms.

Wood and vinyl. You can build inground pools of decay-resistant wood or even of heavy PVC sheet laid on a sand bed. Though such pools may last for years, they're best thought of as temporary. But they do enable you to experiment with the pool's location before you commit yourself to immovable concrete.

Rustic garden pool

Oriental pool with bridge

"Natural" freeform pool

Contemporary raised pool

Pool with stream and waterfall

Wall-mounted spill fountain with pool

Barrel fountain

Formal pool

Including a hot tub or spa

A common feature in many gardens, hot tubs and spas have understandable appeal: an invigorating bath alfresco, usually enlivened by venturi jets, all in a vessel large enough to accommodate both social and solitary soaks with equal aplomb.

Once you've decided to add a tub or spa, you're faced with numerous choices and design decisions. Use the discussion that follows — and the illustrations on the facing page — to guide you in the planning process. For more details on landscaping and design, as well as tips on finding a contractor and shopping for a tub or spa, consult the *Sunset* book *Ideas for Hot Tubs, Spas & Home Saunas.*

Hot tub or spa?

Tubs and spas differ principally in material and form, not function. Hot tubs are made of wood in the manner of large, usually straight-sided barrels. With a proper foundation, tubs are self-supporting, which usually makes them easier and less expensive to install than spas. Tubs must be sited so that air circulates around their sides and bottom; this retards the decay to which all wood is prone.

Spas, on the other hand, are usually made of fiberglass or acrylic, or are custom-built of concrete. These materials generally require less maintenance than the wood used in tubs. The molding techniques used to manufacture spas make possible nearly every conceivable shape — and such amenities as contoured built-in seats and changes in depth. Though spas are rigid, they are not self-supporting, and so must be set in sand which is, in turn, held in place by stable earth or rigid retaining walls. Custom-built concrete spas are usually included as adjuncts to swimming pools, and are built at the same time as the pool.

Tubs are easy to install above grade; often a deck is added at or just below the edge of the tub for lounging. Spas are most easily installed below grade, which makes them suitable for patios and terraces. Above grade, spas must be surrounded by retaining walls to contain the supporting sand.

Either a tub or a spa may be installed on a ledge cut into a hillside. In each case, a retaining wall will be needed: on the uphill side for the tub, on the downhill side for the spa (see the drawings below).

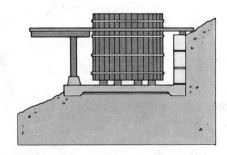

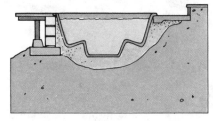

Hillside installations: top, wooden tub with upslope retaining wall; bottom, fiberglass spa with downslope retaining wall.

Choosing the best site

A number of practical considerations enter into your choice of site. You'll need to acquaint yourself with all the code regulations pertaining to tubs and spas. Also, be sure to take into account the microclimate of your property, access from the house, privacy, utility connections, and equipment locations.

Legal requirements. Like a swimming pool, a tub or spa is regarded under law as an attractive nuisance. Be sure to consult local zoning codes regarding covers, fencing requirements, setback limits, and other rules. You will also need a building permit.

Climate considerations. You're probably already familiar with sun and wind patterns in your yard, but now is a good time to take a careful look. Try to anticipate when you're likely to use the tub or spa; then find one or more sites where sun and wind will be to your liking at that time of day. If you

live in a desert region, the shady north side of your house may make a good site, but the sunny south side is usually better in other areas.

At this point, you can begin to consider overheads and screens, too (see pages 68–69). You may want to add an overhead as part of a decking project.

Access and privacy. Give some attention to access and privacy. If the tub or spa will be the hub of social gatherings, or if you plan to use it at night before retiring, you'll probably want to locate it near or on a patio or deck attached to the house. On the other hand, if you want seclusion or a second social area, consider a site away from the house — perhaps an odd, unused corner of your lot.

Regardless of where the tub or spa is located with respect to the house, you'll need to provide a way of getting there that's comfortable even for bare feet. You'll probably want a paved walk from the house, and a deck or patio paving around the tub or spa itself.

Privacy may be a very important factor. You'll probably feel more comfortable in a tub or spa if you're well screened from neighbors' windows and from passersby. Screens and overheads — even outdoor rooms (see pages 70–71) — are often pressed into service to provide the necessary privacy.

Equipment and utilities. Siting is to some extent governed by plumbing. Heaters, pumps, and filters are compact, but they do take up space and require connections to electrical and gas lines. The expense of running these lines to the tub or spa may also limit your choice of location. If you're using solar heating panels, you'll need to find a place for them, usually on the roof; this may dictate a site near the house.

Freeform spa

Freestanding tub

Enclosed spa

Raised poolside spa

Tub set in hillside deck

Spa set in tiled patio

Planning for a swimming pool

Few other elements in your landscape can satisfy as many needs as a swimming pool, whether you're seeking recreation for your family, an area for exercise, a focal point for entertaining, or some combination of these. As a glance at the pools on the facing page shows, you can design and construct a pool to fit almost any life style.

Whether you're thinking about an in-ground pool that will be a permanent part of your landscape, or a temporary aboveground model, careful planning is essential. You'll almost certainly need to deal with one or more professionals—architects, landscape architects and designers, soils and structural engineers, and contractors. You'll be able to communicate your desires more easily if you know about the types of pools available and study possible pool sites on your property.

Before you commit yourself to building a pool, it's important to look into the myriad of legal requirements set forth in deed restrictions, zoning laws, and building, health, and safety codes. Also familiarize yourself with the codes that apply to associated structures such as decks, fences, and overheads. For a complete discussion of pools, see the Sunset book *Ideas for Swimming Pools.*

Which pool for you?

Though budget considerations may make many decisions for you, you still have to decide what size and shape pool best fits your needs and what construction and materials will work best for you.

Size and shape. The architectural axiom that form follows function applies here. Children generally need a wide, shallow area; lap swimmers a long, straight section; and divers a section that's long, wide, and deep. For a full range of activities, most experts agree on dimensions of at least 16 by 32 feet, with a deep end for diving.

In many cases, less may be more. Except for diving, a pool need not be deeper than 4 to 6 feet. For lap swimming, one long axis will suffice. Such

size reductions save not only building costs, but also energy and maintenance expenses later on.

Traditional rectangular and kidney-shaped pools have given way in recent years to new design approaches. Naturalistic pools are probably the most difficult to bring off well; simpler forms derived from geometric shapes can be effective.

Whatever shape or size you choose, consider it part of your overall landscape design. And be sure to plan for a paved area or deck surrounding or adjoining the pool. As a general rule of thumb, the poolside area should be at least equal to the area of the pool itself.

Construction and materials. Pools can be built completely or partially in-ground, or be placed entirely aboveground. Fully in-ground pools are the most accessible from patio areas and the most adaptable to unified landscape schemes, but both aboveground and partially in-ground pools can also be well integrated.

Concrete, either sprayed or troweled, combines workability, strength, permanence, and flexibility of design and application; for these reasons it's often the preferred material. Concrete is always reinforced with steel. Interior finishes include plaster, paint, and tile.

Vinyl-lined pools are usually less expensive than concrete, partly because of the prefabricated liner, and partly because they can be installed very quickly. The liner, generally resting on a bed of sand, is supported by walls made of aluminum, steel, plastic, masonry block, or wood. These walls can extend above grade.

Fiberglass pools consist of one-piece rigid fiberglass shells that are placed on sand beds in excavations which are then backfilled with more sand. These pools also offer speed of installation; choice of shape, however, is usually limited.

Portable pools include the familiar aboveground, vinyl-lined pool, and such "found objects" as vats and tanks. Since no excavation is required, do-it-yourself installation is a real possibility, and substantial cost savings

are virtually the rule when compared with in-ground pools.

Siting your pool

Though you may think you have little choice in siting your pool, especially if your lot is small, you'll derive maximum pleasure from the pool by choosing its exact location very carefully. Here are some points to consider.

Climate and microclimate. In thinking about where to place your pool, keep user comfort foremost in mind. Know your area's climate and the specific microclimate of your property during the seasons of anticipated pool use. You'll need to study the sunlight patterns throughout the swimming season.

Wind can limit pool enjoyment. If regular wind patterns affect your area, look for a spot protected from those winds. If your property offers no such area, plan on adding strategically placed plantings, fencing, or screening to shield swimmers.

Access and privacy. Though the pool doesn't have to be adjacent to your house, access to a changing room and bathroom should be by a direct walk on a comfortable surface. If you're planning to use the pool for entertaining, you'll want it convenient to reach even at night.

Because of the pool's size, you may not be able to make it completely private; but in general, the more secluded it is from neighbors and passersby, the more comfortable you'll be.

Topography. Though you can install a pool on a hillside if you use retaining walls, installation is much simpler and less costly on level ground. Study soil conditions and drainage patterns, too. Parts of your property will be better suited to a pool than others.

Formal pool with integrated patio

Lap pool with spa

Prefabricated above-ground pool

Wooden tank

Freeform pool with waterfall and spa

Ornamental pool

Lighting up your garden

Outdoor lighting serves three general purposes: safety, security, and decoration. Outdoor areas — particularly stairways and hillsides — that may be treacherous after night falls can be made safer by the simple flick of a switch.

Darkness holds its dangers, sometimes imagined, sometimes real. Vulnerable locations include entries, garage doors, curbside areas, and windows out of view from street or yard. Lighting at these points provides a sense of security and can discourage intruders.

Beyond purely practical considerations, garden lighting allows you to create many decorative effects after dark, just by virtue of the patterns of light and shadow produced by night lighting.

To design an outdoor lighting scheme that meets your needs, determine the lighting effect you want in each area of your garden (see below and on the facing page). Information to help you choose between a 12 and 120-volt system follows.

Lighting effects at night

With artificial lighting you have an advantage over daylight — you can control the source of the light. Understanding the effects you can attain will help you decide what kind of lights to use and where to place them.

Before you buy anything, test out your ideas. Use a large flashlight or a bulb and reflector on a long extension cord to go "prospecting" for lighting effects in your garden. Once you've completed your survey, you'll be better equipped to choose among the many fixtures available—or even make your own lighting fixtures.

Downlighting. With downlighting, the source of light is above the subject, just as it is with natural lighting. Lamps near ground level cast concentrated pools of light on steps and paths; tree-mounted lights can give a broad, ethereal moonlit effect.

Uplighting. Here, the light projects upward, causing foliage to glow. Try to position lights just above eye level; if they're mounted below this level, incline them away from the viewer. Uplighting produces intricate light and shadow effects when combined with downlighting.

Diffused lighting. Light filtered through translucent materials, such as plastic and canvas, is useful when you need glare-free illumination over a patio or other large area.

Accent lighting. Night lighting can be used in special ways to accentuate particular landscaping features. Spotlights can focus attention on a plant or sculpture. Grazing light directed along a wall creates visual interest by highlighting surface texture. Underwater lights illuminate garden pools. Strings of bud lights effectively outline step treads; used in a tree, they glitter through the branches. Silhouette lighting accents special plants.

Your lighting choices

Outdoor lighting systems are either 120 volt or 12 volt (low voltage). The equipment available within each category is extensive, and if nothing suits, you can often make your own fixtures from readily available components.

120-volt lighting. You can extend your household electrical circuits into the garden to power a variety of fixtures. You'll need to calculate in advance to see if a given circuit can handle the extra load. As a general rule, a 15-amp, 120-volt circuit can handle up to 1440 watts. From this number, subtract the wattage of fixtures already served by the circuit to get the total wattage you can add.

A 120-volt system is your best choice for situations requiring brilliant illumination, and you can plug power tools and other equipment into the system. But check with your building department before beginning work; codes may require installation by a licensed electrician.

12-volt lighting. Installing low-voltage lighting is easy: you just mount a plug-in transformer outdoors and run two-wire outdoor cable on or in the ground, adding fixtures as you go. Some of the most popular fixtures are illustrated below; for installation instructions, see page 167.

Wide variety and easy installation make 12-volt fixtures popular.

If simplicity is a strong point, limited light production is a weak one. Where you want soft lighting and illumination of smaller areas, a low-voltage system can do the job. Be sure to take your plot plan with you when you buy your equipment so you can accurately estimate the length of wiring runs and the number and size of fixtures and transformers needed.

Uplighting

Accent lighting

Walkway lighting

Downlighting

Backlighting

Diffused lighting

SELECTING THE PLANTS

The effectiveness of any landscape plan depends upon its overall design. Once a design is established, you'll need to select appropriate plants for each area. In this chapter you'll find descriptions of over 200 attractive, dependable and popular trees, shrubs, vines, and ground covers. Two special features, pages 108–109 and 122–123, highlight the landscape roles of fruiting shrubs and trees, and annuals and perennials.

Pages 81–95 contain lists of plants grouped by similar characteristics. Each list gives the botanical names of the plants and the USDA climate zones (see page 96) in which the plants will grow. The lists also chart other helpful information such as season of bloom, growth rate, plant height, or whether plants are deciduous or evergreen.

A plant encyclopedia follows on pages 97–127; it's divided into subchapters—Trees, Shrubs, Vines, and Ground Covers—for easy comparative reference. The descriptions focus on the landscape virtues (and shortcomings, if any) of the plants rather than on their cultural needs.

With this chapter, gardeners from Vancouver to Baltimore, Calgary to Corpus Christi will be able to select appropriate plants to develop gardens that provide lifetime satisfaction.

Vines with showy flowers

In their humblest duty, vines simply hide flaws under a blanket of foliage. But vines can be elevated to greater glory—even becoming work-of-art focal points—through careful training on walls, fences, trellises, pergolas, and house eaves. And what better way to heighten the appeal of such living artwork than with a seasonal show of flowers?

Clematis lawsoniana 'Henryi'

Lonicera japonica 'Halliana'

Bougainvillea 'San Diego Red'

NAME OF PLANT	CLIMATE ZONES	DECIDUOUS	EVERGREEN	SELF-CLINGING	NAME OF PLANT	CLIMATE ZONES	DECIDUOUS	EVERGREEN	SELF-CLINGING
Beaumontia grandiflora	10		●	● (partly)	Passiflora	Varies		●	●
Bougainvillea	9–10		●		Polygonum aubertii	9–10	●	●	●
Campsis	Varies	●	●	●	Solandra maxima	9–10		●	●
Clematis	Varies	●	●	●	Solanum jasminoides	9–10	●	●	●
Gelsemium sempervirens	8–10		●	●	Tecomaria capensis	8–10		●	●
Hydrangea anomala	4–9	●		●	Trachelospermum jasminoides	9–10		●	●
Jasminum	Varies	●	●	● (some)	Wisteria	4–10	●		●
Lonicera	Varies	●	●	●					

Climate zone map is on page 96. Descriptions of plants listed in chart are on pages 120–121.

Flowering shrubs

Flowering shrubs provide the back-
bone for gardens that are designed to
be colorful. By carefully choosing
shrubs according to their bloom season, you can supply plenty of garden
color throughout the growing season.
The shrubs listed below are popular,
widely available, and consistent
performers.

Chaenomeles 'Coral Sea'

Hydrangea macrophylla

NAME OF PLANT	CLIMATE ZONES	SPRING	SUMMER	AUTUMN-WINTER
Deciduous				
Azalea	Varies	●		
Berberis (some)	Varies	●		
Buddleia	5–9	●	●	
Chaenomeles	4–9	●		
Cornus	Varies	●		
Cotinus coggygria	5–10		●	
Cotoneaster (some)	Varies	●		
Cytisus	Varies	●		
Daphne (some)	Varies	Varies		
Deutzia	Varies	●		
Enkianthus	5–9	●		
Forsythia	Varies	●		
Genista	Varies	●	●	
Hibiscus (some)	Varies		●	
Hydrangea	Varies		●	●
Jasminum nudiflorum	6–9	●		●
Kolkwitzia amabilis	5–9	●		

NAME OF PLANT	CLIMATE ZONES	SPRING	SUMMER	AUTUMN-WINTER
Lagerstroemia indica	7–9		●	
Ligustrum (some)	Varies	●	●	
Lonicera (some)	Varies	●	●	
Philadelphus	Varies	●		
Photinia villosa	5–8	●		
Prunus	Varies	●		
Punica granatum	9–10		●	
Rhododendron (some)	Varies	●		
Rosa	Varies	●	●	●
Salix purpurea 'Gracilis'	5–9	●		
Spiraea	Varies	●	●	
Syringa	Varies	●		
Viburnum (some)	Varies	Varies		
Weigela	5–9	●		
Evergreen				
Abelia	6–10		●	●
Arbutus unedo	8–10			●

Climate zone map is on page 96. Descriptions of plants listed in chart are on pages 110–119.

Rhododendron 'Anna Rose Whitney'

Forsythia intermedia

Azalea hybrids

NAME OF PLANT	CLIMATE ZONES	SPRING	SUMMER	AUTUMN-WINTER
Evergreen (cont'd.)				
Azalea	Varies	●		
Berberis (some)	Varies	●		
Callistemon	9–10	Varies		
Calluna vulgaris	4–9		●	●
Camellia	8–10			●
Carissa grandiflora	10	●	●	●
Cistus	8–10	●	●	
Cotoneaster (some)	Varies	●		
Cytisus	Varies	●		
Daphne (some)	Varies	●		
Erica	Varies	Varies		
Escallonia	8–10		●	●
Feijoa sellowiana	9–10	●		●
Fuchsia	8–10	●	●	●
Gardenia	9–10	Varies		
Hebe	Varies	Varies		
Hibiscus rosa-sinensis	10		●	
Ixora coccinea	10	●	●	●
Jasminum (some)	Varies	Varies		

NAME OF PLANT	CLIMATE ZONES	SPRING	SUMMER	AUTUMN-WINTER
Kalmia latifolia	4–9	●		
Leptospermum	9–10	●	●	
Leucothoe (some)	5–9	●		
Ligustrum (some)	Varies	●	●	
Lonicera (some)	Varies	●	●	
Mahonia	Varies	●		
Melaleuca	9–10	Varies		
Myrtus communis	9–10		●	
Nandina domestica	7–10	●	●	
Nerium oleander	9–10	●	●	●
Photinia (some)	Varies	●		
Pieris	Varies	●		
Pittosporum tobira	8–10	●		
Plumbago auriculata	9–10	●	●	●
Prunus (some)	Varies	●		
Pyracantha	6–10	●		
Raphiolepis	8–10	●		●
Rhododendron (many)	Varies	●		
Rosmarinus officinalis	7–10	●		●
Viburnum (many)	Varies	Varies		

Flowering trees

Some trees give you more than just a canopy of foliage. Here's a selection of trees from small to large that offer something extra: some have branches smothered with flowers before their leaves emerge; others display their blossoms against a foliaged back-drop. The seasons of bloom indicated below are general. Where more than one season is shown, it usually means that the bloom season depends on the species or variety.

Magnolia grandiflora

Prunus yedoensis 'Akebono'

NAME OF PLANT	CLIMATE ZONES	SPRING	SUMMER	AUTUMN-WINTER
Deciduous				
Aesculus carnea	5–9	●		
Albizia julibrissin	5–10		●	
Amelanchier	Varies	●		
Bauhinia	9–10	●	●	●
Cassia fistula	10	●		
Catalpa	4–10	●	●	
Cercis canadensis	4–9	●		
Chionanthus	Varies	●	●	
Cladrastis lutea	4–9	●		
Cornus	Varies	●		
Crataegus	Varies	●		
Delonix regia	10	●	●	
Erythrina	9–10	●	●	●
Halesia	5–9	●		
Jacaranda mimosifolia	9–10	●	●	
Koelreuteria	Varies		●	
Laburnum	5–9	●		
Lagerstroemia indica	7–9		●	
Liriodendron tulipifera	4–9	●		
Magnolia	Varies	●	●	
Malus	Varies	●		
Melia azedarach	7–10	●	●	

NAME OF PLANT	CLIMATE ZONES	SPRING	SUMMER	AUTUMN-WINTER
Oxydendrum arboreum	5–9		●	
Parkinsonia aculeata	8–10	●	●	●
Paulownia tomentosa	5–10	●		
Prunus	Varies	●		
Pyrus	Varies	●		
Robinia	Varies	●	●	
Sophora japonica	5–10	●	●	
Sorbus aucuparia	3–9	●		
Styrax	Varies	●		
Evergreen				
Acacia	9–10	●		●
*Arbutus unedo	8–10			●
Callistemon	9–10	Varies		
Citrus	9–10	Varies		
Eucalyptus (some)	Varies	Varies		
Magnolia grandiflora	8–10	●	●	●
Melaleuca	9–10	Varies		
Pittosporum	9–10	●		
Prunus	Varies	●		
Pyrus kawakamii	8–10	●		●

*For plant description, see Shrubs, pages 110–119.

Climate zone map is on page 96. Descriptions of plants listed in chart are on pages 97–107.

Flowering ground covers

Some landscape situations call for a ground cover that's unobtrusive, neat, and unchanging. Other garden areas need to be perked up by a seasonal show of color from a living carpet. Some of the ground covers listed below blaze with color during their seasons; others merely sparkle with it here and there among their greenery.

Cotoneaster congestus

Achillea tomentosa

Ajuga reptans

Hypericum calycinum

NAME OF PLANT	CLIMATE ZONES	SPRING	SUMMER	AUTUMN-WINTER
Achillea tomentosa	4–10		●	
Ajuga reptans	4–10	●	●	
Arctostaphylos uva-ursi	3–10	●	●	
Arctotheca calendula	9–10	●		
Carissa grandiflora	10	●	●	●
Ceanothus	8–10	●		
Ceratostigma plumbaginoides	6–10		●	●
Chamaemelum nobile	3–10		●	
Cistus salviifolius	8–10	●		
Cotoneaster	Varies	●		
Duchesnea indica	3–10	●		
Erigeron karvinskianus	9–10	●	●	●
Fragaria chiloensis	5–10	●		
Galium odoratum	5–10	●	●	
Gazania	9–10	●	●	

NAME OF PLANT	CLIMATE ZONES	SPRING	SUMMER	AUTUMN-WINTER
Hypericum calycinum	6–10		●	
Iberis sempervirens	4–10	●		
Lantana montevidensis	9–10	●	●	●
Liriope spicata	4–10		●	
Mahonia aquifolium	5–10	●		
Ophiopogon japonicus	8–10		●	
Osteospermum	9–10	●	●	
Pelargonium peltatum	10	●	●	●
Polygonum capitatum	7–10	●	●	●
Potentilla tabernaemontanii	4–9	●	●	
Pyracantha	7–10	●		
Rosmarinus officinalis 'Prostratus'	7–10	●		
Santolina	7–10		●	
Teucrium chamaedrys	6–10		●	
Vinca	Varies	●		

Climate zone map is on page 96. Descriptions of plants listed in chart are on pages 124–127.

For colorful fruit

The fruit of some plants is more colorful and showy than their flowers. With hollies, for example, you would scarcely be aware of flowers except for the berries that follow. Some plants with showy fruit or berries give you a bonus: edible produce. For instance, oranges and persimmons are tasty products of highly ornamental garden trees.

Nandina domestica

Ilex aquifolium

Pyracantha

NAME OF PLANT	CLIMATE ZONES	SPRING	SUMMER	AUTUMN-WINTER
Trees				
Citrus	9–10	Varies		
Cornus florida	5–9			●
Crataegus	Varies		●	●
Diospyros	Varies			●
Ilex	Varies			●
Koelreuteria	Varies			●
Malus	Varies		●	●
Melia azedarach	7–10			●
Pistacia chinensis	6–10			●
Pittosporum rhombifolium	9–10			●
Schinus	9–10			●
Sorbus aucuparia	3–9		●	●
Shrubs				
Arbutus unedo	8–10			●
Berberis (many)	Varies			●
Carissa grandiflora	10	Varies		
Cornus mas	4–8			●
Cotoneaster	Varies			●
Elaeagnus	Varies			●
Euonymus (many)	Varies			●
Ilex	Varies			●
Kolkwitzia amabilis	5–9		●	●

NAME OF PLANT	CLIMATE ZONES	SPRING	SUMMER	AUTUMN-WINTER
Shrubs (cont'd.)				
Lonicera (most)	Varies			●
Mahonia	Varies		●	●
Myrtus communis	9–10			●
Nandina domestica	7–10			●
Photinia	Varies			●
Punica granatum	9–10			●
Pyracantha	6–10			●
Raphiolepis	8–10		●	●
Rosa	Varies			●
Taxus	Varies			●
Viburnum (many)	Varies	Varies		●
Vines				
Akebia quinata	4–10		●	●
Ampelopsis brevipedunculata	4–10		●	●
Celastrus scandens	3–8			●
Euonymus fortunei	5–10			●
Ground Covers				
Carissa grandiflora	10	Varies		
Cotoneaster	Varies			●
Mahonia aquifolium	5–10		●	●
Pyracantha	7–10			●

Climate zone map is on page 96. Descriptions of plants listed in chart are on pages 97–127.

For striking foliage colors

Not all garden color comes from seasonal flowers, fruit, or foliage changes. Many plants boast colorful foliage the entire time they're in leaf. Some manage to be assertively different from the green of most plants, flaunting bronze purple, brilliant yellow, or steely blue color. Others are more low-key in soft gray, blue green, or variegated with cream or white. The plants listed below will give these long-term color accents among plainer green-leafed shrubs and trees. You can also use them with one another and with flowering and fruiting plants to achieve pleasing color combinations. Some individuals can be planted in groups, as in hedge, for striking mass color effect.

Pittosporum tobira 'Variegata'

Prunus cerasifera 'Krauter Vesuvius'

NAME OF PLANT	CLIMATE ZONES	GRAY	BLUE	RED	YELLOW	VARIEGATED
Trees						
Abies concolor (some)	4–8	•				
Acacia baileyana	9–10	•				
Acer palmatum (some)	6–9			•		•
Acer platanoides (some)	4–9			•		
Catalpa erubescens 'Purpurea'	4–10			•		
Cedrus deodara 'Aurea'	7–10				•	
Cercis canadensis 'Forest Pansy'	4–9			•		
Chamaecyparis lawsoniana (some)	6–9		•		•	
Cornus florida (some)	5–9					•
Cupressus sempervirens (some)	8–10		•			
Elaeagnus angustifolia	3–9	•				
Fagus sylvatica (some)	4–10			•		•
Gleditsia triacanthos inermis 'Sunburst'	4–9				•	
Ilex aquifolium (some)	7–10					•
Juniperus (some)	Varies	•	•			
Malus (some)	Varies			•		
Picea pungens (some)	3–8		•			
Pinus sylvestris (some)	3–8		•			
Prunus blireiana (some)	6–9			•		
Prunus cerasifera (some)	5–9			•		
Robinia pseudoacacia 'Frisia'	4–9				•	
Thuja plicata 'Aurea'	6–9				•	
Shrubs						
Aucuba japonica (several varieties)	7–10					•
Buxus sempervirens 'Aureo-Variegata'	5–10					•
Chamaecyparis lawsoniana (some)	6–9		•		•	

NAME OF PLANT	CLIMATE ZONES	GRAY	BLUE	RED	YELLOW	VARIEGATED
Shrubs (cont'd.)						
Chamaecyparis pisifera (some)	4–9		•		•	
Cistus (several)	8–10	•				
Codiaeum variegatum	10					•
Cornus alba (some)	2–9					•
Cotinus coggygria	5–10				•	
Dodonaea viscosa (some)	9–10				•	
Elaeagnus 'Coral Silver'	4–10	•				
Elaeagnus pungens (some)	7–10					•
Euonymus (some)	Varies					•
Hydrangea macrophylla 'Tricolor'	6-10					•
Ilex aquifolium (some)	7–10					•
Juniperus (some)	Varies	•	•		•	•
Leucothoe fontanesiana 'Rainbow'	5–9					•
Ligustrum ovalifolium 'Aureum'	6–10					•
Ligustrum 'Vicaryi'	4–10					•
Myrtus communis (some)	9–10					•
Osmanthus heterophyllus 'Variegatus'	7–10					•
Pieris japonica 'Variegata'	5–9					•
Pittosporum tobira 'Variegata'	8–10					•
Prunus cistena	4–9			•		
Rhamnus alaternus 'Variegata'	7–10					•
Taxus baccata (some)	6–9				•	•
Thuja occidentalis 'Rheingold'	2–10				•	
Viburnum tinus 'Variegatum'	7–10					•
Weigela florida 'Variegata'	5–9					•

Climate zone map is on page 96. Descriptions of plants listed in chart are on pages 97–107 and 110–119.

Trees & shrubs for hedges & screens

Some landscape situations demand a hedge planting—whether to screen for privacy, to shut out an objectionable view, or simply to direct foot traffic. In any case, you'll want to use plants that have dense foliage from the ground up, such as those listed below.

Buxus microphylla

Buxus sempervirens

NAME OF PLANT	CLIMATE ZONES	SHORT	MEDIUM	TALL
Deciduous				
Acer campestre	5–8			●
Berberis (some)	Varies	●	●	
Carpinus betulus	6–9			●
Cotoneaster (some)	Varies	●	●	
Elaeagnus (some)	Varies		●	●
Euonymus (some)	Varies	●	●	
Ilex (some)	Varies	●	●	●
Ligustrum (some)	Varies	●	●	●
Lonicera (some)	Varies	●	●	
Photinia villosa	5–8		●	●
Punica granatum (small and dwarf varieties)	9–10	●	●	
Rhamnus (some)	Varies	●	●	
Salix purpurea 'Gracilis'	5–9	●	●	
Viburnum (some)	Varies	●	●	●
Evergreen				
Abelia grandiflora	6–10		●	
Arbutus unedo	8–10		●	●
Bamboo (some)	Varies		●	●
Berberis (some)	Varies	●	●	
Buxus	Varies	●	●	
Callistemon citrinus, salignus	9–10			●
Camellia	8–10	●	●	●
Carissa grandiflora	10	●	●	
Chamaecyparis lawsoniana (some varieties)	6–9		●	●
Cotoneaster (some)	Varies	●	●	
Dodonaea viscosa	9–10		●	●
Elaeagnus (some)	Varies		●	●

NAME OF PLANT	CLIMATE ZONES	SHORT	MEDIUM	TALL
Evergreen (cont'd.)				
Escallonia	8–10		●	
Euonymus (some)	Varies	●	●	
Feijoa sellowiana	9–10		●	
Gardenia jasminoides	9–10	●	●	
Hebe buxifolia	9–10	●		
Hibiscus rosa-sinensis	10		●	
Ilex (some)	Varies	●	●	●
Ixora coccinea	10		●	
Juniperus	Varies	●	●	●
Laurus nobilis	8–10		●	●
Ligustrum (some)	Varies		●	●
Lonicera (some)	Varies		●	
Mahonia (several)	Varies	●	●	
Myrtus communis	9–10	●	●	
Nandina domestica	7–10		●	
Nerium oleander	9–10		●	●
Osmanthus	Varies		●	●
Photinia (some)	Varies		●	●
Pittosporum (several)	9–10		●	●
Prunus	Varies		●	●
Pyracantha	6–10	●	●	●
Raphiolepis	8–10	●	●	
Rhamnus (some)	Varies		●	●
Rosmarinus officinalis	7–10	●	●	
Taxus	Varies	●	●	●
Thuja	Varies	●	●	●
Tsuga (some)	Varies	●	●	●
Viburnum (some)	Varies	●	●	●
Xylosma congestum	9–10		●	●

Climate zone map is on page 96. Descriptions of plants listed in chart are on pages 97–107 and 110–119.

Trees for patios & gardens

Limited size plus good garden manners set these trees apart for use in patios and smaller gardens. These trees have root systems that won't buckle pavements or prevent other plants from growing beneath the trees. Good patio trees have a minimum of litter from leaves, fruits, or blossoms. They also grow slowly and don't need frequent corrective pruning. All possess beauty that bears close-up viewing.

Citrus limon 'Eureka'

Maytenus boaria

NAME OF PLANT	CLIMATE ZONES	FLOWERS	FRUIT	AUTUMN COLOR
Deciduous				
Acer (many)	Varies			•
Amelanchier	Varies	•		•
Bauhinia	9–10	•		
Betula	Varies		•	•
Cassia fistula	10	•		
Cercis canadensis	4–9	•		•
Chionanthus	Varies	•		•
Cladrastis lutea	4–9	•		•
Cornus (some)	Varies	•	•	•
Crataegus	Varies	•	•	•
Erythrina (some)	9–10	•		
Halesia	5–9	•	•	•
Koelreuteria paniculata	5–9	•	•	•
Laburnum	5–9	•	•	
Lagerstroemia indica	7–9	•		•
Magnolia	Varies	•		
Malus	Varies	•	•	•
Parkinsonia aculeata	8–10	•		
Prunus	Varies	•	•	•
Pyrus	Varies	•	•	•
*Rhus typhina	3–9	•	•	•

NAME OF PLANT	CLIMATE ZONES	FLOWERS	FRUIT	AUTUMN COLOR
Robinia (various)	Varies	•		•
Sapium sebiferum	8–10			•
Sorbus aucuparia	3–9	•	•	•
Styrax	Varies	•		•
Evergreen				
Acacia baileyana	9–10	•		
*Arbutus unedo	8–10	•	•	
Callistemon	9–10	•		
Citrus	9–10	•	•	
*Dodonaea viscosa	9–10	•		
Eriobotrya deflexa	9–10	•		
Ficus benjamina	10			
Ilex (many)	Varies		•	
Maytenus boaria	9–10			
Melaleuca	9–10	•		
Pittosporum (most)	9–10	•	•	
Pyrus kawakamii	8–10	•		
Schinus terebinthifolius	9–10		•	
*Xylosma congestum	9–10			

*For plant description, see Shrubs, pages 110–119.

Climate zone map is on page 96. Descriptions of plants listed in chart are on pages 97–107.

Large shade trees

These are the trees that poets praise: majestic, towering, spreading, venerable. Though at maturity they can elicit such words, in the home landscape they are more often praised for offering welcome shade in good quantity. On large properties, of course, you can plant them with an eye strictly for their poetic virtues.

Albizia julibrissin

Quercus phellos

NAME OF PLANT	CLIMATE ZONES	FAST	MEDIUM	SLOW
Deciduous				
Acer (many)	Varies	●	●	
Aesculus carnea	5–9		●	
Albizia julibrissin	5–10	●		
Carpinus caroliniana	3–9	●	●	
Carya illinoensis	5–9	●		
Catalpa speciosa	4–10	●		
Celtis	Varies		●	
Delonix regia	10	●		
Erythrina caffra	9–10	●	●	
Fagus	Varies			●
Fraxinus	Varies	●		
Ginkgo biloba	4–10			●
Gleditsia triacanthos inermis	4–9	●		
Jacaranda mimosifolia	9–10		●	
Juglans	Varies		●	
Koelreuteria bipinnata	8–10		●	
Liquidambar styraciflua	5–10	●		
Malus pumila	4–10		●	
Melia azedarach	7–10	●		
Morus alba	5–10	●		

NAME OF PLANT	CLIMATE ZONES	FAST	MEDIUM	SLOW
Parkinsonia aculeata	8–10	●		
Paulownia tomentosa	5–10	●		
Pistacia chinensis	6–10		●	
Platanus (several)	5–10	●		
Quercus (many)	Varies		●	
Salix (some)	Varies	●		
Sophora japonica	5–10		●	
Tilia	Varies			●
Ulmus	Varies	●		
Zelkova serrata	6–9		●	
Evergreen				
Cinnamomum camphora	9–10			●
Eriobotrya japonica	8–10		●	
Ficus (some)	Varies		●	
Fraxinus uhdei	9–10	●		
Magnolia grandiflora	7–10			●
Pinus (some)	Varies	●		
Pittosporum undulatum	9–10	●		
Prunus	Varies	●		
Quercus (many)	Varies		●	
Schinus molle	9–10	●		

Climate zone map is on page 96. Descriptions of plants listed in chart are on pages 97–107.

Plants for shaded gardens

Any garden is bound to have some shaded spots, whether from trees or because of the sun's position in the sky. Because not all plants thrive in the shade, some people consider shade areas to be a problem. This needn't be the case: the following list presents plants that actually prefer or require some shade.

Camellia japonica 'Kumasaka'

Hedera helix

NAME OF PLANT	CLIMATE ZONES	DECIDUOUS	EVERGREEN	FLOWERS
Trees				
Acer circinatum	5–9	●		
Acer palmatum	4–9	●		
Cornus	Varies	●		●
Ilex	Varies	●	●	
Vines				
Akebia quinata	4–10	●		●
Ampelopsis brevipedunculata	4–10	●		
Celastrus scandens	3–8	●		
Euonymus fortunei	5–10		●	
Hedera	Varies		●	
Hydrangea anomala	4–9	●		●
Lonicera japonica, sempervirens	Varies		●	●
Parthenocissus	Varies	●		
Trachelospermum jasminoides	9–10		●	●
Shrubs				
Arbutus unedo	8–10		●	●
Aucuba japonica	7–10		●	
Azalea	Varies	●	●	●
Buxus	Varies		●	
Camellia	8–10		●	●
Codiaeum variegatum	10		●	
Daphne odora	7–10		●	●
Enkianthus	5–9	●		●
Euonymus fortunei	5–10		●	
Fuchsia	8–10		●	●
Gardenia jasminoides	9–10		●	●

NAME OF PLANT	CLIMATE ZONES	DECIDUOUS	EVERGREEN	FLOWERS
Shrubs (cont'd.)				
Hydrangea	Varies	●		●
Ilex	Varies	●	●	
Kalmia latifolia	4–9		●	●
Laurus nobilis	8–10		●	
Leucothoe	5–9		●	●
Mahonia	Varies		●	●
Myrtus communis	9–10		●	●
Nandina domestica	7–10		●	●
Osmanthus	Varies		●	●
Pieris	Varies		●	●
Rhododendron	Varies	●	●	●
Taxus	Varies		●	
Viburnum (several)	Varies	●	●	●
Ground covers				
Aegopodium podagraria	4–8	●		
Ajuga reptans	4–10		●	●
Duchesnea indica	3–10		●	●
Euonymus fortunei	5–10		●	
Fragaria chiloensis	5–10		●	●
Galium odoratum	5–10		●	●
Hypericum calycinum	6–10		●	●
Liriope spicata	4–10		●	●
Mahonia aquifolium	5–10		●	●
Nandina domestica	8–10		●	●
Ophiopogon japonicus	8–10		●	
Pachysandra terminalis	4–9		●	●
Polygonum capitatum	7–10		●	●
Taxus baccata 'Repandens'	6–10		●	
Vinca	Varies		●	●

Climate zone map is on page 96. Descriptions of plants listed in chart are on pages 97–127.

Plants that tolerate drought

Plants that endure or thrive with limited water are a blessing to water-conscious gardeners. The list below includes plants that prefer little water or that tolerate limited water during the growing season. Most do need routine watering, though, until they become established.

Nerium oleander

Rosmarinus officinalis 'Prostratus'

NAME OF PLANT	CLIMATE ZONES	DECIDUOUS	EVERGREEN	FLOWERS
Trees				
Acacia	9–10		•	•
Albizia julibrissin	5–10	•		•
Cedrus deodara	6–10		•	
Celtis	Varies	•		
Eriobotrya japonica	8–10		•	•
Eucalyptus (most)	Varies		•	•
Ficus carica	7–10	•		
Koelreuteria paniculata	5–9	•		•
Melia azedarach	7–10	•		•
Olea europaea	9–10		•	
Parkinsonia aculeata	8–10	•		
Pinus (many)	Varies		•	
Pistacia chinensis	Varies	•		
Quercus (many)	Varies	•	•	
Robinia	Varies	•		•
Schinus	9–10		•	
Ulmus pumila	5–9	•		
Shrubs				
Arbutus unedo	8–10		•	•
Callistemon citrinus	9–10		•	•
Cistus	8–10		•	•
Cotinus coggygria	5–10	•		•
Cotoneaster	Varies	•	•	•
Cytisus	Varies	•	•	•
Dodonaea viscosa	9–10		•	
Elaeagnus	Varies	•	•	
Escallonia	8–10		•	•
Genista	Varies	•		•
Mahonia	Varies		•	•
Melaleuca (most)	9–10		•	•
Myrtus communis	9–10		•	•
Nerium oleander	9–10		•	•

NAME OF PLANT	CLIMATE ZONES	DECIDUOUS	EVERGREEN	FLOWERS
Shrubs (cont'd.)				
Pittosporum tobira	8–10		•	•
Plumbago auriculata	9–10		•	•
Prunus (evergreen)	Varies		•	
Punica granatum	9–10	•		•
Pyracantha	6–10		•	•
Rhamnus	Varies	•	•	
Rosa rugosa	2–9	•		•
Rosmarinus officinalis	7–10		•	•
Taxus	Varies		•	
Xylosma congestum	9–10		•	
Ground covers				
Achillea	4–10		•	•
Arctostaphylos uva-ursi	3–10		•	•
Arctotheca calendula	9–10		•	•
Baccharis pilularis	8–10		•	
Ceanothus	8–10		•	•
Cistus salviifolius	8–10		•	•
Cotoneaster	Varies	•	•	•
Hypericum calycinum	6–10		•	•
Juniperus (some)	Varies		•	
Lantana montevidensis	9–10		•	•
Mahonia aquifolium	5–10		•	•
Polygonum cuspidatum compactum	4–10		•	•
Pyracantha	7–10		•	•
Rosmarinus officinalis 'Prostratus'	7–10		•	•
Santolina	7–10		•	•
Taxus baccata 'Repandens'	6–10		•	
Teucrium chamaedrys	6–10		•	•

Climate zone map is on page 96. Descriptions of plants listed in chart are on pages 97–107, 110–119, and 124–127.

Plants for hillsides

Hillsides don't always provide the best environment for plant growth. Soil may be poor or shallow, water may run off more rapidly than it penetrates, sun and wind may give plants a regular beating. This list suggests popular plants that are most likely to cope well with unfavorable hillside conditions—and be attractive at the same time.

Abelia grandiflora 'Edward Goucher'

Lantana montevidensis

NAME OF PLANT	CLIMATE ZONES	FLOWERS	EROSION CONTROL
Shrubs			
Abelia grandiflora	6–10	●	
Bamboo (some)	Varies		●
Callistemon phoeniceus, 'Prostratus'	9–10	●	
Carissa grandiflora	10	●	
Chaenomeles	4–9	●	
Cistus	8–10	●	●
Cotoneaster	Varies	●	●
Cytisus	Varies	●	
Elaeagnus	Varies		
Forsythia suspensa	5–9	●	
Genista	Varies	●	
Jasminum (some)	Varies	●	●
Lagerstroemia indica (shrub types)	7–9	●	
Plumbago auriculata	9–10	●	
Prunus laurocerasus 'Zabeliana'	6–10		
Rosmarinus officinalis	7–10	●	●
Xylosma congestum	9–10		
Vines			
Bougainvillea	9–10	●	
Euonymus fortunei	5–10		●
Hedera	Varies		●
Lonicera japonica	5–10	●	●
Parthenocissus	Varies		●

NAME OF PLANT	CLIMATE ZONES	FLOWERS	EROSION CONTROL
Vines (cont'd.)			
Passiflora	Varies	●	
Polygonum aubertii	5–10	●	
Solandra maxima	9–10	●	
Tecomaria capensis	8–10	●	
Trachelospermum jasminoides	9–10	●	●
Ground covers			
Arctostaphylos uva-ursi	3–10	●	●
Arctotheca calendula	9–10	●	
Baccharis pilularis	8–10		●
Ceanothus	8–10	●	●
Cistus salviifolius	8–10	●	●
Cotoneaster	Varies	●	●
Hypericum calycinum	6–10	●	●
Juniperus	Varies		●
Lantana montevidensis	9–10	●	●
Osteospermum	9–10	●	
Pelargonium peltatum	10	●	
Polygonum cuspidatum compactum	4–10	●	
Pyracantha	7–10	●	
Rosa wichuraiana	5–10	●	
Santolina chamaecyparissus	7–10		
Taxus baccata 'Repandens'	6–10		
Vinca	Varies	●	●

Climate zone map is on page 96. Descriptions of plants listed in chart are on pages 110–119, 120–121, and 124–127.

For autumn foliage color

Each autumn the leaves of some plants change color from green (usually) to the bright colors we call "autumnal": red, orange, yellow, gold. This pageant of color is most dramatic in northeastern North America, but a measure of that display is possible in other areas.

Acer palmatum

Acer saccharum

NAME OF PLANT	CLIMATE ZONES	MILD-WINTER COLOR	FLOWERS (IN OTHER SEASONS)
Trees			
Acer	Varies	●	
Amelanchier	Varies		●
Betula	Varies	●	
Carpinus	Varies		
Carya illinoensis	5–9		
Celtis	Varies		
Cercis canadensis	4–9	●	●
Chionanthus	Varies	●	●
Cladrastis lutea	4–9	●	●
Cornus	Varies	●	●
Crataegus	Varies	●	●
Diospyros	Varies	●	
Erythrina coralloides	9–10	●	●
Fagus	Varies	●	
Ficus carica	8–10	●	
Fraxinus	Varies	●	
Ginkgo biloba	4–10	●	
Gleditsia triacanthos inermis	4–9	●	
Halesia	5–9	●	●
Juglans	Varies	●	
Koelreuteria	Varies	●	●
Lagerstroemia indica	7–9	●	●
Larix	Varies	●	
Liquidambar styraciflua	5–10	●	
Liriodendron tulipifera	4–9	●	●
Malus	Varies	●	●
Melia azedarach	7–10	●	●
Morus alba	5–10	●	
Nyssa sylvatica	4–9	●	
Oxydendrum arboreum	5–9	●	●
Pistacia chinensis	6–10	●	
Populus	Varies	●	
Prunus	Varies	●	●

NAME OF PLANT	CLIMATE ZONES	MILD-WINTER COLOR	FLOWERS (IN OTHER SEASONS)
Pyrus	Varies	●	●
Quercus (many)	Varies	● (some)	
Rhus typhina	3–9	●	
Salix	Varies	●	● (some)
Sapium sebiferum	8–10	●	
Sassafras albidum	4–9	●	
Sorbus aucuparia	3–9	●	●
Styrax	Varies		●
Ulmus	Varies	●	
Shrubs			
Berberis (some)	Varies	●	●
Cornus	Varies	●	●
Cotinus coggygria	5–10	●	●
Cotoneaster divaricatus	5–10	●	●
Enkianthus	5–9	●	●
Euonymus alata	3–9	●	
Hydrangea quercifolia	5–9	●	●
Lagerstroemia indica (shrubs)	7–9	●	●
Nandina domestica	7–10	●	●
Photinia villosa	5–8	●	●
Prunus	Varies	●	●
Punica granatum	9–10	●	●
Rhododendron (some)	Varies	●	●
Rhus	Varies	●	
Salix purpurea 'Gracilis'	5–9	●	
Spiraea	Varies	●	●
Viburnum (many)	Varies	●	●
Vines			
Parthenocissus	Varies	●	
Wisteria	4–10	●	●

Climate zone map is on page 96. Descriptions of plants listed in chart are on pages 97–107 and 110–121.

For distinctive foliage textures

Foliage appearance or "texture" can be as important as color in landscape planning. Too much sameness of any sort of leaves produces not just monotony but indistinctness: think of a hedge composed of one kind of plant, for example. Here we single out the foliage extremes—small and fine, large and bold— that can provide contrast, as well as unusual leaf shapes that can add variety and interest to your garden.

Eriobotyra deflexa

Acer palmatum

NAME OF PLANT	CLIMATE ZONES	BOLD	FINE	UNUSUAL
Trees				
Acacia baileyana	9–10		●	
Acer palmatum (cutleaf varieties)	6–9		●	
Aesculus carnea	5–9	●	●	
Albizia julibrissin	5–10	●	●	
Catalpa	4–10	●		
Delonix regia	10		●	
Eriobotrya	Varies	●		
Ficus carica	8–10	●		●
Ginkgo biloba	4–10			●
Gleditsia triacanthos inermis	4–9		●	
Jacaranda mimosifolia	9–10		●	
Juglans regia	7–9	●		
Larix	Varies		●	
Liriodendron tulipifera	4–9			●
Magnolia grandiflora	7–10	●		
Maytenus boaria	9–10		●	
Parkinsonia aculeata	8–10		●	
Paulownia tomentosa	5–10	●		

NAME OF PLANT	CLIMATE ZONES	BOLD	FINE	UNUSUAL
Platanus	5–10	●		
Sassafras albidum	4–9			●
Schinus molle	9–10		●	
Tsuga	Varies		●	
Shrubs				
Buxus	Varies		●	
Calluna vulgaris	4–9		●	
Cytisus	Varies		●	
Erica	Varies		●	
Genista	Varies		●	
Hydrangea	Varies	●		
Ilex crenata	6–10		●	
Leptospermum	9–10		●	
Myrtus communis	9–10		●	
Rhododendron (some)	Varies	●	●	
Rosmarinus officinalis	7–10		●	
Taxus	Varies		●	
Tsuga canadensis (some)	5–9		●	

Climate zone map is on page 96. Descriptions of plants listed in chart are on pages 97–107 and 110–121.

Plant hardiness map for the U.S. & Canada

This plant hardiness zone map, devised by the United States Department of Agriculture, is used in countless nursery catalogs and garden books to indicate where plants can grow. The zones are based on average expected low temperatures in winter. Each zone encompasses a 10°F (approximately 10°C, too) range.

To use the map, locate the hardiness zone in which you live. For each plant you want to grow, check to see if the zone number in the lists and plant descriptions is the same as your zone. If the number is the same or lower, then the plant should survive the winter cold in your zone. *(For instance, if you live in Zone 7, all plants listed for 7, 6, 5, 4, and 3 should survive winters in your zone.)*

In our plant listings, we have followed the standard method of rating hardiness. Besides indicating the coldest zone in which a plant will grow, we have considered its adaptability and usefulness in warmer zones. The zone listings for each plant in this chapter indicate the range of climate zones in which it is adapted.

The map's limitations, however, are obvious. A zone map based only on minimum expected temperatures cannot possibly account for variations in soils or for microclimates within each zone. Furthermore, such a map fails to acknowledge other significant factors in climate that affect plant growth: humidity, expected high temperatures, and wind.

Just consider the differences in Zone 9 and 10 along the Gulf Coast and in Florida compared with those zones in California. The Gulf Coast areas have high humidity and summer rainfall, whereas in the West, rainfall occurs in winter, with summer temperatures likely to be higher and humidity low.

Fortunately for the gardener, many plants can accept a variety of climates and still perform well. But where significant limitations do exist, we have noted them in such phrases as "Zones 5-8, desert only," or "Zone 10, only in Florida."

If you live outside of the map area: Obtain the average winter minimum temperature from a local agricultural office. Then find the USDA zone in which your average winter minimum temperature falls; use that zone as explained in the text above.

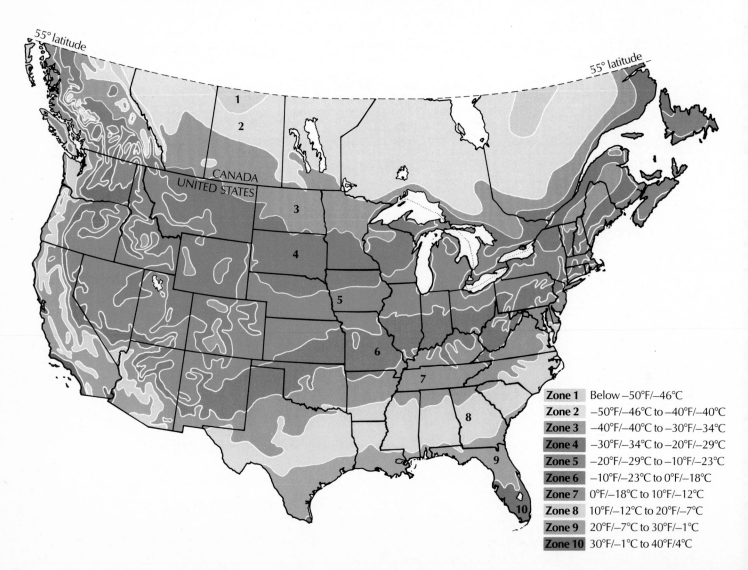

Zone 1	Below −50°F/−46°C
Zone 2	−50°F/−46°C to −40°F/−40°C
Zone 3	−40°F/−40°C to −30°F/−34°C
Zone 4	−30°F/−34°C to −20°F/−29°C
Zone 5	−20°F/−29°C to −10°F/−23°C
Zone 6	−10°F/−23°C to 0°F/−18°C
Zone 7	0°F/−18°C to 10°F/−12°C
Zone 8	10°F/−12°C to 20°F/−7°C
Zone 9	20°F/−7°C to 30°F/−1°C
Zone 10	30°F/−1°C to 40°F/4°C

Trees for permanent character

In many landscape designs, the most important consideration will be the choice of trees. Because trees take more time than other plants to reach mature size, careful selection is critical: to remove a poorly chosen tree can be a tricky task for a professional, and to start anew means further waiting to achieve the desired effect. More than any other plants, trees can establish the general character of a landscape—whether it appears sheltered, shaded, framed by perimeter plantings, or is given perspective by skyline sentinels or by an avenue planting.

ABIES. Fir. Evergreen conifer. Zones vary. Firs are symmetrical, dense cone-shaped trees. Layers of evenly spaced branches radiate from straight, single trunks. In youth firs are handsome, compact shrubs, but all become skyline trees in time, 75–100 feet tall — too tall for many suburban gardens. Use as background trees or specimens on large grounds. With few exceptions, firs grow best in moist, cool climates. Among the most commonly sold are White fir (*A. concolor*), Zones 4–8, with bluish green needles, and Grand or Lowland fir (*A. grandis*), Zones 6–9 (West) and 6–7 (East), with deep green needles.

ACACIA. Evergreen. Zones 9–10. Among the many acacia species, only a few are commonly available. Bailey acacia (*A. baileyana*), Silver wattle (*A. dealbata*), and Green Wattle (*A. decurrens*) have finely cut, fernlike leaves and spectacular displays of small yellow flowers, which are clusters of stamens. Bailey acacia is smallest of the three, a rounded 20–40-foot tree with blue gray foliage (there also is a purple-leafed form); Silver wattle, with silvery gray foliage, is similar but grows to 50 feet. Green wattle also is in the 50-foot range but has dark green leaves. Blackwood acacia (*A. melanoxylon*) is upright and narrower, to 50 feet, with pale flowers and lance-shaped leaves.

All acacias are fast growing, with shallow, aggressive root systems that rule out planting beneath. They are excellent for hillside plantings and for garden fringes where poor soil and drought limit choice of other plants. All are good for massing and screen plantings; Bailey and Blackwood acacias are good specimens.

Acer palmatum

ACER. Maple. Deciduous. Zones vary. Maples cover a great range of sizes and shapes, including the large, round-topped shade tree with sharply lobed leaves and brilliant autumn color. For convenience, we discuss them under the headings "small" and "large." Most have shallow, fibrous root systems that compete with other plantings; lawn and some ground covers will be the most successful beneath.

Small maples. These trees share a general gracefulness that minimizes their size, up to 35 feet. Japanese maple (*A. palmatum*), Zones 6–9 (West), 5–8 (East), is the most widely planted small maple. A round-topped spreading tree, it grows about 20 feet high and wide, and usually branches low to the ground or has several trunks. Leaves have 5–9 deeply cut lobes and branches tend to be horizontally layered. Autumn color is red to yellow.

Named varieties are available with red, variegated, or finely dissected foliage; some named varieties never exceed shrub size. Vine maple (*A. circinatum*), Zones 5–9 (West) and 5–8 (East), may reach 35 feet with somewhat irregular form. Multitrunked specimens are common. Light green leaves, nearly round with lobed margins, turn yellow to red in autumn. Use Japanese and vine maples in part shade to sun. Plant in groves, woodlands, patios, gardens, or lawn.

Other regionally available small maples with similar uses are Trident maple (*A. buergeranum*), David's maple (*A. davidii*), Amur maple (*A. ginnala*), and Rocky Mountain maple (*A. glabrum*). Hedge maple (*A. campestre*), Zones 5–8, forms a dense, rounded crown; autumn color is yellow. This is less graceful than maples mentioned above. Use as patio or garden specimen, as avenue tree, or even as a clipped hedge.

Large maples. These are the typical maples that cast heavy and welcome summer shade, then turn fiery colors in autumn. Use in avenue and background plantings or as lawn specimens. Norway maple (*A. platanoides*) grows in Zones 4–9, but in eastern states the leaves will burn in warmer parts of Zones 7–9. This maple grows 90 feet high and nearly as wide. There are named selections that are smaller trees, some with red to purplish foliage. Red maple (*A. rubrum*), Zones 4–10, is similar but shorter (to 70 feet) with smaller leaves; it, too, has named varieties that have different growth forms and leaf color. Weak wood is subject to storm breakage. Sugar maple (*A. saccharum*), Zones 4–9 (West) and 3–7 (East), is another similar species. Its form is more oval than the previous two, with a short, thick trunk. In time it reaches 120 feet high. Sycamore maple (*A. pseudoplatanus*), Zones 6–9 (West) and 6–7 (East), forms a broad, rounded crown 40–70 feet high and wide; foliage does not turn brilliant colors in autumn. Silver maple (*A. saccharinum*), Zones 4–9, has silvery gray leaf undersides that shimmer in a breeze. Bark on young trees also is silvery gray. Growth is upright, fast, and up to 100 feet high by 75 feet wide — with upright limbs and somewhat drooping branches. It's probably the most graceful of large maples but has weak wood that's highly susceptible to storm damage.

AESCULUS carnea. Red horsechestnut. Deciduous. Zones 5–9 (West) and 5–7 (East). Broad leaves consist of 5 leaflets arranged like an open fan, the longest segments extending up to 10 inches. In midspring, 8–10-inch-long spikes of pink to red flowers grow upright from branch tips. Form is round-headed, to 40 feet high and 30 feet wide; shade is dense. Foliage will scorch in dry heat and wind. Best uses are as specimen shade and street trees with only lawn or low ground cover beneath.

ALBIZIA julibrissin. Silk tree (also called Mimosa in East). Deciduous. Zones 5–10. Silk tree grows with one or more trunks to form a flat-topped canopy up to 40 feet high and spreading wider. Each leaf is composed of so many tiny leaflets that foliage has feathery appearance. The tree casts filtered shade. During summer, fluffy pincushionlike pink to reddish flowers dot the top of the canopy. With regular watering, growth is rapid. Litter from flowers, leaves, and seed pods can be a nuisance in paved areas.

ALDER. See Alnus.

ALNUS. Alder. Deciduous. Zones 5–9. These birch relatives share some family resemblances: smooth trunks and foliage crowns that are taller than wide. Best growth is in moist soil; regular garden watering is necessary where summers are dry. Roots are shallow and invasive, so use alders in backgrounds or grove plantings. White alder (*A. rhombifolia*) may reach 90 feet, bearing 4½-inch-long oval leaves; drooping branch tips give it birchlike grace. Italian alder (*A. cordata*) is smaller (to about 40 feet) with 4-inch, heart-shaped leaves. Both display decorative tassel-like catkins before leaves emerge.

AMELANCHIER. Shadblow, Shadbush, Service berry. Deciduous. Zones vary. All species are lightweight, delicate, often multitrunked trees with good spring display of white or pink flowers, edible fruits in summer, glowing autumn foliage color, and attractive winter branch and twig patterns. Shadblows cast light shade and roots are not

...Amelanchier

invasive. Downy service berry (*A. canadensis*), Zones 4–8, is slender and tall (around 30 feet in gardens), usually with several trunks. Allegany service berry (*A. laevis*), Zones 5–8, grows about as tall but with a spreading habit; new leaves are bronzy purple. A hybrid between the two is the Apple service berry (*A. grandiflora*), Zones 5–8. Growth is smaller — 20-25 feet high and wide — and flowers are larger; new growth also is bronzy purple.

APPLE. See Malus pumila.

ARBORVITAE. See Thuja.

ASH. See Fraxinus.

BAUHINIA. Orchid tree. Deciduous. Zone 10 and warmer parts of Zone 9. Orchid trees form umbrella-shaped canopies and single or multiple trunks. Good-looking two-lobed leaves and spectacular flower display recommend them for patio or other prominent location. Largest flowers (to 6 inches) in autumn and winter are on the 35-foot Hong Kong orchid tree (*B. blakeana*); colors range from pink through purple. Brazilian *B. forficata* bears 3-inch creamy white flowers in spring and midsummer. It also reaches 20 feet, with picturesquely angled trunk and limb structure. Another tall tree, to 35 feet, is Purple orchid tree, *B. variegata*. Winter flowers are pink to purple; 'Candida' is the white-flowered variety, blooming in early spring. Trees produce huge crop of beans after bloom; cut them off to bring earlier new growth.

BEECH. See Fagus.

Betula pendula

BETULA. Birch. Deciduous. Zones vary. These are trees of all-season beauty. When out of leaf, birches are striking, with delicate limb structure, decorative bark, and hanging seed tassels. Clean green foliage of spring and summer turns glowing yellow in autumn. Though some birches may grow to 100 feet high, these graceful trees never seem massive.

All birches need regular watering and have somewhat greedy roots; leaves attract aphids, which drip honeydew. Use in groves and in foreground plantings, especially where dark-leafed evergreens form the backdrop. White-barked species include Euro-

pean white birch (*B. pendula*), Zones 3–10 (West) and 3–7 (East), with pendent branchlets, and Canoe birch (*B. papyrifera*), Zones 3–8, which is taller, more open, and upright. Two choice species with colored bark are Cherry or Sweet birch (*B. lenta*), Zones 4–8, with lustrous red brown bark; and River, Black, or Red birch (*B. nigra*), Zones 5–10, with bark that is pinkish when young and cinnamon brown to black and peeling when trunk and limbs age. Both are in the 75-foot range.

BIRCH. See Betula.

BOTTLEBRUSH. See Callistemon.

CAJEPUT TREE. See Melaleuca quinquenervia.

CALLISTEMON. Bottlebrush. Evergreen. Zone 10 and warmer parts of Zone 9. The common name comes from the appearance of the flowers, which consist mostly of long stamens clustered tightly and uniformly around the stems. Two species — red-flowered Lemon bottlebrush (*C. citrinus*) and pale yellow-flowered White bottlebrush (*C. salignus*) — become massive shrubs unless trained as single or multitrunked trees. Narrow leaves on these species are copper and pink, respectively, when new. Lemon bottlebrush is round-headed to 25 feet and more graceful if grown with several trunks. White bottlebrush grows to same height but is slender. Weeping bottlebrush (*C. viminalis*) is quite different with its sparse foliage, pendulous branches, and red flowers; it may reach 30 feet. All three are good as specimen or patio trees.

CALOCEDRUS decurrens (formerly *Libocedrus decurrens*). Incense cedar. Evergreen conifer. Zones 4–10 (West) and 5–8 East). Rich green foliage consists of overlapping tiny, scalelike leaves arranged in vertical flat sprays. The tree is a neat, dense, narrow pyramid of foliage that may reach 75–90 feet high (slow-growing at first, but growth quickens as plants become established). Trees growing in the open hold branches to the ground. You can remove lower limbs to reveal handsome, red brown, furrowed bark. Incense cedar makes a good specimen tree and a first-rate windbreak or high, hedgelike green wall.

CAMPHOR TREE. See Cinnamomum camphora.

CARPINUS. Hornbeam. Deciduous. Zones vary. Hornbeams are neat, attractive, medium-size shade trees; two species are widely available. European hornbeam (*C. betulus*), Zones 6–9, grows pyramidally to about 40 feet, becoming broader and more rounded only with age. You can plant it as a high screen or hedge (you'll need to shear it); look for narrowly upright 'Fastigiata' for these uses. American hornbeam (*C. caroliniana*), Zones 3–9, forms a rounded crown to about 30 feet high. Smooth gray bark is an

attractive feature. Both species have decorative drooping clusters of nutlets and oval leaves that turn yellow (*C. betulus*) or red (*C. caroliniana*) in autumn.

CARYA illinoensis. Pecan. Deciduous. Zones 5–9. Pecans will reach 70 feet high and wide in deep, rich, moist soil where hot summer weather prevails. They produce tasty nuts and plenty of shade — especially welcome in best-performance regions. Young trees grow fairly quickly, then slow down as they attain size. Foliage is similar to that of the Black walnut (*Juglans nigra*) but has a finer texture with 11–17 narrower leaflets. Autumn color is yellow. For nut production, some varieties require another tree nearby for pollination.

CASSIA. Senna. Evergreen and deciduous. Zones vary. Fast growth and spectacular yellow flower display followed by conspicuous beanlike seed pods characterize three tree species. All have leaves composed of many small leaflets; texture and shade are light. Crown of Gold tree (*C. excelsa*), Zones 9–10, is partly deciduous, reaches 25–30 feet, and blooms in late summer and fall. Gold medallion tree (*C. leptophylla*), Zone 10, is nearly evergreen with main flower display in midsummer. Tree reaches 20–25 feet; branches tend to be low and somewhat pendulous. Deciduous Golden shower tree (*C. fistula*), for Florida only, gives a spring display of hanging flower clusters before new leaves emerge. Form is round-topped, to 40 feet high and wide. All cassias are good specimen and accent trees.

CATALPA. Deciduous. Zones 4–10. Large, heart-shaped leaves and large clusters of bell-shaped white, yellow, and brown flowers on branch ends in late spring suggest a tropical tree. Long, slender beanlike seed pods follow flowers. Common catalpa or Indian bean (*C. bignonioides*) grows 20–50 feet high and wide. Its variety 'Aurea' has yellow leaves. Western catalpa (*C. speciosa*) is a round-headed 40–70-footer. Similar in size to common catalpa is *C. erubescens* 'Purpurea', with blackish purple young leaves and branchlets that turn dark purplish green as they mature. All have open structures and need shelter from strong winds to keep foliage attractive.

CEDAR. See Cedrus.

CEDRUS. Cedar. Evergreen conifer. Zones vary. Graceful Deodar cedar (*C. deodara*), Zones 7–10, grows rapidly into a soft-textured pyramid up to 80 feet high and half that wide. Branch tips are pendulous with soft green to gray green short needles. Atlas cedar (*C. atlantica*), Zones 6–10, grows more slowly and is more angular, stiff, and open; variety 'Glauca' has silvery blue needles. Cedar of Lebanon (*C. libani*), Zones 6–10, is the slowest grower but reaches 80 feet with wide-spreading branches forming an open, irregular crown. All cedars are specimen and background trees for large properties. Once established they are quite drought-tolerant.

CELTIS. Hackberry. Deciduous. Zones vary. Hackberries resemble elms *(Ulmus)* but are better garden trees because of their deep root systems and relative freedom from disease. When established, hackberries tolerate heat, drought, and strong wind. Use them to cast moderate shade over lawn, garden, or home. Yellow is the autumn foliage color. Common hackberry *(C. occidentalis)*, Zones 3–10, is round-headed and about 50 feet high and wide in gardens. Mississippi hackberry *(C. laevigata)*, Zones 6–9, is similar but has slightly smaller leaves and more uniform growth habit. European hackberry *(C. australis)*, Zones 7–9, may reach the same height but is narrower and more upright.

CERCIS canadensis. Eastern redbud. Deciduous. Zones 4–9. A lavish display of small purplish pink, sweat-pea-shaped flowers precedes 3–6-inch heart-shaped leaves; there are also white and pink-flowered varieties; variety 'Forest Pansy' has red purple foliage. Form is slightly irregular and rounded, with one or several trunks; ultimate height is 25–35 feet. Older trees carry branches in horizontal tiers. Use as a feature tree for patio and garden. Autumn foliage color is yellow; flat seed capsules stay on branches after leaves fall.

CHAMAECYPARIS lawsoniana. Lawson false cypress, Port Orford cedar. Evergreen conifer. Zones 6–9, Pacific Coast only. Selected forms of this tree include many shrubs and shrublets, but the basic species is a forest giant over 100 feet high. In the garden it grows at a moderate rate to about 60 feet high and 15–20 feet wide. Shape is conelike or columnar; flat sprays of dense foliage droop gracefully. Typical foliage is blue green but can vary considerably from one plant to another. Selected named varieties range from golden to silvery blue. Height and narrow habit make Port Orford cedar good for background, grove, high hedge, or screen planting.

CHERRY. See Prunus.

CHINABERRY. See Melia azedarach.

CHINESE FLAME TREE. See Koelreuteria bipinnata.

CHINESE PISTACHE. See Pistacia chinensis.

CHINESE SCHOLAR TREE. See Sophora japonica.

CHINESE TALLOW TREE. See Sapium sebiferum.

CHIONANTHUS. Fringe tree. Deciduous. Zones vary. Fluffy clusters of white flowers with narrow petals decorate these small trees like fringe. Male and female flowers are borne on separate trees; male flowers are slightly showier, female trees produce olivelike purple fruit if male tree is nearby. Growth is slow, often with multiple trunks;

oval glossy leaves turn yellow in autumn. Chinese fringe tree *(C. retusus)* reaches about 20 feet and blooms in late spring and early summer. Spring-blooming American native fringe tree *(C. virginicus)* grows taller and has larger leaves. Growth is best in the East; tree is shorter and shrubbier in the West. Tree is very late to leaf out; early spring-blooming flowers planted beneath will receive full sun. Plant in full sun to part shade and use as feature in patio or garden.

CINNAMOMUM camphora. Camphor tree. Evergreen. Zones 9–10. Growth rate is slow to moderate, but mature tree reaches 50 feet high and has a greater spread. Dark bark covers massive trunk and limbs that bear shiny, light green, oval-pointed leaves to 5 inches long. New spring growth is pink to bronzy. Old leaves drop in spring and must be removed from lawns or planted areas; they decompose slowly. Shade is dense; roots are competitive and capable of lifting and breaking pavement. Use as a shade tree in lawn, though lawn beneath it near trunk may not be first-rate.

CITRUS. Includes Orange, Lemon, Grapefruit, Lime, Mandarin orange (Tangerine), Tangelo, and several hybrids. Evergreen. Zones 9 (some) and 10. All are good-looking small trees with glossy oval leaves, fragrant white blossoms, and edible fruit. Time of year for flowering and fruiting varies greatly. Climate controls which types to plant for good fruit production; local advice will determine your choices. Citrus have special watering requirements — a factor in their landscape placement. For best results retain foliage to the ground. If pruned from below to reveal trunk and limb structure, don't plant anything in the soil beneath (though you can group container plants beneath a citrus tree). Citrus make fine patio and small garden trees.

CLADRASTIS lutea. Yellow wood. Deciduous. Zones 4–9. Slow to moderate growth forms rounded crown to about 35 feet high and 20 feet wide. Smooth, gray bark contrasts with bright green, walnutlike leaves that turn vivid yellow in autumn. Late spring blossoming is spectacular: hanging clusters (up to 10 inches long) of intensely fragrant blossoms resemble white Wisteria. Flowering is erratic — usually a heavy crop occurring every 2–3 years — and a tree may not begin to blossom until it is 10 years old. Tree is subject to storm breakage. This is a good feature specimen or medium-size shade tree for close-up planting and general garden use.

CORAL TREE. See Erythrina.

CORNUS. Dogwood. Deciduous. Zones vary. Graceful good looks and a horizontal branching pattern characterize the three most popular dogwoods. Most widely grown is Eastern dogwood *(C. florida)*, Zones 5–9, which may grow 25–30 feet high and wide after many years. Spring display of flowers

(actually colored bracts) comes before leaves emerge; flowers are white, pink, or a deep pink bordering on red. This is a classic choice for patio, garden, lawn, or woodland edge; a dark backdrop shows off flowers in spring and glowing reddish foliage in autumn. The pyramidal Giant dogwood *(C. controversa)*, Zones 6–9, grows more rapidly to 40–60 feet at maturity. Individual white flowers, small but showy, are in large clusters. Autumn color is red. Kousa dogwood *(C. kousa)*, Zones 6–9, is a large multi-stemmed shrub that can easily be thinned to a 20–25-foot tree. Showy white blossoms appear with leaves but are borne prominently along branch tops. Autumn foliage is orange and red.

All three dogwoods have showy fruit liked by birds. The small, red fruit of the Eastern dogwood hang on the tree after leaf drop. Giant dogwood has black fruit that ripen in late summer. Kousa dogwood forms red, strawberrylike fruit that hang from branches in autumn.

Cornus florida

CRABAPPLE. See Malus.

CRAPE MYRTLE. See Lagerstroemia indica.

CRATAEGUS. Hawthorn. Deciduous. Zones vary. There are many species and varieties of hawthorns, but most are small trees to about 25 feet high, dense and thorny with angular branching; many are multitrunked unless trained. Single blossoms—white is the most usual color—are carried in flattened clusters and come in great profusion after the leaves; pink and red-flowered varieties are also available. Fruit that follow usually look like clusters of tiny red apples. They ripen from summer to fall; those that aren't eaten by birds provide striking winter color on bare trees. Autumn foliage is usually red or orange.

Because of small size and attractiveness in all seasons, hawthorns are popular as specimen and accent trees in smaller gardens; they are also good-looking in row plantings. They are not pest and disease-free—aphids, for example, can be a problem almost anywhere—so they are not a top choice as patio trees.

CRYPTOMERIA japonica. Japanese cedar. Evergreen conifer. Zones 6–9. The wild species is a relatively fast-growing timber tree that reaches 100 feet or more. The straight

. . . Cryptomeria japonica

trunk has peeling bark and slightly drooping branches with short needles that give a soft look to the foliage mass. The variety 'Elegans', a slow-growing, dense, pyramid-shaped plant to about 25 feet high, is a more frequently sold variety. Its gray green foliage turns coppery to purplish red in winter. Use as a featured accent plant for its symmetry and soft texture.

CUPRESSOCYPARIS leylandii. Leyland cypress. Evergreen conifer. Zones 5–10. Outstanding traits of this tree are wide climate adaptability, from cool and moist to hot and dry, and rapid growth. Form is upright, almost columnar, with upright branches of flattened, gray green foliage sprays. Several named varieties are sold, varying in foliage color from bluish green to yellowish. Although it can be used as a specimen, its chief value is as a high hedge or screen plant that can be trimmed as needed.

CUPRESSUS. Cypress. Evergreen conifer. Zones vary; best in western states. Smooth Arizona cypress (*C. glabra*), Zones 7–10, is a heat- and drought-tolerant, fast-growing tree to 40 feet high and 20 feet wide. Foliage is gray blue to gray green. It's a good screen planting but tends to lose lower branches or become sparse as plants mature; use foreground shrubbery to maintain screening to ground level. Entirely different is Italian cypress (*C. sempervirens*), Zones 8–10, usually available in one of its upright, pencil-slim varieties. These tall (to 60 feet) columnar cypresses are attractive only on larger properties where they can be used in groves or along driveways and avenues.

CYPRESS. See Cupressus.

DELONIX regia. Royal poinciana, Flamboyant, Flame tree. Deciduous. Zone 10, Florida only. This is one of the most spectacular shade trees for frost-free, warm climates. Growth is rapid and tall to about 50 feet, spreading to 80 feet or more in an umbrella shape. Just after new leaves emerge (between May and July), orange or red blossoms burst open to cover tree. Seed pods — narrow, woody, and up to 2 feet long — develop after bloom. Individual leaves, up to 2 feet long, are actually composed of tiny leaflets and appear light and fernlike.

DIOSPYROS. Persimmon. Deciduous. Zones vary. Persimmons are ornamental in all seasons. Spring and summer foliage is neat and polished, autumn leaves are brilliant, colorful fruit are conspicuous, and winter branch pattern is picturesque. American persimmon (*D. virginiana*), Zones 5–9, reaches 30–50 feet high in gardens and about half as wide. Yellow to orange fruit are round and to 2 inches in diameter; they form on female trees only if there is a nearby male tree for pollination. Oriental persimmon (*D. kaki*), Zones 7–9, is available in several named varieties. Eventual size is about 30 feet high and wide. Orange fruit are usually

oval shaped, to 7 inches long in some varieties; fruit remain on the tree after leaf drop, looking like large holiday ornaments. Fruit drop can be a problem on paved surfaces. Persimmon trees are excellent for accent planting.

DOGWOOD. See Cornus.

DOUGLAS FIR. See Pseudotsuga menziesii.

ELAEAGNUS angustifolia. Russian olive. Deciduous. Zones 3–9. This small tree does well where hot summers, cold winters, drought, and poor soil discourage many other trees. It also grows well under better conditions, disliking only warm winters and humid or cool summers. Narrow, willowlike, silvery gray leaves clothe an upright and angular branch structure; height may be 20–25 feet with equal spread. In early summer small, fragrant, greenish yellow flowers appear; silver yellow berrylike fruit that resemble miniature olives follow. As tree matures, trunk and major limbs develop dark brown, shredding bark. Most plants are thorny, but some nurseries may carry thornless selections. Use as a specimen tree or windbreak hedge.

ELM. See Ulmus.

EMPRESS TREE. See Paulownia tomentosa.

Eriobotrya japonica

ERIOBOTRYA. Loquat. Evergreen. Zones vary. Both species are fast growers with leathery, bold leaves to 4 inches wide and 12 inches long. Taller is *E. japonica*, Zones 8–10, which can become a dense, rounded specimen to 30 feet high and wide. New growth and undersides of leaves are covered with rusty orange fuzz. White autumn and winter flowers produce yellow to orange edible fruit. Bronze loquat (*E. deflexa*), Zones 9–10, has glossier leaves that emerge and retain their copper color for a long time before turning green. Spring flowers are creamy white but produce no edible fruit. Plant needs training to become a tree, either with one trunk or several. This is the better patio tree because of its smaller size and absence of fruit.

ERYTHRINA. Coral tree. Deciduous. Zones 9–10. There are many different coral trees sold in the Southeast and Southwest. They are usually thorny with brilliant blossoms

from greenish white to orange, red, or pink. Strong trunk and branch structure give trees great garden sculpture value. They may have one or more trunks; and though heights vary, most become umbrella-shaped. All have leaves composed of three oval leaflets. Blossoms, often in spikes at branch tips, produce seed pods that contain colorful, but poisonous, beanlike seeds. Use as accent trees; larger ones provide good shade.

EUCALYPTUS. Evergreen. Zones 8–10. This vast group of trees is widely represented in California and parts of Arizona. Growth habits range from shrubby and almost viny types to gigantic skyline types. Foliage varies a great deal, too. All share three features: crisp, leathery, and frequently aromatic foliage; fluffy flowers composed of prominent stamens that surround the flower base; and woody, flat-topped seed capsules. Most trees have distinctly different juvenile and mature foliage.

Root systems of many eucalyptus are shallow and greedy, but usually you can grow lawns and ground covers beneath the greedy ones. Trees shed dead leaves, twigs, and bark year-round. Some are susceptible to storm breakage.

Use as background and skyline specimens, windbreaks, or patio and garden specimens, depending on the species. For detailed descriptions, uses, and climate restrictions for 51 species, refer to the *Sunset New Western Garden Book.*

EUROPEAN MOUNTAIN ASH. See Sorbus aucuparia.

FAGUS. Beech. Deciduous. Zones vary. Majestic and imposing aptly describe beeches. They are not trees to work into a landscape, but rather trees to work a landscape around. Their heavy shade, ground-sweeping lower branches, and surface roots rule out plantings beneath. Use as a specimen tree set in lawn or at background of a garden. American beech (*F. grandifolia*), Zones 4–10 (West) and 4–9 (East), grows slowly to a broad pyramid, up to 90 feet. Oval, 3–5-inch leaves are soft green in spring and golden brown in autumn. More common is European beech (*F. sylvatica*), Zones 4–10 (West) and 4–9 (East), which is a broader tree available in several fancy-leafed varieties. Most popular are the copper and purple-leafed sorts. Many of these named forms are smaller trees that differ from typical shape; all are good accent plants but come with greedy root systems.

FERN PINE. See Podocarpus gracilior.

FICUS. Fig. Deciduous and evergreen. Zones vary. Edible fig (*F. carica*), Zones 8–10, is deciduous. Rough-textured leaves—up to 9 inches long and wide — have 3–5 lobes and clothe gray-barked, knobby limbs. In addition to fruit, tree produces dense shade. Fruit drop can be a problem in paved areas. This tree is valuable as a sculptural accent.

Good evergreen figs are Weeping Chinese banyan (*F. benjamina*), Zone 10, and Indian laurel fig (*F. microcarpa*), Zones 9–10. Both have gracefully drooping branchlets and shiny, oval leaves. Variety *nitida* of the Indian laurel fig has upright branches. All three reach about 50 feet high with rounded crowns. Use them where a neat, polished tree is needed. They can also be clipped as high hedges or screens. Avoid planting near sewer lines or close to pavement.

FIR. See Abies.

FLAMBOYANT. See Delonix regia.

FLAXLEAF PAPERBARK. See Melaleuca linariifolia.

FRAXINUS. Ash. Deciduous and evergreen. Zones vary. There are many ash species and even some named varieties selected for special characteristics; availability varies. In general, ashes are fast-growing, tough, and undemanding; many are popular where heat, wind, heavy or damp soils, or drought limit planting of other trees. All have oval, pointed leaflets composing each leaf, and most turn brilliant yellow or purple in autumn. The one evergreen, Shamel ash (*F. uhdei*), Zones 9–10, will drop some or all foliage in colder areas of its adaptability. Sizes vary, but most ashes are big and round-headed, good for shading streets, lawns, and homes. Surface roots hinder gardening beneath these trees.

FRINGE TREE. See Chionanthus.

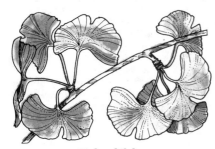

Ginkgo biloba

GINKGO biloba. Ginkgo, Maidenhair tree. Deciduous. Zones 4–10. Individual leaves are fan-shaped, up to 4 inches across the widest part, similar to leaflets of maidenhair fern. Leathery and light green, they turn dazzling yellow in autumn, then drop almost all at once. Tree grows at slow to moderate rate, somewhat assymetrically in youth but to a more uniform shape when mature. Form varies from narrow to spreading, usually 35–50 feet tall. Female trees bear ill-scented fruit; male trees are fruitless. Trees grown from seed may be either male or female, but named selections are male trees. 'Autumn Gold' is upright when young but becomes spreading as it matures; 'Fairmount' is faster growing and pyramidal. All-year attractiveness makes this a tree to feature in lawn or near the house, alone or in groves.

GLEDITSIA triacanthos inermis. Thornless honey locust. Deciduous. Zones 4–9 (West) and 4–7 (East). These trees grow 35–60 feet tall, depending on variety, but appear delicate because branch structure is open and leaves consist of many small leaflets. Shade is not dense. Spring leaf-out is late, autumn leaf-drop (after foliage has turned yellow) is early. Leaflets dry up and filter into plantings or lawn, so you need do little raking. You can buy several named selections. All are rapid growers but differ in size, shape, or leaf color. 'Moraine' is vase-shaped and spreading; 'Shademaster' is more upright. 'Imperial' is tall and spreading with denser foliage; 'Skyline' is pyramidal. 'Rubylace' has dark red new growth that turns green, and 'Sunburst' has yellow new leaves that darken to yellowish green.

GOLDENCHAIN TREE. See Laburnum.

GOLDENRAIN TREE. See Koelreuteria paniculata.

GOLDEN SHOWER TREE. See Cassia fistula.

GRAPEFRUIT. See Citrus.

HACKBERRY. See Celtis.

HALESIA. Deciduous. Zones 5–9. Snowdrop tree or Silver bell (*H. carolina*) and Mountain silver bell (*H. monticola*) are refined trees with charming displays of pendent, bell-shaped flowers in spring just as leaves emerge. The most obvious difference between the two is size. Snowdrop tree reaches 30 or more feet high and wide, tending to have several trunks. Oval leaves are to 4 inches long and flowers are about ½-inch long. Mountain silver bell is distinctly tree-like to 60 feet tall, pyramidal to rounded at maturity. Leaves are larger, and flowers are 1 inch long. Foliage of both turns yellow in autumn; dry, winged fruit remain on branches through winter. Flowers are attractive close up, but trees also are good-looking at a distance, especially with dark background. They cast moderate shade and are good for growing woodland plants beneath.

HAWTHORN. See Crataegus.

HEMLOCK. See Tsuga.

HOLLY. See Ilex.

HONEY LOCUST. See Gleditsia triacanthos.

HORNBEAM. See Carpinus.

HORSECHESTNUT. See Aesculus.

ILEX. Holly. Evergreen. Zones vary. Most hollies are planted as shrubs, but many will become trees in time, holding branches to the ground unless pruned to reveal trunk. Habit is dense, upright, and usually taller than wide. Most hollies are either male or female; females bear berries but require nearby male of the same species for pollination. Attractive year-round, hollies are good background screens or barriers and specimen trees in lawn, garden, and patio. The

typical holly is English holly (*I. aquifolium*), Zones 6–9 (West) and 6–8 (East), with glossy, spine-edged leaves and red berries; many varieties are available, some with variegated foliage. Shape is pyramidal, to 60 feet and half as wide. Wilson holly (*I. altaclarensis* 'Wilsonii'), Zones 7–10 (West) and 7–9 (East), can be trained into a tree of 20 feet or more. Lusterleaf holly (*I. latifolia*), Zones 7–10, has the largest leaves: leathery, to 6 inches long with finely toothed margins. Growth habit resembles English holly but is somewhat more open. American holly (*I. opaca*), Zones 6–9, resembles English holly but grows in colder regions; leaves are not shiny. Yaupon (*I. vomitoria*), Zones 7–10, produces typical berries (without a pollinator) but has untypical foliage: leaves are narrow, to 1½ inches long.

INCENSE CEDAR. See Calocedrus.

INDIAN BEAN. See Catalpa.

JACARANDA mimosifolia. Deciduous to semievergreen. Zones 9–10. Filmy, fernlike foliage forms a broad canopy atop an open, irregular tree to 50 feet high and wide. You can grow it with one or several trunks. Leaves usually drop in late winter and tree remains bare until flowering time (typically late spring but it may occur earlier or later); sometimes, though, a tree will leaf out immediately after shedding one crop of foliage. Blossoms are lavender blue (there is a white-flowered variety), tubular, and about 2 inches long in large clusters; decorative flat, nearly round seed pods follow. Trees cast pleasant shade but also are good to look down upon for best view of flowers.

JAPANESE PAGODA TREE. See Sophora japonica.

JAPANESE SNOWDROP TREE. See Styrax japonica.

JERUSALEM THORN. See Parkinsonia aculeata.

JUGLANS. Walnut. Deciduous. Zones vary. Walnuts leaf out fairly late in spring and drop foliage after it turns tawny gold, before too much of autumn passes. Trees are large and cast dense shade; texture varies according to whether leaflets are large or small. Branch structure is heavy, with relatively few, thick twigs. Largest is Black walnut (*J. nigra*), Zones 5–8, which reaches 100–150 feet with fine-textured foliage. Toxic substance in black walnut roots can inhibit growth of some plants, so do not use with vegetable or ornamental plantings. Butternut (*J. cinerea*), Zones 5–8, is similar but only 50–60 feet high and wide-spreading. Use them on large properties for shading lawn or as background specimens. English walnut (*J. regia*), Zones 7–9, is the source of commercial walnuts. The tree is low-branched and wide-spreading and has the largest leaflets. Best use is in home orchard, not garden (it won't take regular garden watering); keep soil clear beneath canopy.

JUNIPER. See Juniperus.

JUNIPERUS. Juniper. Evergreen conifer. Zones vary. Many junipers sold as ground covers or shrubs are small-size variants of species that are trees in the wild. But nurseries seldom carry the full-size tree forms. More often you will find tall columnar or pyramidal varieties of *J. chinensis*, Zones 5–10; *J. communis*, Zones 3–10; *J. deppeana pachyphlaea*, Zones 7–10; *J. excelsa*, Zones 7–10; *J. scopulorum*, Zones 5–10; and *J. virginiana*, Zones 3–9. Depending on the variety, foliage may be any shade of green, steel blue, gray, or red-tinted in winter. Juvenile leaves are needlelike or spiny; mature foliage is scalelike. Appearance is fine-textured, but because of density, plants always seem bulky. Use large junipers in full sun as vertical accents or group them in small groves. In a small garden they can be somberly overpowering.

KOELREUTERIA. Deciduous. Zones vary. Both species provide patio and garden shade and are deep rooted enough to garden beneath. Chinese flame tree *(K. bipinnata)*, Zones 8–10, grows at a moderate rate, upright but spreading to 20–40 feet. The small leaflets turn yellow in late autumn. Lanternlike 2-inch seed capsules in salmon, orange, or red decorate the tree in late summer and autumn. Goldenrain tree *(K. paniculata)*, Zones 5–9, reaches 20–40 feet high with variable spread, casting light shade. Growth rate is slow to moderate. It has no autumn foliage display, but new spring leaves are salmon red. In late summer, the tree billows with large clusters of yellow blossoms; these become lanternlike fruits—red when young, buff to brown when mature. For a very narrow, upright growth habit, look for varieties 'Kew' or 'Fastigiata'.

LABURNUM. Goldenchain tree. Deciduous. Zones 5–9 (West) and 5–7 (East). Most popular is *L. watereri* and its variety 'Vossii'. Striking spring bloom is the chief reason for growing this tree. Before leaves emerge, the vase-shaped tree is festooned with hanging blossom clusters to 20 inches long, looking like bright yellow Wisteria. Poisonous seed pods follow; they aren't decorative and should be removed to conserve tree's energies. Trunk and limbs are green, and cloverlike leaves are bright green. Use as a garden or patio accent, or as a repeated accent in formal plantings.

LAGERSTROEMIA indica. Crape myrtle. Deciduous. Zones 7–9. As long as the summer is warm to hot, crape myrtle produces its showy, eye-catching flower clusters. Small, crepelike blossoms are carried in dense, foot-long clusters at branch tips, with smaller clusters lower on stems. Color ranges from red to pink, lavender to purple, and white. In autumn, the 2-inch oval leaves turn brilliant yellow, orange, or red. Bark is always attractive: smooth gray to light brown, flaking off to show patches of pinkish inner bark. Grow

as a single-trunked specimen, vase-shaped to about 30 feet, or with multiple trunks. Use as garden or patio focal point—individually or as repeated accent in more formal plantings.

LARCH. See Larix.

LARIX. Larch. Deciduous conifers. Zones vary. Among cone-bearing trees with needles, larches are almost unique in being deciduous. New spring needles are bright green, short, soft, and appear in fluffy clusters. They turn bright yellow to orange in autumn before falling. Small cones resembling brown rose blossoms dot bare winter branches of mature trees. All species form graceful pyramids to 60 feet, sometimes spreading wider in age. They prefer cool summers and cold winters. In the West you may find fast-growing Japanese larch *(L. kaempferi)*, Zones 5–8, most widely sold; in the East, European larch *(L. decidua)*, Zones 3–8, and American larch or Tamarack *(L. laricina)*, Zones 3–6, are more common. Use larches, alone or in groves, for their graceful symmetry. Where space permits they're striking with background of dark evergreen conifers.

LAUREL. See Prunus.

LAWSON FALSE CYPRESS. See Chamaecyparis lawsoniana

LEMON. See Citrus.

LIBOCEDRUS. See Calocedrus.

LIME. See Citrus.

LINDEN. See Tilia.

LIQUIDAMBAR styraciflua. American sweet gum. Deciduous. Zones 5–10. Foliage suggests some sort of maple: each leaf is 3–7 inches across and generally has five pointed lobes. Even the brilliant autumn color is maplelike, in yellow to gold and orange to red, from bright to dark. In moist soils, or with regular watering, trees grow rapidly to about 60 feet in gardens. Form is upright and narrow in young specimens; older trees become about half as wide as high. Mature trees bear fruit that are round, spiny balls; they hang from bare winter branches and drop in the spring. These are favorite street and background trees and are especially lovely when planted in groves. In time, their surface roots may make it difficult to grow lawn or other plants beneath.

LIRIODENDRON tulipifera. Tulip tree. Deciduous. Zones 4–9. The stately tulip tree is immediately recognizable by its lyre-shaped leaves. Growth is tall, straight, and rapid in good, moist soil. It grows 60–90 feet high and half as wide, which rules it out of small gardens. On larger properties it is a handsome specimen, avenue tree, or backdrop. Blossoms, appearing only after trees are at least 10 years old, look like 2-inch, green and gold tulips. They're interesting but not showy because they're borne among the

foliage. And by blooming age the foliage is high above the ground. Autumn leaf color is clear, soft yellow, even in mild-winter climates.

Liriodendron tulipifera

LOCUST. See Robinia.

LOQUAT. See Eriobotrya.

MAGNOLIA. Deciduous and evergreen. Zones vary. Specialist nurseries may carry a number of worthwhile magnolias, but two species and their named varieties predominate in general nurseries.

Evergreen magnolias. Southern magnolia *(M. grandiflora)*, Zones 7–10, is associated with the romance of the South. Big (to 10 inches across), white, strongly fragrant blossoms are outstanding during long bloom season: late spring to autumn. Decorative, cone-shaped seed heads bearing scarlet seeds follow bloom. Leaves are broad, oval, and leathery; upper sides appear varnished and undersides often have rust-colored fuzz. Shade is dense. Slow to moderate growth rate produces a tree to 100 feet high and about half as wide in time. Bloom may come after 10–15 years on seed-grown plants. You can buy various named varieties that are smaller and will bloom when younger. These are trees for avenues, lawns, and (with reservations) patios. Root system should not be disturbed by cultivation of other plants; litter from fallen leaves, flower parts, and seed heads requires regular maintenance from spring to autumn.

Deciduous magnolias. Saucer magnolia *(M. soulangiana)*, Zones 4–10, is often planted as a flowering shrub and ends up as a multi-trunked tree to 25 feet high and wide. Somewhat chalice-shaped, 6-inch flowers (appearing before spring leaf-out) are white to pink or purplish red; a number of named varieties differ in flower color and shape. Oval leaves are light to medium green, to 6 inches long, soft-looking rather than glossy. Gray-barked branches form attractive winter patterns. Use as accent in patio or garden, allowing space for its mature size. Digging can damage shallow, fleshy roots; set out permanent plantings near tree while it's young.

MAIDENHAIR TREE. See Ginkgo biloba.

MALUS. Apple, Crabapple. Deciduous. Zones vary. Traditional eating apples are varieties of *M. pumila*, Zones 4–10 (best fruit-producing zones vary according to variety). This handsome shade tree reaches 40 feet high, and is rounded and spreading. Spring display of pink-tinted white blossoms would justify growing the tree even without the promise of fruit. Dwarf, semidwarf, and 'spur' varieties are suitable for small gardens and patio. Plants that prefer some shade will grow beneath any of the *Malus* species and varieties.

Crabapples are usually smaller trees, to 25 feet high. Before spring leaf-out they're covered with single, double, or semidouble flowers, white through pink shades to red. Many bear decorative fruit — red, yellow, or orange — varying in size from a cranberry to a small apple, depending on species or variety. There are many crabapple species and varieties in the nursery trade: visit a good local nursery to check availability and to learn about individual characteristics. Use crabapples as patio, lawn, foreground, avenue, driveway, or background trees.

MANDARIN ORANGE. See Citrus.

MAPLE. See Acer.

MAYTEN TREE. See Maytenus.

MAYTENUS boaria. Mayten tree. Evergreen. Zones 9–10. Narrow leaves, gracefully drooping branchlets, and dome-shaped outline give mayten tree the appearance of a weeping willow. For the garden, this is a better choice than a weeping willow: growth rate is moderate, eventually to 30–50 feet tall, and the root system is not invasive. Variety 'Green Showers' has slightly broader leaves than do seed-raised plants. Use as a handsome accent specimen, lawn tree, or for patio shade.

MELALEUCA. Evergreen. Zones 9–10. Because of their clustered flowers with prominent stamens, these are sometimes called "bottlebrushes." (For other bottlebrushes, see *Callistemon*.) Leaves are narrow to needlelike and flowers are white, cream, pink, or purplish, depending on the species. Decorative bark is either white or light brown, peeling off in papery strips or thick, spongy sheets. Cajeput tree (*M. quinquenervia*) and *M. styphelioides* are the tallest, reaching 20–60 feet with drooping branches; the latter is the more fine-textured, pendulous of the two. Flaxleaf paperbark (*M. linariifolia*) reaches 30 feet with umbrella-shaped crown; bark and blossoms are white. Pink melaleuca (*M. nesophila*) may reach 20–30 feet but needs training to become single-trunked specimen with regular shape; untrained it will produce heavy, contorted branches that usually sprawl before gaining height. Most melaleucas tolerate heat and drought as well as seacoast wind.

MELIA azedarach. Chinaberry. Deciduous. Zones 7–10. Fast growth (to 30–50 feet high) produces a rounded, spreading crown densely covered with large leaves divided into many small leaflets. Clusters of lavender blossoms in late spring–early summer produce ½-inch round, yellow fruit that hang on tree well into winter. Autumn foliage is yellow. Texas umbrella tree, the variety 'Umbraculiformis', is the form usually sold; it reaches about 30 feet high and has a wide-spreading, flattened crown. These are undemanding shade trees, good where summers are hot and dry and soil is alkaline. Wood is brittle, so limbs in full leaf are subject to storm damage.

MEXICAN PALO VERDE. See Parkinsonia aculeata.

MIMOSA. See Albizia julibrissin.

MORAINE LOCUST. See Gleditsia triacanthos inermis.

MORUS alba. White mulberry. Deciduous. Zones 5–10. For garden planting, be sure to get one of the fruitless forms: 'Fan-San', 'Fruitless', 'Kingan', or 'Stribling' (also sold as 'Mapleleaf'). These grow rapidly to about 35 feet high and wide. Large, bright green, oval to lobed leaves turn brilliant yellow in autumn. Tree grows well in range of climates from seashore to desert. Fruitless mulberry is a fast and first-rate shade producer. Surface roots rule out plantings in soil beneath canopy, but white mulberry makes a good patio tree as long as other plants are in containers.

MOUNTAIN ASH. See Sorbus aucuparia.

MULBERRY. See Morus.

NYSSA sylvatica. Black or sour gum, Pepperidge, Tupelo. Deciduous. Zones 4–9. This is a tall, narrow tree to 50 feet high and 25 feet wide. Foliage reliably turns hot scarlet to coppery red in early autumn even in mild-winter regions. Leaf-out is late in spring; leaves are glossy, dark green, and oblong to 5 inches long. Best growth is with regular garden watering; tree even likes continually damp soil. Use as a specimen lawn or background tree to show off autumn foliage.

OLEA europaea. Olive. Evergreen. Zones 9–10. This is one of the signature plants of the Mediterranean. Gray green, willowlike leaves with lighter undersides are delicate and fine-textured; tree bases and limbs on older trees are thick and gnarled. Young bark is gray, turning dark brown in later years. Ultimate size is 25–30 feet high and wide, and habit tends toward several trunks. Olives are handsome avenue and driveway trees, and a single tree makes a striking feature specimen in lawn or garden as long as you anticipate dense root system near tree's base and the inevitable mess from fruit drop with most varieties. A reliable fruitless variety is 'Swan Hill'; the variety 'Fruitless' may not be entirely so, but at least crop will be less than what commercial varieties produce.

OLIVE. See Olea.

ORANGE. See Citrus.

ORCHID TREE. See Bauhinia.

OXYDENDRUM arboreum. Sourwood, Sorrel tree. Deciduous. Zones 5–9. This elegant, slow-growing tree is attractive year-round. New growth in spring emerges bronzy red, becoming glossy green, lance-shaped leaves to 8 inches long. Midsummer flowers come in clusters shaped like an outspread hand with fingers pointing downward and outward; creamy white, bell-shaped blossoms hang along each 5–10-inch "finger." Autumn foliage is brilliant red to maroon — a bright backdrop to green seed capsules that form after flowering. Later these turn silver gray and hang on late into winter. Slender, pyramidal growth reaches 25–40 feet high and about 20 feet across. Sourwood is a splendid specimen for patio or garden as long as its shallow roots are not covered by lawn or disturbed by digging.

PARKINSONIA aculeata. Jerusalem thorn, Mexican palo verde. Deciduous. Zones 8–10. To many desert dwellers, Jerusalem thorn is indispensable. With practically no care, this drought-tolerant tree grows rapidly to 15–30 feet high and wide, filtering sunlight through an intricate network of branches and leaves. A leaf is 6–9 inches long and consists of many tiny leaflets along the leaf stalk; leaflets fall during drought and cold. But because of yellow green bark, many spiny twigs, and remaining leaf stalks, the tree really doesn't look bare when it is leafless. In spring, loose, 7-inch clusters of yellow blossoms light up the tree for about a month; intermittent flowering occurs at other times of year. Jerusalem thorn won't take regular lawn watering. Use it to shade patio (if you don't mind litter of fallen leaf stalks) and as background planting where it can filter sun over the garden for part of the day.

Paulownia tomentosa

PAULOWNIA tomentosa. Empress tree. Deciduous. Zones 5–10. At a casual glance this could be mistaken for Catalpa: leaves are big and heart-shaped, tree grows rapidly to 50 feet high by 30–40 feet wide, and in spring it bears 2-inch trumpet-shaped

...Paulownia tomentosa

flowers. A notable difference is at flowering time; large, upright clusters of pendent lavender-blue blossoms appear before or during leaf-out. Top-shaped seed capsules follow the flowers and stay on the tree until next spring. Because it casts dense shade and has shallow root system (that can sprout if disturbed by cultivation), Empress tree is best used at the fringes of a garden or as a striking accent tree.

PEACH. See Prunus.

PEAR. See Pyrus.

PECAN. See Carya illinoensis.

PEPPERIDGE. See Nyssa sylvatica.

PEPPER TREE. See Schinus.

PERSIMMON. See Diospyros.

PICEA. Spruce. Evergreen conifer. Zones vary. You could easily mistake a young spruce for a young fir (*Abies*). Both are neat, symmetrical, pyramidal in growth, and short-needled. Spruces also are towering timber trees, too large for most suburban gardens. Spruces generally grow more rapidly than firs, may start to lose lower branches while plants are still young, and become more irregular in shape as they mature, often thinning out to leave gaps between branches.

The most widely planted is Colorado spruce (*P. pungens*), Zones 3–8 (and the only spruce to grow well in lower Midwest and Southwest). In trees raised from seed, foliage ranges from dark green through blue green to icy blue. Several named selections, chosen for foliage color, are available: varieties 'Glauca', the Colorado blue spruce, and 'Koster', the Koster blue spruce, are the most widely distributed (though not the bluest). The tree's striking color and perfect symmetry qualify it for accent use on larger properties where its ultimate development into a bare-trunked tree will look attractive.

Norway spruce (*P. abies*), Zones 3–8, is a fast-growing, tall (to 150 feet), dark green pyramid. Use as windbreak, shelter planting, for slower-growing trees, or skyline specimen. Engelmann spruce (*P. engelmannii*), Zones 3–8, resembles blue green forms of Colorado spruce; growth is narrow and fairly slow, holding branches to the ground for many years. White spruce (*P. glauca*), Zones 3–5, grows at moderate rate. Silvery green needles clothe drooping branchlets.

PINUS. Pine. Evergreen conifer. Zones vary. Pines vary greatly in size and shape. Needles range from scarcely more than an inch to more than one foot long; cones vary from 2 inches to nearly 2 feet in length. You can shape a juvenile pine and restrict its size to some extent, but in time the tree will defy such limitation. Be sure to allow space for ultimate size and character.

Most pines have a single trunk with branches radiating from it in whorls; some pine species are wide-spreading, others nar-

row and upright. A few pines tend naturally toward multiple trunks or will branch low and form a crown with no one central leader. But always the branching radiates in whorls from trunks and limbs. The pines that attain tree stature are usually poor choices for small and medium-size gardens. On larger properties, use pines as specimen accents, background screens, skyline accents, and small forest plantings where their size and competitive root systems won't interfere with other plantings. Most pines, once established, will grow in fairly dry soils. Consult local sources to learn about the pines that grow well in your area.

PISTACIA chinensis. Chinese pistache. Deciduous. Zones 6–10 (West) and 6–8 (East). This is a fairly large tree, to 60 feet high and nearly as wide, but it has an air of delicacy because leaves are divided into many pairs of narrow, 4-inch leaflets. Female trees produce bright red fruit that later turn blue. Tree grows at moderate rate, irregular and lopsided, but becomes symmetrical with age. Variety 'Keith Davey' is fruitless and more regular in growth. Summer shade and drought tolerance are assets, but many people grow this tree for the blaze of autumn foliage color—generally in shades of red or orange. This is the only tree to color red in desert regions.

PITTOSPORUM. Evergreen. Zones 9–10. Pittosporums are valued especially for neat, polished, dense foliage. Bonus attributes with most types are fragrant (but not always showy) flowers and pea-size yellow to orange fruit. Though natural growth habits vary, all pittosporums but one can be used for hedge planting, either sheared or informal, and windbreaks. Largest is Victorian box (*P. undulatum*), which reaches 40 feet high and wide in time; shallow, greedy root system rules out permanent planting underneath. Queensland pittosporum (*P. rhombifolium*) is a bit smaller and more open with the most conspicuous fruit; it's the best of the group as a patio shade tree. Quite similar in narrowly upright form and wavy-edge leaves are *P. eugenioides* and *P. tenuifolium*. Usually you see them as hedges; but if allowed to become trees they can reach 40 feet high by half as wide. Use as accent and background specimens. Willow pittosporum (*P. phillyraeoides*) is the unique individual: slow growing, to about 20 feet, with long, drooping branches. Very narrow leaves are deep dusty green, less dense than others. Use as an accent specimen in patio or garden.

PLANE TREE. See Platanus.

PLATANUS. Plane tree, Sycamore. Deciduous. Zones 5–10. Massiveness and aggressive roots limit use of plane trees to large properties and roadsides. Where space allows, all plane trees are handsome lawn specimens. London plane tree (*P. acerifolia*) and American sycamore or Buttonwood (*P.*

occidentalis) are similar; the latter has whiter bark and has a longer leafless period. Leaves are large (to 10 inches across) and lobed like maple leaves; thick trunks and major limbs are covered with greenish or light brown bark that flakes off in patches to show yellowish or white inner bark. Trees lack autumn color, but when branches are bare you see the brown, round seed clusters that hang on slender stems from branches. The two Western natives California sycamore (*P. racemosa*) and Arizona sycamore (*P. wrightii*), both Zones 7–10, often grow with picturesquely angled trunks and in multi-trunked groups.

Platanus acerifolia

PLUM. See Prunus.

PODOCARPUS. Evergreen conifer. Zones vary. Though related to pines and other evergreens with needles, these trees have narrow, pointed leaves. Fern pine (*P. gracilior*), Zones 9–10, varies depending upon method of propagation. When grown from seed, young plants grow fairly upright, bearing narrow, glossy, dark green 4-inch leaves; this represents the juvenile form of the plant. When the plant reaches the mature phase, leaves are grayish green, half as long, and more dense on fairly pendulous branches. Old trees may reach 60 feet high and about half as wide. Cuttings raised from mature growth maintain mature foliage and pendulous habit, and need considerable training to assume tree uprightness and height. These plants often are sold as *P. elongatus*. Slow-growing *P. falcatus* is similar to fern pine. Yew pine (*P. macrophyllus*), Zones 7–10, has bright green 4-inch leaves, broader than those of fern pine, and stiffer overall appearance. Slow growth takes it to a narrow 50 feet high.

Neat appearance and lack of pests and litter make these good patio trees despite their size after many years. Use them in the garden where you want fairly vertical but softly graceful accent plants, or plant them in a small grove; you can also maintain them as an informal hedge or high screen.

POPULUS. Cottonwood, Poplar, Aspen. Deciduous. Zones vary. Most poplars and cottonwoods have bad garden reputations. They are rapid growing, tough, and have networks of aggressive surface roots that can crack and raise pavement, or clog sewer and drainage lines. Limbs are subject to breakage, and some trees are pest or disease plagued. They are poor choices for town and suburban gardens; on large properties and in country landscapes, though, they can shine. In some dry plains and desert states, they constitute the majority of trees. Most widely planted is Lombardy poplar (*P. nigra* 'Italica'), Zones 3–10, which is rigidly upright to 40–100 feet with bright green triangular leaves that turn luminous yellow in autumn. Bolleana poplar (*P. alba* 'Pyramidalis'), Zones 3–10, has similar growth habit but bears lobed leaves. Use as windbreaks, as roadside or driveway trees, as single or clustered vertical accents. Quaking aspen (*P. tremuloides*), Zones 3–7, is prized for its fluttering leaves, smooth gray to white trunks and limbs, and vibrant yellow autumn color. Though it can reach 60 feet under most favorable conditions, it is usually much shorter and slighter. Grove plantings are especially attractive.

PRUNUS. Deciduous and evergreen. Zones vary. Included in the deciduous *Prunus* group are the familiar cherries, peaches, plums, apricots, and almonds. The deciduous trees are famous for their spring flower display on leafless limbs. For strictly ornamental use you can choose from many flowering but fruitless varieties. These are small to medium-size trees that vary from quite upright to rounded, according to species or variety, but are usually no wider than their height. Best for garden use are flowering cherries and plums; flowering peaches (and nectarines) are subject to too many pests and diseases to make their planting worthwhile for most gardeners.

Flowering cherries may have single, semidouble, or double blossoms in white or pink according to species or variety; many carry their blossoms in pendent clusters. Young bark is often a feature: birchlike but in lustrous mahogany brown.

Flowering plums carry smaller blossoms along branches of previous year's growth; flowers may be white, blush, or pink. Most widely planted are various purple-leafed selections (foliage ranges from dark purplish red to coppery red). Some of these will produce fruit (cherry-size plums), which can be a nuisance if they fall on pavement. Both flowering cherries and plums are fine accent specimens for patio and garden. They are frequently planted in rows as driveway or backdrop trees. They are easy trees to garden beneath.

Most evergreen *Prunus* species and varieties are dense, glossy-leafed plants that will endure heat, wind, and some drought. Usually they start out as shrubs branched to the ground and grow 30–40 feet high and sometimes as wide; train them to one trunk or let several develop. Root systems are aggressive, ruling out planting beneath. Best uses are as windbreak and background plantings; with regular pruning you can maintain them as hedges. Trained as trees they are polished, but fruit-drop on pavement rules them out for

patio or street planting. All produce tiny cream white blossoms clustered in spikes and small, cherrylike fruit. Largest leaves (7–9-inch ovals) are on English or Cherry laurel (*P. laurocerasus*), Zones 7–10; it also flowers so profusely as to be called showy. Carolina cherry laurel (*P. caroliniana*), Zones 7–10, has 4-inch oval leaves; Portugal laurel (*P. lusitanica*), Zones 7–10, has slightly larger oval leaves and prominent flower spikes in late spring into summer. Hollyleaf cherry (*P. ilicifolia*), Zones 9–10, has the broadly oval, spiny-margined leaves the name suggests; similar but with few or no marginal leaf spines is Catalina cherry (*P. lyonii*), also Zones 9–10.

PSEUDOTSUGA menziesii. Douglas fir. Evergreen conifer. Zones 6–9 (West) and 6–8 (East). Native range extends from Alaska into Mexico, and east into the Rocky Mountains. Appearance and adaptability vary somewhat, depending on point of origin. The Rocky Mountains bluish-needled form, *P.m. glauca*, grows in Zones 4–8. Forest size is statuesque — 70–250 feet high — but trees have a soft, graceful appearance that mitigates their massiveness. Growth is rapid, regular, and dense. Young trees are cone-shaped and bear foliage to the ground; as trees age, the conical form remains but lower branches die. Main limbs vary from slightly upright to slightly drooping. Soft, densely set needles, to 1½ inches long, surround branches in bottlebrush fashion; typically they are dark green, but new spring growth is bright apple green. Use on large properties as backdrop or skyline trees, windbreak, or isolated specimen.

Pyrus communis

PYRUS. Pear. Deciduous and evergreen. Zones vary. Common or fruiting pear (*P. communis*), Zones 5–9, is a highly ornamental garden tree: 30–40 feet tall at maturity, pyramid shaped with an obvious vertical branching pattern. Dark green, glossy oval leaves turn glowing red in autumn; spring flower display is white. Trees are deep rooted and long lived; you can easily garden beneath them. Other pears are strictly ornamental, producing insignificant or inedible fruit. Several widely sold varieties of *P. calleryana*, Zones 5–9, are 'Bradford', with upward-sweeping branches to 50 feet high and 30 feet wide and 'Aristocrat', of similar

height and pyramidal in outline, with purple red autumn color. Sand pear (*P. pyrifolia*), Zones 6–9, resembles common pear but has more leathery, glossy leaves that in autumn turn purplish red. Evergreen pear (*P. kawakamii*), Zones 8–10, is a favorite feature tree in patios and small gardens. Shape and spread are determined more by pruning than by natural habit. Grow as single or multi-trunked tree; willowy, drooping branches need guidance to form good framework. Height is less than that of other pears — to about 25 feet. Glossy leaves are backdrop for good show of white flowers in late winter to spring.

QUERCUS. Oak. Deciduous and evergreen. Zones vary. Though all oaks bear acorns, the trees vary greatly — from the 90-foot, broad-spreading, deciduous Red oaks (*Q. rubra*), Zones 4–10, to the enormously spreading, evergreen Southern live oaks (*Q. virginiana*), Zones 8–10. Some have opaque canopies (Holly oak, *Q. ilex*, Zones 7–10), making them seem larger than they are, whereas others (Scarlet oak, *Q. coccinea*, Zones 5–9) are variably open in growth, the see-through quality reducing the effect of their actual mass.

With some exceptions, oaks are large trees, given good conditions. They contribute majestic beauty and shade to a garden. They are good lawn specimens as well as sturdy avenue, backdrop, or skyline trees. You can even use oaks for shade in small gardens and patios — most have deep root systems that allow other plants to grow beneath. Deciduous kinds offer autumn color (rusty yellow, orange, or red) and good winter branch pattern.

Popular deciduous oaks are White oak (*Q. alba*), Zones 4–9, to 90 feet; Swamp white oak (*Q. bicolor*), Zones 4–9, to 60 feet; Scarlet oak (*Q. coccinea*), Zones 4–9, to 80 feet; Oregon white oak (*Q. garryana*), Zones 6–9, to 90 feet; Pin oak (*Q. palustris*), Zones 4–9, to 80 feet; Red oak (*Q. rubra*), Zones 4–10, to 90 feet; and Shumard oak (*Q. shumardii*), Zones 5–9, to 80 feet. You have fewer choices among evergreen oaks, and they may be more difficult to find in nurseries. Among them are Coast live oak (*Q. agrifolia*), Zones 9–10, to 70 feet; Holly oak (*Q. ilex*), Zones 7–10, to 70 feet; Cork oak (*Q. suber*), Zones 8–10, to 70 feet; and Southern live oak (*Q. virginiana*), Zones 8–10, to 60 feet.

REDBUD. See Cercis canadensis.

REDWOOD. See Sequoia sempervirens.

RHUS. Sumac. Deciduous and evergreen. Zones vary. Evergreen African sumac (*R. lancea*), Zones 9–10, is an especially graceful small tree to 25 feet, single or multitrunked. Growth is fairly slow; habit is spreading and open, with weeping outer branchlets. Leaves consist of 3 dark green, narrow, drooping leaflets to 5 inches long. Female trees may bear pea-size yellow or red berrylike fruits— a maintenance problem on pavement. Use as

. . . Rhus

a patio or lawn tree, or as a filmy screen planting. It's especially useful in desert regions for filtering sunlight.

Staghorn sumac *(R. typhina)*, Zones 3–9, is often considered a weed tree or shrub where it grows wild—frequently in poor soils. Liabilities are brittle wood (subject to breakage from snow and ice) and a shallow root system that suckers profusely if roots are cut or broken. But with regular water in decent soil it grows rapidly into an attractive, light-structured tree from 15 to 30 feet high and sometimes as wide. Stems branch in "Y" fashion, forming an open crown with essentially no twigs. Each large leaf is composed of 11–13 narrow leaflets, to 5 inches long, that turn brilliant orange to red in early autumn. Plant in garden or patio where roots won't be disturbed. Use as a backdrop or in a grove; it's particularly attractive with a background of needle-leafed evergreens. Also use it as a single-trunked specimen, or multi-trunked or low-branched shrub-tree.

ROBINIA. Locust. Deciduous. Zones vary. Open structure and small, rounded leaflets of fresh green color give locusts a graceful appearance that belies their toughness. Individual blossoms look like small sweet peas and come in conspicuous clusters even though bloom comes after leaf-out. Trees grow fairly rapidly and succeed even in hot and dry regions. Garden drawbacks are aggressive surface roots and brittle wood. Black locust *(R. pseudoacacia)*, Zones 4–9, is better in western North America out of its native range where it has numerous insect problems. It grows up to 75 feet high, with attractive open branching pattern and deeply furrowed dark brown bark. Branches are armed with paired thorns. Fragrant white blossoms in 4–8-inch hanging clusters later develop 4-inch, beanlike seed pods. Variety 'Frisia' has yellow to chartreuse foliage; variety 'Pyramidalis' is narrow and columnar. Use black locust wherever you need filtered shade over ground that won't be intensively gardened. Idaho locust *(R. ambigua* 'Idahoensis')*, Zones 5–10, reaches about 40 feet high and half as wide. Leaves are more plentiful than on black locust and bright magenta flowers come in 8-inch clusters. Very similar is *R.* 'Purple Robe' with darker flowers and bronzy new growth. Both are good garden background trees or accent specimens.

ROWAN. See Sorbus aucuparia.

ROYAL POINCIANA. See Delonix regia.

RUSSIAN OLIVE. See Elaeagnus angustifolia.

SALIX. Willow. Deciduous. Zones vary. Water-loving willows present a garden problem because their roots are shallow and will invade nearby drainage lines and septic tanks. Other drawbacks are continuous leaf drop during growing season; brittle, easily broken wood; and susceptibility to several pests. Nevertheless, gardeners still plant weeping willows, in particular, for their beauty and rapid growth. These include *S. babylonica*, Zones 5–10, the smallest (30–50 feet high and wide) and most pendulous; Golden weeping willow *(S. alba* 'Tristis')*, Zones 3–10, to 70 feet high with bright yellow year-old branches; Wisconsin weeping willow *(S. blanda)*, Zones 5–10, to 50 feet high with shorter weeping branches; and Thurlow weeping willow *(S. elegantissima)*, Zones 5–10, also to 50 feet but with much longer pendent branches. The classic site for weeping willow is overhanging water: beside pond, lake, or stream. If you want one as a lawn or patio shade tree, you must train it so the tree structure will be high enough to keep branches from hanging too low to walk or sit beneath.

SAPIUM sebiferum. Chinese tallow tree. Deciduous. Zones 8–10. Though the tree's form—rounded to 35 feet high and wide—may not suggest a poplar, the foliage certainly does. Three-inch, light green leaves are roundish, tapering to slender point, and they flutter in the breeze. In autumn the foliage changes to blazing red, yellow, orange, plum purple, or even a mixture of colors. With regular watering, growth is rapid. Natural habit is almost shrubby, with several trunks. Use as patio or lawn specimen, or as screen planting.

SASSAFRAS albidum. Sassafras. Deciduous. Zones 4–9. Here is a tree with plenty of character. A sturdy, thick trunk supports rather short branches that often grow nearly horizontally from the trunk; from these main branches, smaller branches angle upward. The trunk branches tend to be randomly placed and sparse, creating an open, almost patchwork crown. Form is pyramidal, eventually to 60 feet. Aromatic leaves 3–7 inches long are irregularly shaped; leaf shape may be oval, lobed on one side (mitten shaped), or lobed on both sides. In autumn they turn orange to scarlet. Plant sassafras where gardening won't disturb its roots: cut or broken roots sprout profusely. Use as an accent specimen in lawn or background, alone or in small groves.

SCHINUS. Pepper tree. Evergreen. Zones 9–10. The two pepper trees differ greatly in appearance and in uses. California pepper tree *(S. molle)* combines pendent grace of weeping willow with heavy, gnarled trunk and limb structure reminiscent of ancient olive trees. Rapid growth takes it to 40 feet high and wide. Foliage is narrow and light green; inconspicuous yellowish white flowers produce decorative hanging clusters of rose-colored berries in autumn. Roots are close to the surface and greedy; they'll crack nearby pavement, penetrate drainage and sewer lines, and prevent growth of all but tough lawn beneath the tree. Plant as a specimen where suitable or along a country road.

Brazilian pepper *(S. terebinthifolius)* is usually planted as a shade tree for patio or garden. It reaches about 35 feet high with equal spread, forming a rounded crown without pendulous branches. Leaflets are much broader, coarser, and darker green than those of California pepper tree, and the winter berries are larger and bright red. Grow it as a single-trunk specimen or as a multitrunked clump.

SENNA. See Cassia.

SEQUOIA sempervirens. Coast redwood. Evergreen conifer. Zones 8–10 (8 only in the East). Though famous as the world's tallest tree, the coast redwood is also a surprisingly good garden candidate. It's fast growing (3–5 feet a year), pest free, and almost always fresh looking and woodsy smelling. To over 300 feet high in the wild, it is likely to be only 70–90 feet high and 15–30 feet wide in the garden after 25 years. Typical shape is a symmetrical narrow pyramid of soft-looking foliage. Branches usually grow straight out from trunk and curve upward at tips; branchlets hang down slightly from main branches. The trunk is covered with red brown fibrous bark. Flat, pointed, narrow leaves—medium green on top, grayish underneath—grow in one plane on both sides of stem, giving a featherlike appearance. Small round cones are 1 inch long. Use a single tree for a bold accent specimen in the lawn or garden background, or plant a grove for an emphatic vertical statement. Tree retains branches to the ground for many years unless you remove them to reveal the tree's sturdy, red brown trunk.

Sequoia sempervirens

SERVICE BERRY. See Amelanchier.

SHADBLOW. See Amelanchier.

SILK TREE. See Albizia julibrissin.

SILVER BELL. See Halesia carolina.

SNOWBELL. See Styrax.

SNOWDROP TREE. See Halesia carolina.

SOPHORA japonica. Japanese pagoda tree, Chinese scholar tree. Deciduous. Zones 5–10 (West) and 5–8 (East). Normal growth is moderate to about 20 feet, then quite slow; tree eventually may reach 40–50 feet in height and width. Rounded canopy consists of small oval leaflets borne on smooth, green-barked limbs; shade is moderate and overall effect is graceful. In mid to late summer come foot-long clusters of yellowish white, sweet-pea-like blossoms (which can stain concrete paving). Normally bloom comes only when tree is 5 or more years old, but variety 'Regent' will bloom at an early age. In autumn, foliage color does not change, but leaves drop and disintegrate quickly, eliminating need for raking. This is a good tree to use for shading patio, lawn, or garden.

SORBUS aucuparia. European mountain ash, Rowan. Deciduous. Zones 3–9 (West) and 3–7 (East). This tree and the smaller American mountain ash (*S. americana*) offer something of interest in all seasons. Five-inch clusters of small white flowers bloom in spring, followed by hanging clusters of pea-size to cranberry-size red orange fruit that will remain on the tree through winter, birds permitting. Each leaf consists of 2-inch oval leaflets arranged in featherlike formation; in autumn, leaves turn yellow, ochre, or orange red. Branches rise upward to form an oval to rounded crown reaching 40–50 feet high. Use as a specimen tree for lawn or garden. Red orange fruit in winter are especially showy against a backdrop of needleleafed evergreen trees.

SOUR GUM. See Nyssa sylvatica.

SPRUCE. See Picea.

STYRAX. Snowbell. Deciduous. Zones vary. Attractive growth habit, flowers, moderate size and deep, noncompetitive roots make these first-rate trees for patio and small garden planting. Japanese snowbell or snow-drop tree (*S. japonicus*), Zones 5–9, has a strongly horizontal branching pattern that results in a broad, flat-topped crown to 30 feet high. Oval, 3-inch leaves angle upward from branches, and in late spring the white, bell-like blossoms hang below leaves. Autumn foliage is yellow. Fragrant snowbell (*S. obassia*), Zones 7–9, differs in its narrow spread, larger leaves, and flowers that come at ends of branches in 6–8-inch drooping clusters. Prune to control shape; plant tends to be shrubby unless lower side branches are suppressed. It's a nice tree to look up into; plant it in raised beds near outdoor entertaining areas, or on high bank above path.

SWEET GUM. See Liquidambar styraciflua.

SYCAMORE. See Platanus.

TANGELO. See Citrus.

TANGERINE. See Citrus.

THUJA. Arborvitae. Evergreen conifer. Zones vary. The most familiar arborvitaes are symmetrical shrubs, but two North American species are trees. Both have overlapping scalelike leaves on branches carried in flat sprays. American arborvitae (*T. occidentalis*), Zones 3–8 (East), 6–9 (West), is a narrow, conical 60-footer in its wild form. Leaf sprays are bright green to yellowish green. Foliage turns brown in severe cold and will scorch badly in the coldest, windiest gar-

dens. Its varieties 'Douglasii Pyramidalis' and 'Fastigiata' form dense, slim cones to about 25 feet tall; they're the most widely sold. Use them as vertical accents, backgrounds, or screens. Western red cedar (*T. plicata*), Zones 6–9 (West), 5–8 (East), is a 200-foot timber tree in its native West Coast forests; it will reach about half that height in gardens, with widely spreading lower branches. Dark green foliage on drooping branchlets gives graceful, lacy appearance. Cinnamon brown cones are ½ inch wide. Use as lawn or background specimen, but allow plenty of room. You can also plant it as a high hedge or screen and control size by trimming.

TILIA. Linden. Deciduous. Zones vary. Lindens are dense, compact trees, usually taller than wide, with irregularly heart-shaped leaves and drooping clusters of small, fragrant flowers. They're popular street, park, and lawn trees because of their neat appearance. Autumn foliage is yellow only where winters are cold. American linden (*T. americana*), Zones 4–9, may reach 60 feet high by 25 feet wide with dense crown of dark foliage; narrowly upright varieties are available. Little-leaf linden (*T. cordata*), Zones 4–9, forms a slightly shorter and broader pyramidal crown; its varieties 'Greenspire' and 'Rancho' are more narrow and upright. Crimean linden (*T. euchlora*), Zones 5–9, casts less shade from a tree that reaches 35–50 feet high and wide. Its variety 'Redmond' has a pyramidal shape. Silver linden (*T. tomentosa*), Zones 6–9, takes its name from dark leaves with silvery undersides that flutter in breeze. It grows 60 feet high and about half as wide.

TSUGA. Hemlock. Evergreen conifer. Zones vary. Gracefulness is the hallmark of all hemlocks: small, needlelike leaves are dense on slightly pendulous branches. All are narrowly pyramidal and tall (from 40 feet); use on larger properties as specimens, backdrop, or skyline trees. In smaller gardens, train and clip them as hedges. Hemlocks need high humidity in summer. Canada hemlock (*T. canadensis*), Zones 5–9, may become a broad 90-foot pyramid in its native territory and tends to grow 2 or more trunks. Dark green needles, banded in white beneath, are about ½ inch long and are arranged in opposite rows on branchlets. Oval, ¾-inch-long, medium brown cones grow on short stalks, hang down from branches. Many dwarf or pendulous varieties exist; availability varies locally. Carolina hemlock (*T. caroliniana*), Zones 5–7, is similar but shorter (to 40 feet) and narrower. Western hemlock (*T. heterophylla*), Zones 5–9 (West only), is a fast-growing, narrowly pyramidal 200-footer that succeeds only within its native range. Foliage, dark green to yellowish green, gives the tree a fernlike quality.

ULMUS. Elm. Deciduous or partially evergreen. Zones vary. The majestic vase-shaped American elm (*U. americana*), Zones 3–9,

has long been part of classic Americana — famous for shading streets and lawns, regally adorning parks and fields. But now, throughout most of the country, the American elm is being destroyed by Dutch elm disease. No longer is it a safe planting recommendation. All elms are in some degree susceptible to the disease and shouldn't be planted where the disease is or has been active.

Elms provide great shade. They are best used where their shallow and aggressive roots won't compete with garden plantings, other than lawn or ground covers. For tall, dense shade choose Smooth-leafed elm (*U. carpinifolia*), Zones 5–9; Scotch elm (*U. glabra*), Zones 5–9; Dutch elm (*U. hollandica*), Zones 5–9; and English elm (*U. procera*), Zones 5–9. All turn yellow in autumn. Siberian elm (*U. pumila*), Zones 5–9, is worthwhile in regions of heat, drought, and cold winters where tree choice is limited; liabilities are greedy roots, brittle wood, and susceptibility to storm damage. Chinese elm, also sold as Lacebark elm, (*U. parvifolia*), Zones 5–10, is evergreen in mild regions but partly evergreen to deciduous in colder zones. Long, arching, semiweeping branches produce a tree 40–60 feet tall and up to 70 feet across; older specimens have attractive patchwork bark. This is the best choice for shading smaller properties, but it requires training to establish a high crown. Chinese elm is highly resistant to Dutch elm disease.

YELLOW WOOD. See Cladrastis lutea.

Zelkova serrata

ZELKOVA serrata. Sawleaf zelkova. Deciduous. Zones 6–9. This tree is closely related to the elms (*Ulmus*), and like them finds its best use as a shade provider along streets and driveways and in lawns. Mature tree may be 60 feet tall and wide with a distinctive, bulky structure. The trunk is short and thick, and from it come many ascending branches that emerge at nearly the same point. Form ranges from urn-shaped to quite spreading: variety 'Village Green' comes close to duplicating the vase shape of American elm (*Ulmus americana*) and is resistant to Dutch elm disease. Train young trees to develop a strong framework. Leaves are 5-inch ovals with toothed edges; autumn color is rusty yellow, occasionally orange, red, or dull reddish brown.

Fruit-bearing shrubs & trees for your garden

Just because a plant bears a crop of edible fruit, you need not assume it has to be set aside in a special plot — the back-40 farm — where it can be productive without interfering with garden attractiveness. All the fruit and berry-producing plants presented here are good-looking enough to incorporate into ornamental plantings without appearing out of place or having their cultural demands short-changed; and to satisfy home needs, you don't usually need farm-quantity plantings. Even if you yearn for a home farm or orchard, don't imagine that it must be a strictly utilitarian plot segregated from the main garden. Crop-producing areas can be worked into the overall landscape plan so that they're an attractive and integral part of the garden.

A few of the popular fruiting shrubs and trees are grown as much for garden ornamentation as for fruit production. These are listed below but their full descriptions appear in the Encyclopedia on pages 97–107, 110–119.

SHRUBS

BLUEBERRIES (*Vaccinium*). Deciduous. Zones vary. Best climates are found in Zones 8 and 9 of the Pacific Northwest, and Zones 4–9 east of the Mississippi River. Plants need cool, moist, acid soil and some humidity. In the South, varieties of rabbiteye blueberries are best; in other areas, highbush varieties are grown. Most varieties are upright plants to about 6 feet. New growth is bronzy, turning to dark green; oval leaves color yellow or red in autumn. Blueberries are good for filmy hedge plantings or for massing in woodland gardens. Tiny white to pinkish blossoms produce showy fruit in summer.

CANE BERRIES (*Rubus*). Deciduous. Zones vary. Represented here are blackberries (including boysenberry, dewberry, loganberry, olallieberry, youngberry) and the various raspberries (red, black, purple, and yellow). Of all the fruits and berries described on these pages, the cane berries are the most obvious crop plants. Regardless of the various growth types and handling techniques, they are best planted in rows or narrow strips and trained on or between wires; for landscape planting they are useful as a hedge or backdrop. Foliage is attractive, robust (each leaf contains several broadly oval, serrated leaflets); clusters of white flowers, colored fruit are ornamental in spring and summer.

CURRANTS and GOOSEBERRIES (*Ribes*). Deciduous. Zones vary. These are similar plants 3–5 feet high and spreading as wide; leaves are lobed to maplelike, about 3 inches wide, and stems of some gooseberries are spiny. Bushes are attractive specimen or hedge/barrier/backdrop plantings. The summer fruit are somewhat showy: currants have drooping clusters of red or white fruit, and gooseberries may be green, pink, or red — larger fruit but in smaller clusters. Both grow best in regions where winter is cold, soil and air moisture high in summer; Zones 3–8 or 9 (West), Zones 3–6 (East) for currants; same Western Zones and Zones 3–7 (East) for gooseberries.

GRAPES (*Vitis*). Deciduous vines. Zones vary. A healthy grape vine is a ruggedly handsome, bursting-with-vigor landscape adornment. Any overhead structure is suitable for displaying its lush beauty, and on a wire fence you can display a grape vine as an espalier. Older stems have shaggy brown bark, contrasting with large rounded to lobed leaves that may be bright green or gray green (shape and color vary according to variety). Blossoms are inconspicuous, but the hanging grape clusters are highly decorative. There are various types of grapes that have different regional climate preferences. European wine and table grapes thrive in the West and selected areas of the Northeast; American and American hybrid varieties grow in the East and in central states as well as in the West; the South has a different selection, based on native species.

KIWI (*Actinidia chinensis*). Deciduous. Zones 7–10 (West), 7–9 (East). For fruit production you need a female, fruit-producing variety and a male variety for pollination. Fruit are egg-size and egg-shaped, covered with brown fuzz that disguises lime green interior; autumn is harvest season. Once established, a vine is tremendously vigorous, climbing by twining. Overheads and fences are natural supports for the heavy stems. Bold foliage is 5–8 inches long and broadly oval to roundish, dark green on upper side but velvety white beneath.

STRAWBERRY (*Fragaria*). Evergreen. Zones 3–10; select varieties adapted to your local climate. The fruiting strawberries make an attractive border planting or can be used as ground cover: clumps of good-looking, deeply veined leaves send out runners to extend the area covered. Their need for regular watering suits them to many garden spots.

Blueberry

Currant

Grape

Apple

Apricot

Cherry

Fig

Peach

Plum

TREES

APPLE. See *Malus pumila*, page 103.

APRICOT (*Prunus armeniaca* varieties). Deciduous. Zones 5–9; individual varieties vary in their climate preferences. Trees will withstand −10°F/−23°C, but late frosts are likely to destroy blooms. The apricot is a good-looking tree with glossy, leathery, rounded leaves; it provides good shade and tawny yellow autumn color. Mature trees are round-topped, to 20 feet high and 30 feet wide, with rugged bark. Many varieties available, adapted to different climates and with different ripening times. Dwarf varieties are shrubby to about 6 feet high, 8 feet across.

CHERRY (*Prunus*). Deciduous. Zones vary, but climate preferences are marked; check with county farm advisor or agricultural extension agent for local recommendations. Sweet cherries (*P. avium*), Zones 5–7, have upright branch structure but may spread equal to height, 30–35 feet. Sour cherries (*P. cerasus*), Zones 4–7, are fairly spreading, more irregular in shape, to about 20 feet at most. Both have handsome young bark, oval leaves, spring display of

white flowers. Duke cherries, a hybrid of the two, are somewhat larger trees than sour cherries. All sweet cherry varieties need another variety as pollinizer for fruit production; sour and duke cherries are self-fruitful.

CITRUS. See *Citrus*, page 99.

FIG. See *Ficus carica*, page 100.

PEACH and NECTARINE (*Prunus persica*). Deciduous. Zones 6–9, generally. Most varieties need some winter chill but are at risk where winter cold drops below −15°F/−26°C, (there are varieties that will thrive in coldest parts of Zone 10). These can be highly ornamental trees and very dependable fruit producers if you are willing to spray for peach leaf curl, which seriously disfigures foliage and weakens trees, and if you realize that trees decline in vigor and health after about 15 years. Spring flower display—pink through red—is spectacular; there are flowering varieties that produce no fruit. Leaves are long, narrow, and curved, on trees that can reach 25 feet unpruned but are usually kept to around 15 feet high and as wide. Dwarf forms of popular varieties are available, growing to about 6–8 feet high; genetic dwarf varieties produce shaggy-leafed 4-foot shrubs.

The fast-growing full-size trees need careful early guidance to form good branch framework; in following years they need annual dormant-season pruning to maintain productivity, shapeliness, and health. Their annual labor requirements are higher than for other home fruit trees. Consult with county farm advisor or agricultural extension agent for varieties best suited to your locality.

PEAR See *Pyrus communis*, page 105.

PLUM and PRUNE (*Prunus*). Deciduous. Zones vary. The most commonly grown plums and prunes are of two types: European and Japanese; each is somewhat different in climate preference, growth habit, fruit. Both types have white blossoms in early spring, oval leaves that turn rusty yellow in autumn. European plums (Zones 5–9, West; 5–7 or 8, East) include all prunes, which are particular varieties that can be dried without fermenting at the pit. Height is 15–20 feet with equal or slightly greater spread; fruit range from green to yellow through purple to nearly black. Japanese plum trees (Zones 6–9, West; 6–8, East) reach about the same size but make long, vigorous growth that requires more pruning.

Shrubs for shaping the landscape

Shrubs form the framework of a landscape — the stable plantings that influence views and direct circulation. They also provide seasonal focal points such as flowers, fruit, foliage, and branch pattern. The bonus is that they remain largely unchanged from one year to the next. Within the shrubs category is a rich assortment of plants ranging from the unobtrusively neutral to the inescapably flamboyant, from knee-high to house-tall.

ABELIA grandiflora. Glossy abelia. Evergreen. Zones 6–10. Though it has no moment of spectacular showiness, glossy abelia is always good-looking. Main and secondary branches arch up and out from the ground. Plant builds gracefully to 8 feet high and wide, well-furnished with glossy, oval, ½–1½-inch leaves. Foliage takes on bronzy to purplish tints in autumn. Small, tubular, white to pinkish flowers appear in profusion from late spring to early autumn. Variety 'Edward Goucher' is somewhat shorter and more fine-textured, with lilac pink flowers.

ARBORVITAE. See Thuja.

ARBUTUS unedo. Strawberry tree. Evergreen. Zones 8–10. After many years with no restraint, this slow-growing tree may reach 35 feet high and wide. Prune it to maintain it as a medium to large shrub. Oblong, 2–3-inch, glossy leaves with red leaf stalks densely clothe branches; shreddy, red brown bark covers trunk and branches. Strawberry tree is unusual because bloom comes in autumn and early winter, and fruit matures at the same time. Drooping clusters of small, urn-shaped, white blossoms contrast with ¾-inch, round, yellow to red fruits. Use as a specimen, or group for screen, barrier, or unclipped hedge planting. Tolerance is remarkable: it grows from desert to seashore, and takes little water to regular watering. Variety 'Compacta' is much shorter and dependably shrubby.

Arbutus unedo

AUCUBA japonica. Japanese aucuba. Evergreen. Zones 7–10. Ability to thrive in shade and tolerance of poor soil are two outstanding attributes. Plant is a dense, bulky shrub usually to 10 feet high and nearly as wide; glossy, tooth-edged leaves may reach 8 inches long by 3 inches wide. Inconspicuous flowers in early spring produce bright red berries on female plants (if a male plant is nearby for pollination) in autumn and winter. Nurseries carry selected varieties with variegated foliage; 3-foot-high 'Nana' has pinkish buff berries.

AZALEA. See Rhododendron.

BAMBOO. Evergreen grass with woody stems. Zones vary. The many bamboos encompass a great range in height — from slightly over a foot tall to over 40 feet — and in growth habit — from compact clumps to those that spread widely by underground stems. The most useful bamboos for general garden purposes are the clump-forming types, 4–16 feet high. These are essential parts of oriental-style landscapes, can be attractive accents regardless of theme, and excel as hedge and screen plantings. Several varieties of *Bambusa glaucescens*, Zones 9–10, meet the criteria of limited height and clumping growth, and boost plentiful foliage carried to the ground. 'Alphonse Karr' and 'Fernleaf' are upright, 'Golden Goddess' and *B. g. riviereorum* have fountainlike habit. *Sinarundinaria murielae*, Zones 7–10, can be held to 6–8 feet; unrestrained, it reaches 15 feet with arching top growth.

BARBERRY. See Berberis.

BEAUTY BUSH. See Kolkwitzia amabilis.

BERBERIS. Barberry. Deciduous and evergreen. Zones vary. Among the many species and selected varieties of barberry are some of the most widely planted shrubs. Availability varies according to region (some are forbidden in grain-growing areas because they are hosts for black rust of wheat); visit a good local nursery to make a selection. Small spring flowers are yellow to orange, usually showy, and often in large clusters; fruit that follow turn red, dark blue, or black in autumn, depending on the species. Deciduous barberries put on a show of yellow to red autumn foliage. Most have small, oval leaves, often with marginal spines; virtually all have spiny branches. Use these undemanding and attractive plants in sun or light shade for screen, hedge, border, and barrier planting. Deciduous Japanese barberry (*B. thunbergii*), Zones 4–9, has several varieties with bronzy red to purplish red foliage and one with yellow leaves.

BOTTLEBRUSH. See Callistemon.

BOXWOOD. See Buxus.

BRIDAL WREATH SPIRAEA. See Spiraea prunifolia.

BROOM. See Cytisus, Genista.

BUCKTHORN. See Rhamnus.

BUDDLEIA. Butterfly bush. Deciduous. Zones 5–9. Fountain butterfly bush (*B. alternifolia*) has long, arching branches covered with small clusters of lilac purple blossoms in spring. Narrow, willowlike leaves are dark green on upper surface, gray beneath, to 4 inches long. As a large shrub, to 12 feet high, the form may be irregular. Trained as small tree, the branches droop with the grace of weeping willow. Common butterfly bush (*B. davidii*) bears long spikes of small flowers in midsummer; many named varieties come in white, pink, lilac, purple, and blue. Fast growth produces open, rangy plant 4–10 feet high and wide with lance-shaped leaves 4–12 inches long, dark green above and white beneath. Best use is as background accent in mixed planting.

BUTTERFLY BUSH. See Buddleia.

BUXUS. Boxwood, Box. Evergreen. Zones vary. English boxwood (*B. sempervirens*), Zones 5–10 (West) and 5–9 (East), is a classic for clipped hedges. Shiny, oval, dark green leaves are no more than 1¼ inches long; foliage is dense. The basic species may reach a billowy 15–20 feet high and wide if not clipped, and is suitable for large hedge work; selected small and slow-growing varieties are better for low hedges such as along pathways. This species won't succeed in alkaline soil or where summer is hot and dry. Japanese boxwood (*B. microphylla japonica*), Zones 5–10, is similar to English boxwood, grows in climate and soil where English boxwood fails. Round-tipped leaves, up to 1 inch, turn bronze to brown in winter in coldest regions. Korean boxwood (*B. microphylla koreana*) is slightly more cold-tolerant, slower growing, and smaller in stature and leaf size than the Japanese form.

CALLISTEMON. Bottlebrush. Evergreen. Zone 10 and warmest parts of Zone 9. Fast growth, showy color, and a tough constitution are chief assets. Actual flowers are quite small, but long, colorful stamens make a conspicuous display. Leaves of most are usually narrow and linear. Use bottlebrushes as accent specimens, screens, or windbreaks. Many have red flowers: Narrow-leafed bottlebrush (*C. linearis*) blooms in summer, reaches 8 feet high and 5 feet wide; Fiery bottlebrush (*C. phoeniceus*) is stiffly upright and dense, with bloom in spring and autumn; Stiff bottlebrush (*C. rigidus*) has gray green leaves sparsely covering an erect plant that may reach 20 feet high, blooming in spring and summer; *C. cupressifolius* grows

5 feet high, spreading wider, with gray green leaves and summer flowers; *C. citrinus* 'Compacta' is less than 6 feet tall and blooms on and off year-round. For pink flowers on a 6–8-foot plant, choose *C.* 'Rosea'; *C. citrinus* 'Jeffersii' is similar but with blossoms of red purple fading to lavender. Needlelike dark green leaves of *C. pachyphyllus viridis* contrast strikingly with light green flowers.

CALLUNA vulgaris. Scotch heather. Evergreen. Zones 4–9 (West) and 4–7 (East); best in Northwest and Northeast. Many named varieties have been selected from the one species — a billowy plant to 3 feet high with tiny, needlelike leaves and small, bell-shaped, pink flowers. Specialists offer heathers ranging from ground covers to stiffly upright plants. Flowers come in white, shades of pink, lavender, and purple, and foliage can be varying shades of green, chartreuse and yellow, gray, rusty red, with many types changing color in winter. Flowering occurs between late spring and midautumn. Feathery texture, small sizes, and year-round good looks make heathers a fine choice for foreground planting. Use different varieties to compose attractive planting entirely of heathers, or interplant with other shrubs having same soil and moisture needs.

CAMELLIA. Evergreen. Zones vary somewhat; generally 8–10. Most camellias are outstanding foliage plants that give a spectacular flower display. Thick leaves are pointed ovals, usually dark green and glossy on dense plants. "Dignified" and "formal" aptly describe these shrubs. The most widely planted camellias are varieties of *C. japonica.* Plants may be slow to moderately fast growing, depending on variety; in time all may become treelike but can easily be kept as shrubs indefinitely. Bloom season spans midautumn through midspring; flowers range from 2 to 6 inches across, single to fully double including various special formations, in white, pink shades, red shades, and variegated combinations. Camellias are excellent hedge and backdrop plants as well as accent specimens. Varieties of *C. reticulata* are more definitely treelike than japonicas, with sparser, less glossy foliage. Blossoms are largest of all: to 8 inches, often informally double, in pink through crimson, many with white variegations. Use the reticulatas as specimen plants or with lower and better-foliaged plants. Sasanqua camellias are varieties of *C. sasanqua* plus those of *C. vernalis; C. hiemalis* is similar. These start flowering in early autumn and usually finish by midwinter. Blooms are small and rather flimsy, but come in great profusion on more limber-stemmed plants. The more vinelike varieties are useful as ground covers and espaliers; stiffer, more upright ones are excellent for hedges and mass plantings as high ground cover. The expanding group of hybrid camellias includes many hybrids of *C. saluenensis;* these are less rigid, often faster growing plants than the japonicas, with less spectacular individual blossoms.

There are *C. reticulata* hybrids with other species that capture some reticulata flower magnificence on more full-foliaged plants.

CARISSA grandiflora. Natal plum. Evergreen. Zone 10 and Zone 9 with protection. Natal plum offers year-round attractiveness. Lustrous, leathery, oval 3-inch leaves are backdrop for highly fragrant, 2-inch, starlike white blossoms and red, plum-shaped, edible fruit that appear throughout the year. Growth is upright but rounded, about 6–10 feet high, (to 20 feet in most favorable locations) with branched spines along branches and at branch tips. Best uses are as barrier hedge and screen, clipped or natural. Smaller-growing varieties are available.

CHAENOMELES. Flowering quince. Deciduous. Zones 4–9. During growing season these shrubs offer no outstanding beauty of leaf or habit, but their late-winter to early-spring flowering cannot be overlooked. Most nursery offerings are hybrids differing in color, size, and growth. Some are dense and upright to 10 feet, some are more rounded and to 5 feet, and others are angular and spreading. Flowers, usually 1½–2 inches across, may be single, semidouble, or double, in white, pink and white, pink, salmon, orange, or red. Flowering is profuse at a time when almost nothing else is in bloom. Use as specimen accents or as hedges, screens, or barriers; most are somewhat thorny.

CHAMAECYPARIS. False cypress. Evergreen. Zones vary. The various tree-size *Chamaecyparis* species have produced many shrub-size variants. Many of these are rock garden shrublets, but several varieties from 6 to 20 feet high are useful as accent or background specimens and as hedge or screen plantings. Fine-textured, feathery appearance comes from tiny scalelike leaves or needles. Foliage color ranges from silvery gray, bluish, and many shades of green to yellow or chartreuse; depending on variety, plant habit may be columnar, pyramidal, rounded, weeping, or spreading. Varieties of *C. lawsoniana* and *C. nootkatensis* grow in Zones 6–9, Pacific Coast only; varieties of *C. obtusa* and *C. pisifera* grow in Zones 4–9 (West) and 4–8 (East).

CISTUS. Rockrose. Evergreen. Zones 8–10 (West) and Zone 8 (East). *Cistus* species and hybrids are invaluable components of dry gardens, used as flowering accents interplanted with other drought-tolerant plants. They also mass well on sloping land. Foliage is somewhat rough-textured, wavy-edged, and aromatic. Late spring and early summer bring heavy show of open, circular flowers with silky texture. Orchid rockrose, *C. purpureus,* has 3-inch reddish purple blooms on a 4-foot plant; purplish pink-flowered *C. incanus* is 3–5 feet tall; *C.* 'Doris Hibberson' has clear pink, 3-inch blossoms, and gray foliage on 3-foot plant. White rockrose, *C. hybridus,* may reach 5 feet high, its 1½-inch flowers white with yellow centers; Crimson-

spot rockrose, *C. ladanifer,* may reach 5 feet, with 3-inch white blossoms spotted dark red at petal bases.

Cistus purpureus

CODIAEUM variegatum. Croton. Evergreen. Zone 10, Florida only. Variable is the key word for croton. Among the many varieties, leaves may be narrowly to broadly lance-shaped, linear, deeply lobed, even spiral. Even more varied are the leaf markings and color combinations: green, yellow, red, purple, bronze, pink, ivory — and almost any combination of these. Usual height is 6–15 feet, but dwarf varieties are available. Use as an accent.

COFFEEBERRY. See Rhamnus californica.

CONFEDERATE ROSE. See Hibiscus mutabilis.

CORNELIAN CHERRY. See Cornus mas.

CORNUS. Dogwood. Deciduous. Zones vary. Largest of the shrubby dogwoods is Cornelian cherry (*C. mas*), Zones 4–8, with attractive, twiggy growth to 15 feet. (You can also train it as small tree.) In late winter, bare twigs carry many clusters of small yellow flowers; these form ¾-inch-long edible fruit that turn bright red in early autumn. Shiny green, oval leaves turn yellow or red before falling. The three species below are valued for brilliant color of bare branches in winter — especially showy against background of snow. Tatarian dogwood (*C. alba*), Zones 2–9, forms a spreading thicket of upright stems to about 10 feet that are blood red in winter; variety 'Sibirica' is shorter, less rampant, with coral red stems. Deep green, pointed leaves to 5 inches long turn red in autumn; small, fragrant, creamy white flowers in 2-inch clusters appear in spring. Redtwig dogwood or Red-osier (*C. stolonifera*), Zones 4–9, is similar but taller (to 15 feet) with leaves half the size; variety 'Flaviramea' has yellow twigs and branches. Bloodtwig dogwood (*C. sanguinea*), Zones 4–9, forms a multistemmed plant to 12 feet high; leaves turn dark red in autumn, twigs and branches are dark red to purplish throughout winter. Flowers and foliage are similar to Redtwig's.

COTINUS coggygria. Smoke tree. Deciduous. Zones 5–10. In time, and without restriction, this forms a massive shrub to 25

…Cotinus coggygria

feet high and wide; prune to keep it smaller or train as a small tree. Roundish leaves to 3 inches long are blue green, turning rusty yellow to orange red in autumn; some purple-leafed varieties retain color until autumn. Large, loose clusters of tiny flowers form the "smoke" as they fade and develop a haze of fuzzy purple hairs. These are striking accent shrubs for sparsely watered background and garden fringe areas.

COTONEASTER. Evergreen and deciduous. Zones vary. All cotoneasters have a conspicuous spring display of small white to pink flowers in clusters. The real display comes from ¼–½-inch berries that turn red in autumn and may last through winter. Leaves of deciduous species color yellow, orange, or red before falling. Among the many species and several hybrids are shrubs from as low as 2 feet to shrub-trees that may reach 15-20 feet; many have arching main stems or erect stems with arching branches. Choose the right size cotoneaster for its intended location: though many can be trimmed as hedges, any heading back of limbs to fit a space almost always detracts from the natural beauty of the plant's graceful form. Among the large types (over 10 feet tall) are evergreen *C. franchetii*, Zones 7–9; Parney cotoneaster (*C. lacteus*, formerly *C. parneyi*), Zones 6–10; Willowleaf cotoneaster (*C. salicifolius*), Zones 6–10; and *C. watereri*, Zones 7–9, a group of hybrids having unusually large fruits and leaves to 5 inches long. *C. henryanus*, Zones 7–10, is semievergreen; *C. multiflorus*, Zones 6–10, is deciduous. Those under 10 feet include evergreen *C.* 'Hybridus Pendulus', Zones 6–10, and Wintergreen cotoneaster (*C. conspicuus*), Zones 7–10. Deciduous species include Cranberry cotoneaster (*C. apiculatus*), Zones 5–10; Spreading cotoneaster (*C. divaricatus*), Zones 5–10; and *C. integerrimus*, Zones 6–10. Other species, both large and small, may be available locally.

CROTON. See Codiaeum variegatum.

CYTISUS. Broom. Evergreen and deciduous. Zones vary. Where they are well adapted, two species have become roadside weeds, giving the group a bad name. But even those two have their garden uses if you control their seed-setting. All brooms have clusters of small, sweet-pea-like flowers; leaves or leaflets are tiny ovals. Young branches are green, so deciduous kinds really don't look bare when leaves drop. Use brooms as individual accents and as mass planting, screen, or hedge. All are drought-tolerant. Canary Island broom (*C. canariensis*), Zones 9–10, is one of the "weeds" — a dense, attractive plant to 8 feet high with bright yellow flowers in spring and early summer. Similar, but with larger leaflets and looser flower spikes, is *C. racemosus*, Zones 9–10. Deciduous Warminster broom (*C. praecox*), Zones 5–10, mounds to about 5 feet high and 6 feet wide; flowers are pale yellow or creamy white, but there are varieties with other colors: 'Albus' (white), 'Allgold' (bright yellow), and 'Hol-

landia' (pink). Scotch broom (*C. scoparius*), Zones 7–10, is the other species that has naturalized widely. Upright, wandlike stems (almost leafless) may reach 10 feet tall, decorated in spring and early summer with intense yellow flowers. Named varieties come in interesting colors: cream, red, white, red and yellow, pink and red, orange and apricot.

DAPHNE. Evergreen and deciduous. Zones vary. Two of the three popular daphnes are prized for their fragrant flowers. All are usually used in the foreground as individual accent plants. Winter daphne (*D. odora*), Zones 7–10, is the most fragrant and also the most difficult to grow. Leathery, 3-inch, lance-shaped leaves are glossy dark green, covering a spreading plant to about 4 feet high. Flowers are a combination of purplish red and creamy pink, in clusters at branch tips in late winter. Of two white-flowered varieties, one has leaves outlined in yellow. *D. burkwoodii*, Zones 5–9, ranges from evergreen to deciduous, depending on winter cold. Plant is upright to about 4 feet, dense with many small, narrow leaves. Flowers are white fading to pink, in late spring and late summer. Variety 'Somerset' grows a bit taller and has deeper pink flowers. Scentless Lilac daphne (*D. genkwa*), Zones 6–9, is deciduous, with upright stems to about 4 feet. Before leaves emerge, lilac blue blossoms cover the stems. White fruits and 2-inch oval leaves follow.

Daphne burkwoodii

DEUTZIA. Deciduous. Zones vary. Masses of pretty flowers decorate plants in mid to late spring. During the rest of the growing season, plants are unobtrusive; there is no autumn foliage color. Slender deutzia (*D. gracilis*), Zones 4–9, is a graceful, arching, 3-foot shrub featuring masses of snow white blossoms. *D. lemoinei*, Zones 4–9, reaches about 6 feet high with broad, upright clusters of pink-tinged flowers. *D. rosea*, Zones 5–9, reaches 3–4 feet with arching stems; varieties have flowers of white or pink and white. Tallest — 7–10 feet — is *D. scabra*, Zones 5–9; erect plant has upright clusters of white, pink, or purple-tinted blossoms.

DODONAEA viscosa. Hop bush, Hopseed bush. Evergreen. Zones 9–10, West only. From ocean to desert, with ample or little water, hop bush thrives. Blunt-tipped leaves

are narrow and willowlike, to 4 inches long, densely covering a billowy-upright plant eventually 12–15 feet high and nearly as wide. Variety 'Purpurea' has bronzy green leaves; 'Saratoga' has leaves of rich purple. Purple-leafed forms make good accent plants; all kinds are excellent screens, unclipped hedges, and windbreaks. They can also be trained to grow as small trees. Flowers are inconspicuous.

DOGWOOD. See Cornus.

ELAEAGNUS. Evergreen and deciduous. Zones vary. These are large, fast-growing, dense, tough plants useful for mass planting as unclipped hedges and screens, barriers (some are thorny), and windbreaks. Tolerance is great: seashore to desert, little to average watering. All foliage has a silvery cast. Flowers are inconspicuous but usually fragrant; berrylike fruit that follow are, with one exception, red or orange. Two deciduous species are 12-foot Silverberry (*E. commutata*), Zones 1–7, with silvery rather than red berries, and 6-foot *E. multiflora*, Zones 4–10. *E.* 'Coral Silver', Zones 4–10, may be evergreen in Zones 9–10, but deciduous in colder regions; foliage is silvery gray. Thornless, evergreen *E. ebbingei*, Zones 7–10, has silvery new growth that turns dark green on upper surface. Another Silverberry, evergreen *E. pungens*, Zones 7–10, has grayish olive foliage; several varieties have gold, yellow, or white variegation.

ENKIANTHUS. Deciduous. Zones 5–9 (West) and 5–8 (East). Elegant, refined plants are good-looking in all seasons. Main stems are upright; secondary branches project in nearly horizontal layers. Glossy, oval leaves cluster toward branch tips and turn brilliant orange or red in autumn. In spring, bell-shaped blossoms hang in clusters beneath leaves. Tallest, to 20 feet, is *E. campanulatus*; yellowish green flowers (red in *E. c. palibinii*, white in variety 'Albiflorus') appear in midspring. Half as tall is white-flowered *E. cernuus*, which has a red-flowered form *rubens*. White flowers appear before leaf-out in 6–8-foot *E. perulatus*.

ERICA. Heath. Evergreen. Zones vary. Often incorrectly called "heather," these relatives of true heather (*Calluna*) offer a greater range of plant sizes and shapes. Also, like true heather, they are most at home in the Northeast and Northwest; heat and dry air challenge their ability to thrive. Tiny leaves are needlelike; small flowers are bell-shaped, urn-shaped, or tubular. Flowering time varies, depending on the species or hybrid; there can be a heath flowering in every month of the year. Flower colors include lilac, purple, pink shades, rosy red, bright red, and white. Plants range from ground cover types to shrubs of all sizes to small trees. Ground cover and shrub types are useful as individual accents or in massed plantings, from foreground to background depending on height. Availability varies; among the more widely distributed are *E.*

carnea and varieties, Zones 5–10 (West) and 5–8 (East); these are low growing (under 1½ feet), bloom in winter and spring. Dorset heath (*E. ciliaris*) and varieties, Zones 7–9 (West) and 7–8 (East), are in the same height range and bloom in summer into autumn. Twisted heath (*E. cinerea*) and varieties, Zones 7–9 (West) and 7–8 (East), may be low-spreading or low-shrubby, flowering in summer and autumn. Cross-leafed heath (*E. tetralix*) is similar. *E. darleyensis* and varieties, Zones 7–10 (West) and 7–8 (East), flower from late autumn through spring on bushy plants to 2 feet high. Biscay heath (*E. mediterranea*), Zones 7–10 (West), 7–8 (East), is an upright shrub to about 6 feet, blooming in winter and spring. Summer to autumn-flowering Cornish heath (*E. vagans*), Zones 5–9 (West) and 6–8 (East), is bushy to about 3 feet but its varieties grow about half that height. For West Coast only are the large shrubs *E. canaliculata*, Zones 9–10, Spanish heath (*E. lusitanica*), and Southern heath (*E. australis*), both Zones 8–10.

ESCALLONIA. Evergreen. Zones 9–10 (safe) and Zone 8 (subject to freeze damage). Small, glossy leaves and dense growth give these plants a healthy appearance. A number of species and named varieties are sold, ranging from 3-foot shrubs to 15–20-foot shrub-trees. Tubular to trumpet-shaped small blossoms come in clusters at branch tips; colors are pink through red and white. Bloom times are late spring, summer, and autumn; many flower throughout that period. Shortest, to about 3 feet, are *E.* 'Compakta' with rose red blossoms and *E. rubra* 'C.F. Ball', with red flowers. Tallest (to about 15 feet) are Pink escallonia (*E. laevis*) and White escallonia (*E. bifida*); the latter can be trained as a small tree. Between these extremes are *E. exoniensis* 'Balfouri' (10 feet) and 'Frades' (6 feet); *E.* 'Jubilee' (6 feet); *E. langleyensis* 'Apple Blossom' (5 feet); *E. rosea* (7 feet). *E. virgata* and varieties (6 feet) are partially deciduous, better able to withstand Zone 8 winters. Use escallonias as hedges, screens, or specimens.

EUONYMUS. Evergreen and deciduous. Zones vary. Deciduous types are noted for their stunning display of red autumn color (warm pink in shade) and usually conspicuous pink or red seed capsules that open to show orange-covered seeds. European spindle tree (*E. europaea*), Zones 3–9, may reach about 20 feet high and can be trained as a small tree; variety 'Aldenhamensis' has more and larger fruits. Winged euonymus or Burning bush (*E. alata*), Zones 3–9, reaches about 10 feet high and 15 feet across with strongly horizontal branch pattern; variety 'Compacta' will make a dense, rounded plant to 6 feet tall, excellent for hedging. Burning bush or Wahoo (*E. atropurpurea*), Zones 6–9, is similar to European spindle tree; autumn color is darker red. Use deciduous types as specimen accents (for autumn foliage and fruit color), screens, or hedges. Shrubby varieties of *E. fortunei* (often sold as varieties of *E.*

radicans), Zones 5–10, are dense evergreen plants 2–4 feet high (depending on variety) with thick, roundish leaves 1–2½ inches long; some have yellow or white variegation. Use as short, neat hedge and barrier plantings. Evergreen euonymus (*E. japonica*), Zones 8–10, and its varieties are larger and bulkier, 8–10 feet high—even treelike in old, unpruned specimens. Many variegated-leaf varieties are popular as specimen plants and hedges; variety 'Microphylla' is a tiny-leafed 2-foot plant. Broadly rounded, to about 9 feet high, *E. kiautschovica*, Zones 6–10, has lighter green, less leathery leaves, and showy, red-seeded pinkish fruit. Two selected varieties, 'DuPont' and 'Manhattan' have darker leaves on compact, upright plants; good for hedge and screen plantings.

EUROPEAN SPINDLE TREE. See Euonymus europaea.

FEIJOA sellowiana. Pineapple guava. Evergreen. Zones 9–10. Although it can be trained as a small tree, pineapple guava is usually grown as a specimen shrub or hedge or screen planting kept as low as 6 feet or allowed to grow to 20 feet high and as wide. Stiff, 3-inch oval leaves are glossy dark green on upper surfaces and feltlike gray white beneath. In May and June come conspicuous flowers: each an inch wide with four purple-tinged white petals and a tuft of red stamens. Edible, egg-shaped gray green fruits 1–4 inches long come 4–7 months later.

FIRETHORN. See Pyracantha.

FLOWERING QUINCE. See Chaenomeles.

FORSYTHIA. Deciduous. Zones vary. With their bare stems densely covered with bright yellow blossoms in late winter and early spring, forsythias become a dominant element in the garden. But after their pointed-oval, rich green leaves emerge, plants blend into the general landscape as unobtrusive, often gracefully arching shrubs. Earliest to flower is *F. ovata*, Zones 4–9, with small amber yellow flowers on a 6-foot, spreading plant. Other kinds grow in Zones 5–9. Varieties of *F. intermedia* are hybrids ranging from 6 to 10 feet tall (depending on variety), upright to spreading, and light to intense deep yellow. Weeping forsythia (*F. suspensa*) sends up strong stems to 10 feet; side branches are pendent. Other uses are as bank cover, espalier, or small tree. Last to bloom is Greenstem forsythia (*F. viridissima*), a stiffly erect plant with greenish yellow blossoms; variety 'Bronxensis' grows only about 1½ feet high.

FUCHSIA. Evergreen to deciduous. Zones 8–10 (reliable outdoor shrubs in West only). The countless named varieties of *F. hybrida* create a summertime spectacle of showy, distinctively shaped blossoms. Somewhat quilted, pointed-oval to heart-shaped leaves are 2–5 inches long; upright varieties reach 3–12 feet depending on the variety, amount of pruning, and frost. Pendent flowers come

continuously from late spring into autumn. Best appearance is where summers are cool and humid. Use as accent or mass plantings especially in patios and small gardens. *F. magellanica*, Zones 6–10, forms a woody shrub 6–20 feet high (tallest only in frost-free areas) with arching branches that carry 1½-inch long red and purple blossoms.

GARDENIA. Evergreen. Zones 9–10. Gardenias are famous for their penetrating fragrance. Of the two available species, the more widely grown is Cape jasmine (*G. jasminoides*) in its several named varieties. Leaves are glossy bright to deep green about 4 inches long and densely clothe a rounded plant. Double white blossoms come in late spring, and continue into summer and even into autumn with some varieties. Best known is 'Mystery' with 4–5-inch flowers on a plant to 8 feet. Other large-flowered varieties with more compact plants are 'August Beauty' and 'Golden Magic' (flowers age to golden yellow). 'Veitchii' (to 4½ feet) has many 1½-inch blooms over long period; 'Veitchii Improved' is a bit taller with larger flowers. Single, 3–4-inch flowers in winter decorate *G. thunbergia*, a robust plant to 10 feet high and twice as wide with nearly black green, 6-inch leaves. Because of their good looks, fragrance, and need for heat, gardenias are good patio plants where heat is reflected.

GENISTA. Broom. Deciduous. Zones vary. So similar and closely related are these plants to *Cytisus* (see page 112) that many have been sold as such. Most widely grown is spreading-arching *G. lydia*, Zones 7–9, a foreground plant to 2 feet high with bright yellow flowers at branch tips in late spring. Mt. Etna broom (*G. aethnensis*), Zones 7–9, is a 15-foot shrub or shrub-tree, its fragrant yellow blossoms coming in summer at ends of slender, green stems. Bridal veil broom (*G. monosperma*), Zones 9–10 (West only), has silvery new growth and slender, gray green branches; plant is upright to about 20 feet high and 10 feet wide, bearing fragrant white flowers in late winter and early spring.

HEATH. See Erica.

HEATHER. See Calluna.

HEAVENLY BAMBOO. See Nandina domestica.

HEBE. Evergreen. Zones 9–10, except where noted, West Coast only. Once classed as *Veronica*, many of these plants may still be sold under that name. Dense, rounded shrubs with shiny foliage bear spikes of tiny flowers at branch tips. The plants mass well as borders or hedges but also make attractive individual specimens. Best performance is near seacoast. Showy hebe (*H. speciosa*) grows 2–5 feet high with narrow 2–4-inch leaves. Summer flowers are red purple in 3–4-inch spikes. *H. andersonii* is a similar shrub, slightly taller, with summer flower spikes that are white at base turning to violet at the tip. Boxleaf hebe (*H. buxifolia*) is more

...Hebe

fine-textured, to 5 feet high and wide, with summer clusters of white flowers. Several hybrid varieties are available, all roughly 3-foot plants with different bloom times and flower colors: 'Autumn Glory', Zones 8–10, (lavender blue, late summer and autumn); 'Carnea' (rosy red, late summer); 'Desilor' (deep blue purple, spring to autumn); 'Patty's Purple' (purple, summer); 'Reevesii' (red purple, summer).

HEMLOCK. See Tsuga.

Hibiscus rosa-sinensis

HIBISCUS. Evergreen and deciduous. Zones vary. These are among the most conspicuous of flowering shrubs. Individual blossom is medium-size to very large, consisting of five overlapping petals that form a nearly circular, flat flower; stamens, like a bottlebrush on a stem, arise from flower's center. Two species have double-flowered varieties. Deciduous Confederate rose (*H. mutabilis*), Zones 7–10, is a large woody shrub or small tree in Zones 9–10 but is smaller in Zones 7–8 where freezing kills part of the branch structure. Broadly oval, lobed leaves are backdrop for 4–6-inch flowers that open white or pink and change to deep red (there also is a red-flowered variety). Rose of Sharon or Shrub althaea (*H. syriacus*), Zones 5–10, is a compact, upright, deciduous plant to 12 feet, broadening with age; it, too, can be trained as a small tree. Single or double flowers to 3 inches across come in white, pink shades, red tones, and purple, often with contrasting stain of color in flower center — many named varieties are sold. The most flamboyant of the group is Chinese hibiscus (*H. rosa-sinensis*), Zone 10 and warmest parts of Zone 9. Many named varieties are sold where this plant thrives; plants range from 6-foot, spreading shrubs to robust 15–25-foot shrub-trees. Leaves are glossy bright green, broadly oval and pointed, against which are displayed 4–10-inch wide flowers in white, pink, red, orange, and yellow as well as blended shades of yellow, pink, and orange. Visit a local nursery to make a selection, choosing carefully according to variety's ultimate size and inherent vigor. Main bloom season is summer, but bloom may appear all year in warmest regions. These are indispensible accent specimens, and screen and hedge plants.

HILLS OF SNOW. See Hydrangea arborescens 'Grandiflora'.

HOLLY. See Ilex.

HOP BUSH. See Dodonaea viscosa.

HYDRANGEA. Deciduous. Zones vary. These shrubs derive their texture and mass from large leaves and flower heads. Two kinds of flowers are produced: fertile (tiny, starlike) and sterile (conspicuous because of large petal-like sepals). Where both types appear in one cluster, sterile flowers in a ring around fertile ones, the type is called "lace cap." Familiar Big-leaf hydrangea (*H. macrophylla*), Zones 6–10, may reach 8 feet high and wide, with thick, shiny 8-inch leaves and foot-wide rounded clusters of sterile flowers. French hybrids (the hydrangeas usually found in florist shops) grow about half as large. Colors range from light pink to crimson, light blue to intense blue purple, and white. Acid soils promote blue blossoms; alkaline soils can turn the same variety pink to red. There are many named varieties including 'Domotoi', with double sterile flowers, and various lace cap types, one with variegated foliage. Smooth hydrangea (*H. arborescens*), Zones 4–9, is best known through its variety 'Grandiflora' (Hills of Snow) — a dense, upright 10-foot plant with 8-inch, broadly oval, gray green leaves and rounded 6-inch clusters of creamy white sterile flowers. Peegee hydrangea (*H. paniculata* 'Grandiflora'), Zones 4–9, has conical, foot-long clusters of mostly sterile white flowers that age to pinkish bronze. Plant is fast-growing to a 10–15-foot shrub or even larger as a small tree; leaves turn bronzy in autumn. Oakleaf hydrangea (*H. quercifolia*), Zones 5–9, makes a rounded 6-foot plant with deeply lobed, oaklike 8-inch leaves that turn bronze to red in autumn. White flowers, turning purplish when mature, come in loose clusters to 8 inches long.

ILEX. Holly. Evergreen and deciduous. Zones vary. Many hollies that begin as shrubs eventually become trees; see page 101 for discussion of these larger representatives. These are dense, polished-looking plants useful as specimens, screens, formal hedges, and — for those with spiny leaves — barrier plantings. They are justifiably renowned for their showy red berries; most berry-producing female plants need a male pollen producer nearby. *I. aquipernyi* 'Brilliant', Zones 7–10, forms a dense cone of spine-edged foliage to 10 feet or more and sets a heavy berry crop without pollination. Chinese holly (*I. cornuta*), Zones 7–10, forms a rounded to dome-shaped 10-foot plant. Leaf form and number of spines vary according to variety; popular Burford holly ('Burfordii') generally has a spine at each leaf tip. Variety 'Jungle Garden' has yellow fruit. Japanese holly (*I. crenata*), Zones 6–10, looks least like holly: oval, spineless leaves are under an inch long, berries are black rather than red. It and its varieties, ranging from 1 foot to 6 feet tall, are excellent hedge plants. The hybrid *I. meserveae*, Zones 6–10, resembles English holly (see page 125) with its spiny leaves and good crop of red berries.

Dense 6–7-foot plants have purple stems; several named varieties are available. Yaupon (*I. vomitoria*), Zones 7–10, forms a large shrub or small tree with narrow, spineless, inch-long leaves; berries form without pollinator. This is another good hedge plant; several named varieties are sold, including dwarf forms less than 2 feet high. Deciduous Winterberry (*I. verticillata*), Zones 4–8, sets heavy berry crop that colors before foliage turns yellow and then remains on the stems into winter. Variety 'Winter Red' is selected form with dark foliage and large berries.

INDIA HAWTHORN. See Raphiolepis indica.

IXORA coccinea. Evergreen. Zone 10 (Florida only). Dense growth and all-year attractiveness make this a popular plant for hedges and mass planting. Compact plant to 12 feet is clothed in broadly oval, glossy 4-inch leaves. Red, orange, yellow, pink, or white starlike blossoms are grouped together in dense clusters at branch tips; bloom comes during much of the year.

JASMINE. See Jasminum.

JASMINUM. Jasmine. Evergreen and deciduous. Zones vary. The most widely grown shrubby jasmines are midway between shrub and vine: plants are sprawling to mounding, and send out long, arching stems. Grow them as large, billowy mounds, or as bank cover; trim into large hedges; or train upward to cascade from an overhead. Primrose jasmine (*J. mesnyi*), Zones 8–10, has 3-inch lance-shaped leaflets on stems to 10 feet long. Its 2-inch bright yellow flowers are scentless; they bloom from autumn into spring in mildest regions, from late winter into spring where winter is colder. Deciduous Winter jasmine (*J. nudiflorum*), Zones 6–9, has 10–15-foot stems, 1-inch scentless blossoms in winter, before leaves emerge. Least vinelike is evergreen *J. floridum*, Zones 7–10. Leaflets to 1½ inches long cover a 4-foot, somewhat sprawling plant. Scentless golden yellow flowers less than an inch across appear from spring into autumn.

JUNIPER. See Juniperus.

JUNIPERUS. Juniper. Evergreen. Zones vary. From coast to coast and border to border, junipers are among the most adaptable and widely planted shrubs. A few basic species have produced countless varieties that differ in foliage color and growth habits. Foliage—scalelike or tiny, prickly needles — may be steel blue to gray green, bright to olive green, yellow green to golden, and variegated. Plant shapes range from vase-shaped or arching to conical or pyramidal, to irregularly upright. Your best selection guide will be a well-stocked local nursery. You're likely to find varieties of the following species: *J. chinensis* (Zones 4–10), *J. communis* (Zones 2–9), *J. sabina* (Zones 4–10), *J. squamata* (Zones 4–10), *J. scopulorum* (Zones 4–10), and *J. virginiana* (Zones 3–10).

KALMIA latifolia. Mountain laurel, Calico bush. Evergreen. Zones 4–9. Given humidity, acid soil, and regular watering, this is one of the most handsome shrubs throughout the year. Growth is rounded, to 8 feet or more, and well-clothed in glossy, leathery, lance-shaped leaves. In late spring, plants burst forth with large clusters to 5 inches across of 1-inch saucer-shaped blossoms; dark pink buds open to pale pink (sometimes white) flowers with dark markings inside. Specialists carry varieties selected for different colorings and markings. Plant as an individual accent or in a group for barrier or screen effect. It's attractive at the edge of a woodland associated with dogwood, rhododendron, or azalea.

Kalmia latifolia

KOLKWITZIA amabilis. Beauty bush. Deciduous. Zones 5–9. Beauty bush sends up gracefully arching stems 10–12 feet high clothed in pointed-oval, 3-inch gray green leaves. In mid to late spring come thick clusters of flowers at branch tips; each bloom is a small flaring trumpet shape, pink with a yellow throat. Bristly, pinkish brown fruit follow and remain decorative throughout summer and autumn. Reddish autumn leaves drop and reveal attractive structure and peeling brown bark. This is an obvious choice for specimen placement and is also good as backdrop to flower borders.

LAGERSTROEMIA indica. See Trees, page 102.

LAUREL. See Laurus, Prunus.

LAURUS nobilis. Sweet bay, Grecian laurel. Evergreen. Zones 8–10. Sweet bay—source of the culinary bay leaf—offers nothing but foliage, but it does that very well. Aromatic leaves are leathery, glossy, pointed ovals to 4 inches long. They densely cover a slow-growing, broadly conical shrub that has been used for centuries as a formal accent plant. Other uses are for hedge and screen planting; ultimately it will become a good-size tree unless you restrict growth. You can also clip it into ornamental shapes.

LAURUSTINUS. See Viburnum tinus.

LEPTOSPERMUM. Tea tree. Evergreen. Zones 9–10 (West only). More widely planted of the available species are varieties

of *L. scoparium*, the New Zealand tea tree. These have tiny, almost needlelike leaves and conspicuous flower display in winter, spring, or summer, depending on the variety. Blossoms resemble ½-inch semidouble roses and come in great profusion along stems. Colors range from light to dark pink, vivid crimson red, and white. Most grow in the 5–10 foot range, upright and spreading with age. A larger, coarser-appearing plant, *L. laevigatum*, the Australian tea tree, becomes a gnarled, picturesque tree to 30 feet high and wide; grow many together as clipped hedge, screen, or windbreak. More useful are varieties 'Compactum' (to 8 feet tall) and 'Reevesii' (to 4–5 feet high with larger, more plentiful leaves). Spring blossoms are white.

LEUCOTHOE. Evergreen. Zones 5–9. For partly shaded woodland gardens, leucothoes contribute polished appearance and graceful form. Drooping leucothoe (*L. fontanesiana*, sometimes sold as *L. catesbaei*) sends up arching stems eventually to 6 feet high; plant forms spreading clump, new stems arising from underground. Polished, leathery leaves are pointed ovals to 6 inches long, turning bronzy purple during coldest months. In mid to late spring come drooping clusters of flowers from previous year's growth; each creamy white blossom looks like a lily-of-the-valley. Variety 'Rainbow' has foliage marked with yellow and pink and grows to about 4 feet high. Very similar to drooping leucothoe is *L. axillaris*; leaves are more sharply pointed and plant is shorter.

LIGUSTRUM. Privet. Evergreen and deciduous. Zones vary. Privets are well-suited as hedge plants, though this use masks the natural beauty of some species. These lilac relatives produce clusters of white flowers in spring or summer; small, blue black, berrylike fruit follow. California privet (*L. ovalifolium*), Zones 6–10, grows rapidly to 15 feet or more if untrimmed; leaves are dark green ovals to 2½ inches long, partly deciduous in colder regions. As a large shrub or shrub-tree it has attractive form: branches arch outward to create nearly horizontal layers. Similar privets are deciduous Common privet (*L. vulgare*), Zones 4–10; deciduous Amur privet (*L. amurense*), Zones 3–10; and semideciduous *L. ibolium* 'Variegata', Zones 4–10, which has leaves margined with creamy yellow. Deciduous *L. obtusifolium* 'Regelianum', Zones 5–10, reaches about 5 feet high with striking horizontal branch pattern. Japanese or waxleaf privet (*L. japonicum*, often sold as *L. texanum*), Zones 7–10, is a dense, compact plant to 12 feet high but easily kept lower; leaves are rounded ovals to 4 inches long— dark green, glossy, and thick. It makes a neat hedge, clipped or natural, and individual plants can be clipped into formal geometrical shapes. Variety 'Rotundifolium' has nearly round leaves on a plant half as high. The variety sold as 'Texanum' grows to about 9 feet tall and provides very dense foliage cover. 'Silver Star' has leaves mottled gray

green and edged in creamy white. Deciduous Vicary golden privet (*L.* 'Vicaryi'), Zones 4–10, has startlingly bright yellow leaves (color is strongest on plants in full sun) on a plant to 4-6 feet high.

LILAC. See Syringa.

LILY-OF-THE-VALLEY SHRUB. See Pieris japonica.

LONICERA. Honeysuckle. Evergreen and deciduous. Zones vary. Compared with vining relatives (see page 121), the shrubby honeysuckles are quite refined and restrained. Most bear showy, fragrant blossoms in typical honeysuckle pattern (tubular with flaring upper and lower lips), and most produce showy fruit attractive to birds. Use as specimen plants, background, and hedges. Evergreen Box honeysuckle (*L. nitida*), Zones 7–10, has glossy, oval, ½-inch leaves that turn purplish in winter; small white blossoms produce blue purple fruit. Privet honeysuckle (*L. pileata*), Zones 5–10, may drop some of its privetlike 1½-inch leaves in colder regions. Plant is low with definite horizontal branch habit; it produces small white flowers, and violet berries. The following four deciduous species are popular in the colder Zones. Tatarian honeysuckle (*L. tatarica*), Zones 3–9, is dense, upright to 9 feet, and well clothed in dark green, 2-inch leaves. Bright red fruit follow small pink blossoms. *L. korolkowii*, Zones 5–9, carries blue green 2-inch leaves on arching stems to 12 feet high; it also has pink flowers and red fruit. Winter honeysuckle (*L. fragrantissima*), Zones 5–10, is partly evergreen in Zones 9–10. Inconspicuous but highly fragrant flowers come from late winter through spring; berries turn red in summer. Stiffly arching plant bears dark green, 3-inch oval leaves. *L.* 'Clavey's Dwarf', Zones 5–10, produces showy red fruit (from inconspicuous blossoms) on 3-foot plant with blue green foliage.

Lonicera fragrantissima

MAHONIA. Evergreen. Zones vary. All mahonias are distinguished by handsome, durable foliage, the leaves consisting of several to many spine-edged leaflets. Conspicuous clusters of small yellow blossoms appear in spring; small, grapelike blue black fruit follow. Most widely planted is Oregon grape (*M. aquifolium*), Zones 5–10 (West) and 5–8 (East). Main stems are upright, form-

...*Mahonia*

ing gradually spreading clumps to 6 feet high or greater unless restricted. Bright copper-colored new growth follows bloom; holly-like leaflets mature to glossy bright to dark green, then turn purplish or reddish bronze in cold weather. This makes a fine specimen plant, mass planting, or even hedge. The hybrid *M.* 'Golden Abundance' resembles Oregon grape but is shorter and more spreading with denser foliage. The following two species are striking as accent plants because of strong form and foliage texture. Leatherleaf mahonia (*M. bealei*), Zones 6–10, sends up vertical stems to 12 feet; foot-long leaves project horizontally and are divided into broad, leathery, 5-inch, yellowish green leaflets. *M. lomariifolia*, Zones 9–10, has nearly branchless stems to 10 feet with 2-foot leaves held almost horizontally near stem ends; each leaf consists of 3-inch glossy leaflets with needle-sharp spines. Plant flowers in winter to early spring.

MELALEUCA. Evergreen. Zones 9–10. Close relatives of bottlebrushes (*Callistemon*, see page 98), melaleucas bear flowers consisting chiefly of showy stamens, but in general their blossom clusters are smaller, and foliage more fine-textured, than bottlebrushes. Best uses are as screens, unclipped hedges, and windbreaks. Dotted melaleuca (*M. hypericifolia*) grows to 10 feet with drooping branches of 1½-inch leaves; orange red, 2-inch blossom clusters come from late spring through winter. The remaining species are large shrubs or small shrub-trees. Heath melaleuca (*M. ericifolia*) reaches 10–25 feet high, with 1-inch needlelike leaves and 1-inch spikes of creamy white spring blossoms. Lilac melaleuca (*M. decussata*) may reach 20 feet high and wide. Arching, drooping branches are covered with ½-inch bluish green leaves; in late spring come lavender to purple flowers in 1-inch spikes. Drooping melaleuca (*M. armillaris*) grows 15–30 feet with prickly, needlelike, 1-inch light green leaves on drooping branches. White flowers on short spikes come from spring to autumn.

MOCK ORANGE. See Philadelphus.

MOUNTAIN LAUREL. See Kalmia latifolia.

MYRTLE. See Myrtus.

MYRTUS communis. Myrtle. Evergreen. Zones 9–10. The basic species is a rounded dense plant reaching about 6 feet high and wide, covered in shiny, 2-inch narrow-pointed leaves. Very old specimens may be spreading small trees. Many ¾-inch fluffy white flowers dot the plant in summer; small blue black berries follow. Variety 'Variegata' has leaves margined with white. These are good hedge, screen, and background shrubs. A number of named varieties offer different forms and sizes. 'Boetica' has larger, darker green, upward-pointing leaves on a 6-foot plant with heavy, gnarled branches. 'Buxifolia' has small, oval leaves. Dwarf myrtle, variety 'Compacta', is a slow-

growing, low plant useful for border plantings and clipped hedges; 'Compacta Variegata' has leaves edged in white. 'Microphylla' is another dwarf with the same uses; leaves are tiny and overlapping.

NANDINA domestica. Heavenly bamboo, Sacred bamboo. Evergreen. Zones 7–10 (West) and 7–9 (East); deciduous in Zone 7. This is not a bamboo, but the long, canelike stems and fine-textured foliage suggest it. Many stems grow directly from the ground, usually unbranched unless cut back; they can reach 8 feet tall unless pruned. An individual leaf may be quite large — to 2 feet wide and long — but is composed of so many 1½–4-inch pointed-oval leaflets that the effect is almost lacy. New growth in spring is pinkish to bronzy red; leaves take on red to purple tints in autumn and may turn brilliant red in winter. In late spring come small creamy white flowers in loose, foot-long clusters at branch ends; when more than one plant is present, pea-size fruit form that turn bright red in autumn. Growth is upright to almost vase-shaped. Use Heavenly bamboo as individual accent plant, hedge, or screen, and in areas where planting space is narrow.

NANNYBERRY. See Viburnum lentago.

NATAL PLUM. See Carissa grandiflora.

NERIUM oleander. Oleander. Evergreen. Zones 9–10. From seashore to desert to near-tropical humidity, oleander thrives. Narrow, leathery, dark green leaves to a foot long clothe a bulky, rounded plant that usually grows with many stems from ground level. Height varies, according to variety, from 4 to 20 feet. Showy flowers, each 2–3 inches across, come from late spring into autumn; colors are red, pink, salmon, yellowish, white; some varieties have double flowers. Use this tough, colorful plant as a specimen, hedge, barrier, or windbreak. Grow where poor soil and lack of water rule out other plants. With diligence, you can train one of the taller varieties into a handsome tree. All parts of the plant are highly poisonous.

OLEANDER. See Nerium oleander.

OREGON GRAPE. See Mahonia aquifolium.

OSMANTHUS. Evergreen. Zones vary. Most *Osmanthus* offer just good-looking foliage to the landscape; flowers are inconspicuous. Nevertheless, you know when they're in bloom by the sweet fragrance floating in the air. Delavay osmanthus (*O. delavayi*), Zones 8–10, is the only one with conspicuous blossoms. Plant reaches about 6 feet high, its gracefully arching branches spreading wider; leaves are 1-inch dark green ovals with toothed margins. During early spring, clusters of ½-inch white flowers appear along branches. Sweet olive (*O. fragrans*), Zones 9–10, reaches 10 feet or more (it can be trained as a small tree), forming a fairly broad, dense plant with 4-inch glossy leaves.

Peak flowering time is spring and early summer; variety 'Aurantiacus', with narrower, duller leaves and tiny orange blossoms, flowers in autumn. Hollyleaf osmanthus (*O. heterophyllus*), Zones 7–10, is densely foliaged and useful for hedges and screens. Nurseries sell a number of named varieties with hollylike foliage; all bloom from late autumn to early spring. 'Gulftide' and 'Ilicifolius' reach about 8 feet; 'Purpureus', 'Rotundifolius', and 'Variegatus' (with leaves margined cream) grow to about 5 feet. *O. fortunei* is a hybrid between Sweet olive and Hollyleaf osmanthus. Hollylike 4-inch leaves are dense on a tall, upright plant that flowers in spring and summer.

PHILADELPHUS. Mock orange. Deciduous. Zones vary. These trouble-free shrubs, give a bountiful display of fragrant white flowers in late spring. All have thin-textured, pointed-oval leaves, somewhat quilted in appearance. Sweet mock orange (*P. coronarius*), Zones 4–10 (West) and 4–9 (East), is a vigorous old favorite to about 10 feet; main stems are upright and branches arch outward. Leaves reach 4 inches long and blossoms are single, about 1½ inches across. Variety 'Aureus' has bright yellow new growth and is a shorter plant. *P. lemoinei*, Zones 5–9, includes a great number of named hybrids. In general they are arching to spreading plants to about 6 feet tall, with 2-inch leaves and single or double flowers. *P. purpureomaculatus*, Zones 5–9, is another hybrid group of similar appearance to the preceding, but flowers have purple centers. *P. virginalis*, Zones 5–9, is another hybrid group with several varieties widely available. Tallest, to about 8 feet, are 'Minnesota Snowflake' (Zones 4–9) and 'Virginal' with double 2-inch blossoms. Shorter are 'Glacier' (double, 4–5 feet) and 'Dwarf Minnesota Snowflake' (double, about 3 feet).

PHOTINIA. Evergreen and deciduous. Zones vary. Bulky shrubs are good screen and background plantings. New growth is conspicuously colorful and flattish clusters of small white flowers appear in spring. Evergreen *P. fraseri*, Zones 7–10, has glossy, oval, 5-inch leaves (bright bronzy red new growth) on a dense plant to 10 feet high and wider. Red berries follow 4-inch flower clusters. Japanese photinia (*P. glabra*) is similar but has 3-inch leaves (copper-colored new growth) and red berries that later turn black. Deciduous *P. villosa*, Zones 4–8, may reach 15 feet tall and 10 feet across; it can be grown as a small tree. Dark green leaves, to 3 inches long, are pink-tinted gold when new and turn bronzy red in autumn. Small flower clusters produce ½-inch red fruit in autumn.

PIERIS. Evergreen. Zones vary. These elegant shrubs boast glossy narrow-pointed leaves, colorful new growth, and clusters (usually drooping) of lily-of-the-valleylike flowers. Nurseries sometimes sell them as *Andromeda*. Lily-of-the-valley shrub (*P. japonica*), Zones 5–9, forms an upright plant with horizontally layered growth to about 10 feet; 3-inch leaves emerge bright red to pink. Bloom comes in late winter to midspring; flowers are white, but named selections offer pink or red blooms. Other varieties have variegated leaves and shorter growth. Chinese pieris (*P. forrestii*, Zones 8–9), may reach 10 feet with greater spread. Leathery leaves reach 6 inches long and are bright red to pink when young. Spring flowers are white. Mountain andromeda or Fetterbush (*P. floribunda*), Zones 4–9 (West), 4–8 (East), has upright flower clusters in midspring on a rounded 6-foot-tall plant; 3-inch leaves have a dull finish.

PINE. See Pinus.

PINEAPPLE GUAVA. See Feijoa sellowiana.

PINUS. Evergreen. Zones vary. Two shrubby pines are popular as specimen shrublets and low border or mass plantings. Mugho pine (*P. mugo mugo*), Zones 3–10 (West) and 3–8 (East), has dark green needles in bundles of two, densely covering a rounded to spreading plant that may reach 4 feet high. Plants raised from seed may vary, those with shortest needles usually making smallest plants. Dwarf white pine (*P. strobus* 'Nana'), Zones 3–8, has soft blue green needles in bundles of five; shrub grows slowly, to 7 feet, spreading about twice as wide as high.

PITTOSPORUM tobira. Tobira. Evergreen. Zones 8–10. You can use this as a specimen plant, hedge, screen, or small tree. Height is 6–20 feet (occasionally taller) with equal spread. Handsome leathery leaves are glossy dark green, rather narrow to 5 inches long with rounded tips; they grow radially around stems, clustering toward branch tips. Orange-blossom-scented white blossoms come in spring, clustered at ends of branches; round, green fruit follow, turn brown in autumn, and open to reveal sticky orange seeds. Variety 'Wheeler's Dwarf' is a 2-foot replica of the species. Variety 'Variegata' reaches 5 feet high and wide, its leaves a soft gray green margined in white.

Plumbago auriculata

PLUMBAGO auriculata. Cape plumbago. Semievergreen. Zones 9–10. Where not "pruned" by frost, this becomes a mounding, almost vinelike plant to about 10 feet

high and wider. Oval, 2-inch light green leaves are evergreen in frost-free regions but partially shed elsewhere. Over a long season — spring to winter — come clusters of inch-wide flowers that resemble *Phlox*; usual color is blue, but choose plants in bloom to get desired shade (there is also a white-flowered form). Use as background shrub, or to cover a bank or fence.

POMEGRANATE. See Punica granatum.

POTENTILLA fruticosa. Bush cinquefoil. Deciduous. Zones 2–9 (West) and 2–8 (East). The various bush cinquefoil varieties are fine-textured shrubs that put on a cheery display of wild-roselike flowers throughout summer. Depending on the variety, plant height ranges from 2 to nearly 5 feet, usually spreading wider. Stems are upright to arching, clothed in narrow-oval leaflets an inch or less in length. Flower size varies from under an inch across to about 2 inches, and colors include white, cream, yellow shades, orange, and red. Use in foregrounds of mixed plantings, as low border shrubs.

PRIVET. See Ligustrum.

PRUNUS. Evergreen and deciduous. Zones vary. Two of the tree-size evergreen *Prunus* species (see page 105) have distinctly shrubby varieties useful for hedge and border plantings. Carolina cherry laurel (*P. caroliniana*), Zones 7–10, and varieties 'Bright 'n Tight' and 'Compacta' form dense plants to 12 feet high if untrimmed; leaves are glossy 2–4-inch ovals. Tiny white spring flowers are clustered on 1-inch spikes. English laurel (*P. laurocerasus*), Zones 6–10, has several shorter varieties. 'Otto Luyken' and 'Schipkaensis' reach 6 feet high, spreading wider; both have glossy, narrow leaves to about 4 inches long. Prominent spikes of tiny white flowers in late spring are followed by purplish black fruit. Zabel laurel, variety 'Zabeliana', is a narrow-leafed form with distinctive branching habit: main stems grow at wide angle from plant's base, sometimes almost horizontally. In time it may build to 6 feet high with greater spread. Deciduous *P. glandulosa*, the Dwarf flowering almond, Zones 4–9, is a spreading 4–5-foot shrub with slender branches covered in early spring with fluffy double pink or white blossoms about an inch across. Light green leaves that follow are narrow and pointed, to 4 inches long. Dwarf red-leaf plum (*P. cistena*), Zones 4–9, is an airy plant 6–10 feet high with striking, purple red oval leaves. Flowers are white or pink-tinted before leaves emerge. Both deciduous types are good for accent plantings and untrimmed hedges or screens.

PUNICA granatum. Pomegranate. Deciduous. Zones 9–10. The fruiting varieties (best known is 'Wonderful') are large shrubs or small trees, depending on training. As shrubs they reach 10 or more feet high with upright, arching branches. Bronzy new growth

matures to glossy bright green or yellowish green, narrow 3-inch leaves. Autumn color is yellow. Flowers are about 4 inches across, a single row of ruffled orange red petals surrounding stamens; rusty red fruit ripen in autumn. A number of dwarf to moderate-size varieties are sold. 'Chico' (about 1½ feet) has double flowers; 'Nana' (to about 3 feet) has single flowers and small, inedible fruit. In the 6–10-foot range are 'Legrellei' (double flowers, cream striped red) and 'Alba Plena' (double creamy white flowers). 'Double Red' resembles 'Wonderful' but has double flowers and no fruit. All make good specimen, border, or hedge plants; they are especially useful where summers are hot and the water supply limited.

PYRACANTHA. Firethorn. Evergreen. Zones vary. In Zones 6–10, firethorns are heavily laden with orange to red berries from as early as summer to the end of winter. Nurseries offer many different species and varieties of varying sizes, growth habits, and cold tolerance. Conspicuous flat clusters of small white flowers in spring are followed by brilliant berries that, in some kinds, ripen by late summer. Glossy leaves are small and oval to pointed, on thorny stems. Growth may be upright to 15 feet in some kinds, or tall and spreading, or under 10 feet; some are angular or have pendent branches — habit depends on the variety (or seedling plant). Use as specimen shrubs, barrier or fence plantings, and espaliers. Selection of available kinds varies regionally.

Raphiolepis indica

RAPHIOLEPIS. Evergreen. Zones 8–10. Excellent for mass planting and hedges, these shrubs are dense, rounded, and symmetrical, with leathery, glossy, pointed-oval 3-inch leaves and a good show of flowers. India hawthorn (*R. indica*) and its varieties are most widely sold. Spring flowers, ½–1 inch across, come in loose clusters and are followed by dark blue berrylike fruit. Plant size and flower color vary according to variety. Shortest is 'Ballerina' — 2 feet by 4 feet across, with deep pink blossoms. In the 5–7-foot height range are 'Bill Evans' (light pink), 'Enchantress' (medium pink), 'Pink Lady' (deep pink), and 'Springtime' (deep pink). From 3 to 6 feet tall are 'Clara' (white), 'Coates Crimson' (reddish pink), 'Fascination' (deep pink), 'Jack Evans' and 'Pink

...Raphiolepis

Cloud' (deep pink), and 'Snow White' (white). Less widely sold is *R. umbellata*, a larger plant (to 6 feet or more) with white flowers and more rounded, darker leaves.

RHAMNUS. Evergreen and deciduous. Zones vary. Included here are the Buckthorns — good-looking foliage shrubs that perform well under less than ideal conditions. They're attractive as specimen plants but are used more often as hedges and high screens. Evergreen Italian buckthorn (*R. alaternus*), Zones 7–10 (West), is dense and fast-growing to 20 feet with equal spread if not restricted; glossy oval leaves reach 2 inches long. A variegated form has leaves edged creamy white. Evergreen Coffeeberry (*R. californica*), Zones 7–10 (West), reaches 15 feet high. Leaves are glossy to dull deep green, to 3 inches long; cherry-size fruit (from inconspicuous flowers) turn from green to red to black when ripe. Varieties 'Eve Case' and 'Seaview' are much lower with larger leaves. Deciduous Common buckthorn (*R. cathartica*), Zones 3–8, reaches Italian buckthorn size. Leaves are to 2½ inches long and turn yellow in autumn; stems often have spiny tips. Alder buckthorn (*R. frangula*), Zones 3–8, reaches about 15 feet with rounded, glossy, 3-inch leaves that turn yellow in autumn. More often grown is variety 'Columnaris', the Tallhedge buckthorn. This is a first-rate hedge plant, growing no more than 4 feet wide and to 15 feet high (but can be kept much lower).

RHODODENDRON. Rhododendron and Azalea. Evergreen and deciduous. Zones vary. It is impossible to generalize in any meaningful way about rhododendrons. There are tree types from the Himalayas, and ground cover types, as well, from the same area. There are tropical species from Southeast Asia, deciduous species from northern Asia, southeastern Europe, and both eastern and western United States. Flowers are basically funnel-shaped in tightly knit clusters called "trusses," but some have practically flat flowers while others are tubular. Color range includes almost everything but true blue, but some lavender blue varieties give a blue effect in the garden. Foliage varies from thumbnail size to well over a foot long, with textures from glossy to matte, veined and rough-appearing to absolutely smooth.

All rhododendrons and azaleas are prized for their color display during bloom season from late winter through spring. The majority of plants are landscape assets when out of bloom, too. In general, azaleas are more fine-textured, lightweight appearing, and informal, whereas rhododendrons are more massive and dominant, but when you explore the specialists' world of rhododendrons you'll discover an exciting array of hybrids and species quite different from the usual, limited retail nursery selection of tough, reliable varieties. For detailed information on types, varieties, and culture, see the *Sunset* book *Azaleas, Camellias, Rhododendrons*.

RHUS. Sumac. Deciduous. Zones vary. Fragrant sumac (*R. aromatica*), Zones 3–9, spreads by underground stems to form large clumps of upright stems 3–5 feet high. Dense foliage consists of pointed-oval 3-inch leaflets, 3 to a leaf; autumn color is bright yellow to red. Use to cover sloping ground or as a foreground plant at garden outskirts. Smooth sumac (*R. glabra*), Zones 2–9, is a shorter version (to 10 feet, sometimes taller) of Staghorn sumac (*R. typhina*) described on pages 105–106. It makes an interesting character plant for its branch structure, and is spectacular in its red early autumn color.

ROCKROSE. See Cistus.

ROSA. Rose. Deciduous to nearly evergreen. Zones 3–10, depending on variety. Most roses sold in nurseries and garden centers are modern hybrid teas, grandifloras, floribundas, and climbers. Specialty mail-order nurseries carry many other kinds of old roses, species, and modern shrub roses.

Modern hybrid teas and grandifloras bear "typical" rose blossoms — large, well-formed, and often fragrant — on bushes 3–8 feet high depending on the variety and climate. Some varieties are well-foliaged, well-branched shrubs, but many are less valuable as shrubs than as flower factories. Floribundas usually are 2–4 feet tall, bushy, and well-foliaged, with clusters of smaller flowers often as individually attractive as hybrid tea blooms. Climbers produce long, somewhat limber canes that can be fanned out on walls, trellises, fences, or trained on overheads; blossoms may be large to fairly small. Many are climbing sports of favorite hybrid tea, grandiflora, and floribunda varieties.

Many gardeners segregate the modern bush roses into separate beds — a sort of monotypic cutting garden. This is a practical approach — special care is concentrated in one space — and the result can be attractive, depending on garden design and choice of varieties. But roses can also be components of mixed plantings with annuals, perennials, and shrubs as long as they receive good light, water, and nutrients. In a mixed planting the deficiencies of gaunt or awkward plants, such as those with sparse foliage, are less noticeable.

Old garden roses — types that were popular in the past — shrub roses, and some species are becoming increasingly popular. Some flower less frequently than modern roses but many are good-looking shrubs at all times. Depending on sizes of individual varieties, these can be used as foreground or background shrubs, and even as hedge plantings. Some climbing types — large-flowered natural climbers and climbing sports of bush roses — can thread their way through other shrubs or trees with a charming effect. For detailed information on types, varieties, and culture, see the *Sunset* book *How to Grow Roses*.

ROSEMARY. See Rosmarinus.

ROSE OF SHARON. See Hibiscus syriacus.

ROSMARINUS officinalis. Rosemary. Evergreen. Zones 7–10. Many upward-sweeping stems rise to 4–6 feet, carrying narrow to needlelike inch-long leaves along their length. Foliage is aromatic, usually glossy green on upper surface and grayish beneath. Pleasant show of ½-inch lavender blue blossoms comes from late winter to spring. Variety 'Tuscan Blue' is larger, more rigidly upright, with broader leaves and brighter, darker-colored flowers. These tolerate drought and must have a well-drained soil. Use in dry gardens, massed or as specimens, and at garden fringes.

SACRED BAMBOO. See Nandina domestica.

SHRUB ALTHAEA. See Hibiscus syriacus.

SILVERBERRY. See Elaeagnus.

SMOKE TREE. See Cotinus coggygria.

SNOWBALL. See Viburnum.

SPIRAEA. Deciduous. Zones 4–9. The spiraeas are fine-textured plants noted for showy display of small, clustered flowers in white, pink, or red. The common ones fall into two categories: upright, arching shrubs to around 6 feet, and low, mounded plants to about 3 feet. Taller kinds have white flowers in clusters all along branches. Spring-blooming Bridal wreath spiraea (*S. prunifolia*) has good red autumn foliage color on upright plant; double-flowered form is showiest. Arching, billowy *S. thunbergii* has less conspicuous flowers and very narrow leaves that turn reddish brown. Summer-flowering Reeves spiraea (*S. cantoniensis*) is upright and arching. Most widely planted of all is *S. vanhouttei*, a fountain-shaped plant with blue green foliage and large, flattish flower clusters. The shorter spiraeas have blooms clustered at branch tips of new growth in summer. Most popular is *S. bumalda* 'Anthony Waterer'; its carmine red, flat clusters come on a dense, rounded 2–3-foot plant with narrow, 4-inch leaves. Variety 'Goldflame' may reach 4 feet, has bronzy new growth that turns yellow by summer; blooms are rosy red. A similar species is *S. japonica*, to about 4 feet; variety 'Atrosanguinea' has deep crimson blooms in late spring.

STRAWBERRY TREE. See Arbutus unedo.

SWEET BAY. See Laurus nobilis.

SWEET OLIVE. See Osmanthus fragrans.

SYRINGA. Lilac. Deciduous. Zones vary. To most gardeners, the word "lilac" means just one plant: Common lilac (*S. vulgaris*), Zones 3–9, with its fat, spiked clusters of intensely fragrant blossoms. This species and its many named varieties grow into large (sometimes to 20 feet), bulky plants with rounded-oval pointed foliage to 5 inches long. In bloom they are beautiful; flowers are single or double, in white, lavender, blue, purple, red, and pink. Out of bloom they are of no special beauty; use as a backdrop for other showy plantings or as hedge or screen. Other large lilacs include the Preston hybrids (*S. prestoniae*), Zones 2–8, which have smaller individual flowers in a more limited color range, blooming several weeks later, and slightly shorter plants with narrower foliage. Chinese lilac (*S. chinensis*), Zones 5–9, is a more graceful plant with smaller foliage than common lilac; open clusters of fragrant flowers come at the same time, in rose purple or white. Persian lilac (*S. persica*), Zones 5–9, is a graceful, arching 6-foot plant with fine-textured foliage; fragrant lavender flowers appear along branches in midspring. Similar is *S. laciniata*, Zones 5–9, which has finely dissected leaves. Korean lilac (*S. patula*), Zones 3–8, reaches little more than 5 feet as a rounded plant; lavender to pink fragrant flowers blossom after hybrid common lilacs.

Syringa vulgaris

TAXUS. Yew. Evergreen. Zones vary. Dark, dense, formal, massive — all describe yews to some extent. Best known is Irish Yew (*T. baccata* 'Stricta'), Zones 6–9, which forms a bulky, flat-topped column to 20 feet or more. Like the basic species and other varieties, it may be shrublike in habit but of tree size in the garden. The yews following are of a better size for most gardens. Yew foliage is narrow, linear, and often dark green. *T. baccata* 'Adpressa', Zones 6–9, forms a rounded, wide-spreading, dense plant 4–5 feet high with ½-inch leaves. *T. media*, Zones 5–9, represents a group of named hybrids many of which are upright and columnar to pyramidal. 'Hicksii' is narrow and upright to 10–12 feet; 'Hatfieldii' forms a broad dark green column or pyramid to 10 feet or more. 'Brownii' is compact and rounded, eventually to 8 feet if not kept lower by shearing. Many other varieties of various growth habits may be available from local sources.

TEA TREE. See Leptospermum.

THUJA. Arborvitae. Evergreen. Zones vary. Arborvitaes are symmetrical plants with scalelike leaves usually carried in flat, vertical sprays. American arborvitae (*T. occidentalis*), Zones 2–10, has numerous named varieties that are globe-shaped to columnar and are useful as specimens and for hedge or border planting. Tallest are 'Douglasii Pyra-

midalis' (pyramidal) and 'Fastigiata' (columnar), which may reach 20 feet but can easily be kept lower. 'Rheingold' is a yellow-foliaged cone-shaped plant to 6 feet high. Short globular forms include 'Globosa', 'Nana', 'Umbraculifera', and 'Woodwardii'. Western red cedar (*T. plicata*), Zones 4–8, is a towering tree that has produced several good shrubby varieties. Hogan cedar, variety 'Fastigiata', forms a dense, slender column useful as accent or tall screen. 'Striblingii' has same uses, reaches only 12 feet high by 3 feet wide.

TOBIRA. See Pittosporum tobira.

TSUGA canadensis. Canada hemlock. Evergreen. Zones 5–9. The densely pyramidal forest tree has several small varieties that retain the same soft, graceful appearance. Leaves are dark green needles about ½-inch long. Most widely planted variety is 'Pendula', the Sargent weeping hemlock. Its drooping branches build up a mounded plant to 3 feet high and 6 feet wide (twice as big after many decades). Grow it in a feature position with room to gradually enlarge.

VIBURNUM. Deciduous and evergreen. Zones vary. The viburnums constitute a large and diverse assortment of valuable garden shrubs and small trees. Most are medium-size to large plants useful for background, screen, and specimen situations; smaller plants usually are dwarf variants of larger species. Many are noted for showy bloom clusters, bright display of sometimes-edible fruit, and good autumn foliage color. Among the best-liked are the various "snowball" types. Common snowball (*V. opulus* 'Roseum'), Zones 3–9, produces rounded white bloom clusters to 2½ inches in diameter; plant reaches 15 feet with lobed, maplelike leaves that color red in autumn. Fragrant snowball (*V. carlcephalum*), Zones 5–9, adds fragrance to its 4–5-inch white flower clusters; oval leaves have good autumn color on upright plant to 10 feet. Chinese snowball (*V. macrocephalum macrocephalum*), Zones 6–9, is a broadly rounded plant 12–20 feet high with dull green, 4-inch oblong leaves that are not completely deciduous in warmer regions; bloom clusters reach 8 inches across. Japanese snowball (*V. plicatum plicatum*), Zones 4–9, has a strongly horizontal branch pattern and prominently veined leaves that turn purplish red in autumn; bloom clusters are 2–3 inches across, carried along branches. Other deciduous species that produce showy flowers and good autumn leaf color are Arrowwood (*V. dentatum*), Zones 3–9; Nannyberry (*V. lentago*), Zones 3–9; Black haw (*V. prunifolium*), Zones 3–9; and Cranberry bush (*V. trilobum*), Zones 3–9. Linden viburnum (*V. dilatatum*), Zones 5–9, produces fine display of red fruit that last long after leaves have fallen.

Among evergreen species are several outstanding for foliage beauty. Sweet viburnum (*V. odoratissimum*), Zones 9–10, has highly

glossy, 3–8-inch leaves on a wide-spreading 10–20-foot plant; flowers are white, and berries that follow turn red, then black. Laurustinus (*V. tinus*), Zones 8–10, produces its pink-budded white flowers from late autumn to spring on a 6–12-foot plant densely covered in dark, glossy 2–3-inch foliage. There are several named varieties including larger-leafed 'Lucidum', 3–5-foot-high 'Dwarf', and 'Variegatum' with foliage marked white and yellow. All have metallic blue fruit. *V. davidii* is worthwhile for foliage alone. A shrub to about 3 feet high and 4 feet wide carries dark, glossy, prominently veined 6-inch leaves. Flowers are not showy, but produce metallic blue fruit. It is good for massing or as a well-groomed specimen. Many other good viburnums may be available locally.

Viburnum carlcephalum

WEIGELA. Deciduous. Zones 5–9. The various weigelas are among the showiest of spring-blooming shrubs; flowers come in midspring after leaf-out. Nurseries offer several species and numerous hybrids ranging from 4 to 10 feet tall. All have funnel-shaped 1-inch flowers (like foxgloves) in small clusters all along stems formed the previous year; colors are pink and red shades, and white. Leaves are pointed ovals to 4 inches long and have no particular autumn color. Pink to rose red *W. florida*, a vigorous 10-footer, is widely grown; its variety 'Variegata' has cream-variegated foliage. Red-flowered varieties include 'Bristol Ruby', and 'Newport Red', all in the 6-foot range, and 'Eva Supreme', about 4 feet tall. Variety 'Java Red,' to 6 feet, has pink flowers opening from red buds; foliage is tinted purple. 'Bristol Snowflake' and 'Candida' are white-flowered and reach about 9 feet. These are fine background specimen shrubs.

XYLOSMA congestum. Evergreen to deciduous. Zones 9–10. What it lacks in flowers (they are inconspicuous) *Xylosma* makes up for in foliage beauty and garden usefulness. Plant is somewhat loose, spreading, and a bit angular, to about 10 feet high and wide; branches arch or droop gracefully. Shiny pointed-oval leaves are yellowish green coming from bronzy new growth. Uses are many: background shrub, screen, or hedge; bank cover; espalier; small tree.

YEW. See Taxus.

Vines for decorative accent

Vines can be highly decorative elements in the garden, in the manner of trimming on a hat: perhaps not essential, but certainly enhancing the appearance of the basic supporting structure. Train a vine on a wall or fence and the vine becomes a living fresco or painting. The stark angularity of an arbor or a pergola can be relieved by vine growth, the picture made more interesting by contrast between softness of foliage and flowers and hard edges of structure. And yes, some vines can completely conceal an unsightly wall.

AKEBIA quinata. Fiveleaf akebia. Deciduous to evergreen. Zones 4–10 (West) and 4–9 (East). Plentiful leaves create a fine texture; each leaf consists of 5 deep green, oval leaflets 2–3 inches long arranged in clover fashion at the end of a 3–5-inch leaf stalk. Vigorous twining stems climb easily to 30 feet. Spring clusters of small purple flowers may produce purplish sausagelike fruit. Where winter temperatures drop below freezing, leaves fall late in the year; in mild-winter regions, some or all may remain on the plant until spring.

AMPELOPSIS brevipedunculata. Blueberry climber, Porcelain vine. Deciduous. Zones 4–10. The large, deeply lobed leaves resemble those of grape and Boston ivy. Conspicuous clusters of greenish white pea-size berries turn metallic blue from late summer into autumn. Strong-growing vine (to 20 feet) has forked tendrils. Foliage cover is medium dense; leaves turn brilliant red in autumn. In mild climates this deciduous vine drops some leaves; new leaves grow, redden, and drop all winter.

BEAUMONTIA grandiflora. Herald's trumpet, Easter lily vine. Evergreen. Zone 10. Vigorous growth can take plants to 30 feet high and wide (and larger in Florida). Climbing stems arch and loosely twine. Shiny, broad, oval leaves reach 9 inches long and form dense foliage cover. Many highly fragrant 5-inch trumpet-shaped white blossoms with green veins appear in spring and summer. Heavy growth requires sturdy supports and protection from strong wind.

BITTERSWEET. See Celastrus scandens.

BLUEBERRY CLIMBER. See Ampelopsis brevipedunculata.

BOSTON IVY. See Parthenocissus tricuspidata.

BOUGAINVILLEA. Evergreen. Zone 10 and warmest parts of Zone 9. Vibrant colors make bougainvillea a favorite vine in frost-free areas. Brightly colored bracts surrounding the flowers provide the display. Purple and shades of red are the most common. Medium-size leaves are rich green and heart-shaped; most varieties offer dense foliage cover. Plant grows long, lax, thorny stems that must be tied to supports in order to climb. Vigor depends on the variety.

CAMPSIS. Trumpet creeper, Trumpet vine. Deciduous. Zones vary. The three trumpet vines bear showy trumpet-shaped blossoms in arching clusters during summer. All have leaves divided into many oval, toothed leaflets that form a dense cover. Stems cling to any surface by means of aerial rootlets, but tie stems in place to support vine's weight.

The most vigorous (to 40 feet) is North American native *C. radicans*, Zones 5–10, with 2-inch-wide orange and scarlet flowers; a bit less rampant growing (and for the same zones) is its hybrid *C. tagliabuana* 'Mme. Galen', which has slightly larger salmon orange blossoms. The least vigorous vine (to about 20 feet), Chinese trumpet creeper (*C. grandiflora*), Zones 7–10, has 3-inch brilliant scarlet flowers.

Campsis tagliabuana 'Mme. Galen'

CAPE HONEYSUCKLE. See Tecomaria capensis.

CAROLINA JESSAMINE. See Gelsemium sempervirens.

CELASTRUS scandens. American bittersweet. Deciduous. Zones 3–8. Clusters of inconspicuous female flowers produce small yellow to orange rounded capsules that split open in autumn and winter to show red-coated seeds. These are conspicuous before the 4-inch oval leaves turn yellow in autumn, and fruit usually decorate bare branches into winter. Male and female flowers are on separate plants; plants that bear female flowers need a nearby male plant for fruit formation. American bittersweet climbs easily to 20 feet by twining. The ropelike branches can kill shrub branches or young trees by girdling.

CLEMATIS. Evergreen and deciduous. Zones vary. The *Clematis* species and varieties climb by twining their leaf stalks around any slender support. Many of the popular clematises are hybrids discussed below under "Hybrid clematis."

Evergreen clematis (*C. armandii*), Zones 7–10 (West) and 7–8 (East), is a potential tree climber. Each leaf contains 3 pendent, glossy, dark green leaflets to 5 inches long. Large clusters of fragrant, starlike white flowers, each up to 2½ inches wide, bloom in early spring. Of somewhat similar appearance (but only semievergreen) is Sweet autumn clematis (*C. dioscoreifolia*), Zones 6–10 (West) and 6–8 (East). Flowers and foliage are smaller and bloom comes in late summer and autumn; blossoms fade and give way to decorative seed heads. Deciduous Anemone clematis (*C. montana*), Zones 6–10 (West) and 6–8 (East), will also head for the treetops. Tooth-edged, pointed leaves emerge bright red and turn bronzy green when mature. In spring 2-inch pink blossoms (resembling Japanese anemones) cover plant. *C. m. rubens* has blossoms of rose red changing to pink.

Hybrid clematis. These large-flowered types have long oval "petals" (actually sepals) arranged around the true flower, which has no petals. Colors include shades of violet and purple, as well as red, pink, blue, and white. "Flowers" appear in spring, summer, or both seasons and are 4–9 inches wide. Most are of restrained growth.

CREEPING FIG. See Ficus pumila.

CUP-OF-GOLD-VINE. See Solandra maxima.

EASTER LILY VINE. See Beaumontia grandiflora.

EUONYMUS fortunei. See Ground Covers, page 125.

FICUS pumila. Creeping fig. Evergreen. Zones 9–10. Young plants have a dense clothing of bright green, heart-shaped, crinkled leaves ½–¾ inch long. But after some years when the plant is well established, it sends out mature growth: leathery, 2–4-inch oblong leaves on short, stubby stems from the flat, hugging framework. Unrestricted old vines can climb and cover four-story buildings, developing arm to leg-thick stems. Though vines cling tightly to any surface, avoid hot south and west-facing walls.

GELSEMIUM sempervirens. Carolina jessamine. Evergreen. Zones 8–10. Paired leaves are glossy, light green, pointed ovals to 4 inches long. Fragrant trumpet-shaped flowers — bright yellow, 1½-inches long — bloom along stems in winter and early spring. Lax, slender stems climb by twining but need some help to grow upward. All parts of this plant are poisonous.

HEDERA. See Ground Covers, page 125.

HERALD'S TRUMPET. See Beaumontia grandiflora.

HONEYSUCKLE. See Lonicera.

HYDRANGEA anomala. Climbing hydrangea (usually sold as *H. a. petiolaris*). Deciduous. Zones 4–9 (West) and 4–8 (East). Small, clinging roots along stems adhere to any surface and can reach great heights. Glossy, broad, heart-shaped leaves are up to 4 inches long. After vine becomes well established, the clinging stems send out short, shrubby stems that bear late spring flowers. Each "flower" is a 6–10-inch broad cluster of two kinds of blossoms: a ring of conspicuous white sterile blossoms an inch or more wide and small fertile flowers in the center.

JASMINE. See Jasminum.

JASMINUM. Jasmine. Evergreen, semievergreen, and deciduous. Zones vary. The following four jasmines are vining plants with fragrant blossoms.

Spanish jasmine (*J. grandiflorum*), Zones 8–10, is only semievergreen in Zone 8 and parts of Zone 9. Glossy leaves consist of 5–7 narrow 2-inch leaflets; clusters of 2½-inch white flowers bloom through summer. Its long green stems need tying to support. Common white jasmine (*J. officinale*), Zones 9–10, has a similar appearance but is a larger plant (to 30 feet) with flowers only 1 inch wide. Angelwing jasmine (*J. nitidum*), Zone 9 (warmest parts) and Zone 10, loses some of its leaves during winter in all but frost-free gardens. Glossy green leaves are pointed ovals to 2 inches long, on stems to 20 feet that twine but still need tying. Pinwheel-shaped 1-inch flowers come in late spring and summer, white from purple buds. Rampant *J. polyanthum*, Zones 9–10, has narrow leaflets that give plant a fine texture. Inch-wide flowers, in clusters, are white with pink undersides; bloom may start in late winter and last into summer.

LONICERA. Honeysuckle. Evergreen and semievergreen. Zones vary. Vigor and fragrance are associated with most honeysuckles. Though vine, leaf, and flower sizes vary, all have the same configuration: clustered flowers are individually tube-shaped, usually splitting toward the apex into two lobes (the upper one larger than the lower); oval leaves are in opposite pairs and are often a bluish green. Those described here are widespread in the nursery trade; others may be locally available.

Japanese honeysuckle (*L. japonica*), Zones 5–10, can smother a fence, top of arbor, or the ground. Most common form is 'Halliana' (Hall's honeysuckle); white flowers come in late spring. Variety 'Aureoreticulata' (Gold-net honeysuckle) has leaves strikingly veined

yellow. Equally vigorous is Trumpet honeysuckle (*L. sempervirens*), Zones 4–10, which has scentless, 2-inch, trumpet-shaped summer blossoms in yellow orange to bright red; scarlet berrylike fruit follow in autumn. Less rampant (to 12–15 feet) and longer blooming (spring to frost), Gold Flame honeysuckle (*L. heckrottii*), Zones 6–10, bears flowers that are coral pink outside and yellow inside. The largest in its parts is the Giant Burmese honeysuckle (*L. hildebrandiana*), Zones 9–10, with thick, ropelike stems, 6-inch leaves, and 6–7-inch summer blossoms that turn from white to yellow and orange.

PARTHENOCISSUS. Deciduous. Zones vary. Included here are two of the vines most renowned for brilliant autumn foliage color. Boston ivy (*P. tricuspidata*), Zones 4–10, clings tenaciously by means of small roots on stems. In time a plant will create a solid, shinglelike cover of glossy leaves to 8 inches wide, usually with 3 pointed lobes. Varieties with consistently small leaves and slower growth are 'Lowii' and 'Veitchii'. Virginia creeper (*P. quinquefolia*), Zones 3–10, has leaves that are divided, fanlike, into 5 tooth-edged, 6-inch leaflets. Compared with Boston ivy, this is a more open, meandering vine. It attaches by disc-tipped tendrils.

PASSIFLORA. Passion vine. Evergreen and semievergreen. Zones vary. Rampant passion vines are grown for their unusual blossoms and fast, dense growth. Vines climb by means of tendrils, to 30 feet or more unchecked, and need support to climb. Flowers have 10 identical petals and sepals arranged circularly, a ring of contrasting filaments in the center, and prominent stamens and pistils. Largest blossoms, to 4 inches wide in white and purple, come all summer on *P. alatocaerulea*, Zones 8–10. Three-inch-long leaves have 3 deep lobes. Passion fruit (*P. edulis*), Zones 9–10, produces 2-inch white and purple flowers; egg-shaped, 3-inch-long edible fruit follow. All passion vines are good ground covers on sloping terrain.

Passiflora alatocaerulea

PASSION VINE. See Passiflora.

POLYGONUM aubertii. Silver lace vine. Deciduous (below about 15°F/−9°C) or evergreen. Zones 5–10 (West) and 5–9 (East).

Twining stems grow easily to 30 feet in a year. Glossy, bright green leaves are arrowhead-shaped with wavy edges, to 2½ inches long. Many tiny white flowers appear in foamy clusters from late spring to autumn.

PORCELAIN VINE. See Ampelopsis brevipedunculata.

POTATO VINE. See Solanum jasminoides.

SILVER LACE VINE. See Polygonum aubertii.

SOLANDRA maxima. Cup-of-Gold vine. Evergreen. Zones 9 (warmest parts) and 10. Fast growth produces a thick-stemmed vine that can cover a 40-foot wall. Heavy stems require tying to support. Leaves are glossy, leathery ovals to about 6 inches long. Bowl-shaped 8-inch blossoms are golden yellow with brownish centers and a few purple stripes; main bloom time is late winter into spring.

SOLANUM jasminoides. Potato vine. Evergreen. Zones 9–10. This rampant-growing vine never loses its delicate appearance. Twining stems bear wavy-edged oval or arrowhead-shaped leaves to 3 inches long, rich green often tinged purple. Threadlike stalks carry inch-wide, star-shaped blossoms in fluffy clusters of 8–12; heaviest bloom is in spring, but flowers may appear all year.

TECOMARIA capensis. Cape honeysuckle. Evergreen. Zones 8–10. Vigorous, sprawling stems must be tied to the supports for cape honeysuckle to climb. Glossy foliage consists of many 1–2-inch oval leaflets that form a fine-textured backdrop for brilliant blossoms in autumn and winter. The most common form has orange red tubular flowers in compact clusters at branch tips.

TRACHELOSPERMUM jasminoides. See Ground Covers, page 127.

TRUMPET CREEPER. See Campsis.

VIRGINIA CREEPER. See Parthenocissus quinquefolia.

WISTERIA. Deciduous. Zones 4–10. Great beauty and vigor are the hallmarks of *Wisteria*. Long, drooping clusters of sweet-pea-like flowers appear before graceful leaves and long streamers of new growth emerge. Each leaf is composed of paired oval leaflets plus one at the tip. Stems extend a vine's territory by twining. Old stems become thick and heavy, so permanent supports should be sturdy. Most common kind is Chinese wisteria (*W. sinensis*), which has foot-long clusters of violet blue, lavender, or white flowers depending on the variety; leaves contain 7–13 leaflets. Japanese wisteria (*W. floribunda*) carries flower clusters 18 inches and longer; selected varieties have white, blue, lavender, purple, and pink flowers, and double-blossom lilac flowers. The 12–16 leaflets per leaf are broader than those of Chinese wisteria.

Annuals & perennials for seasonal color

Annuals and perennials are just as important in the landscape picture as the usually permanent plantings of trees and shrubs. Most annuals and perennials are grown for the beauty of their flowers and the color impact these blossoms provide. In this respect they are no different from many shrubs. But annuals last for just one flowering season, and the majority of perennials must be periodically divided and replanted — and therein lies their special landscape advantage: you can paint a new garden image easily by changing plants or by planting a different color of the same plant. Changing the color accents in your garden can be like moving furniture to give new life to a room — the room, in this case, being the framework established by trees, shrubs, vines, ground covers, and structural elements.

Nurseries and mail-order plant suppliers carry a wide selection of annuals and perennials. On this and the facing page, we have profiled many of the most popular kinds.

ANNUALS

AGERATUM (*Ageratum houstonianum*). Bushy, hairy-leafed plants 6 inches to 2 feet, depending on variety. Tiny flowers — shades of lavender, pink, white — in showy clusters.

BACHELOR'S BUTTON (*Centaurea cyanus*). Fringy flowers 1½ inches across, blue, white, pink, reddish on 1–2½-foot plant with narrow, gray green foliage.

CALENDULA (*Calendula officinalis*). Double daisy flowers 2½–4½ inches across, in cream, yellow shades, orange, apricot. Fall through spring bloom where winter is mild.

CINERARIA (*Senecio hybridus*). Late-winter bloom in mild climates — broad clusters of single daisy flowers in white, brilliant blues, violet, red. Lush, broad leaves on 1½-foot plant.

COCKSCOMB (*Celosia argentea*). Dwarf to 3-foot kinds; rough, bright green leaves. Two flower types, plumelike and crested (fan-shaped), in bright pink, yellow, orange, red.

COSMOS (*Cosmos bipinnatus*). Tall (3–6 feet) but delicate with finely divided leaves. Single daisy flowers in lavender, pink, rose, purple.

FAIRY PRIMROSE (*Primula malacoides*). Winter, early spring bloom where winter is mild. Oval leaves in clumps of rosettes; loose flower clusters (white, lavender, pink, red) on thin, 12–15-inch stems.

FOXGLOVE (*Digitalis purpurea*). Biennial. Clumps of hairy, tongue-shaped leaves giving rise to 4–6-foot stems of drooping bells: purple, white, cream, pastel shades, spotted.

GAILLARDIA (*Gaillardia pulchella*). Single daisy flowers or fully double and pincushionlike 2–3 inches: cream, gold, maroon, and bicolor combinations. Low foliage, stems 1–2 feet tall.

HOLLYHOCK (*Alcea rosea*). Biennial. Foliage mound of large, rounded to lobed leaves. Flower spike 6–9 feet high with saucer-shaped or double flowers: white, cream, pink to red, purple, apricot.

ICELAND POPPY (*Papaver nudicaule*). Perennial grown as annual. Slender, hairy stems to 2 feet above foliage clump. Cup-shaped flowers to 3 inches: cream, yellow, orange, red, pink, white.

IMPATIENS (*Impatiens wallerana*). Bushy, succulent plant, dwarf (8 inches) to tall (2 feet). Showy 5-petaled flat flowers: red, orange, pink shades, violet, white, variegated.

LOBELIA (*Lobelia erinus*). Fine-textured low plants, compact or spreading, with small flowers in brilliant blue shades, white, pink. 'Crystal Palace' has bronze leaves.

MARIGOLD (*Tagetes*). Finely divided, usually strong-smelling leaves; varieties range from dwarf (6 inches) to tall (3 feet). Double flowers with many florets in white, cream, yellow, orange, rust.

PANSY and VIOLA (*Viola*). Winter, spring bloom in mild regions. Low plants with flat, rounded flowers: violas (smaller) in solid colors, pansies (larger) combine colors.

PETUNIA (*Petunia hybrida*). Low, sprawling plants with large, funnel-shaped flowers, single or double, in white, pink, red, purple, blue, cream, yellow.

PHLOX (*Phlox drummondii*). Short (6–18-inch) bushy plants with large clusters of flat flowers in white, pastel shades, red, violet at tops of stems.

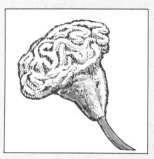

Cockscomb

Foxglove

Pansy

Snapdragon

Columbine

Cottage pink

Daylily

Iris

PINCUSHION FLOWER (*Scabiosa atropurpurea*). Tall (to 3 feet) slender plants with wiry stems. Clustered flowers with prominent stamens: white, pink shades, lavender to purple.

SNAPDRAGON (*Antirrhinum majus*). From 8-inch dwarf types to 3-foot strains. Upright plants with spikes of distinctively shaped flowers in broad range of colors.

SWEET ALYSSUM (*Lobularia maritima*). Fine-textured, low, spreading plants with profuse clusters of tiny blossoms in white, pinkish lavender, dark violet.

VERBENA (*Verbena hybrida*). Low, wide-spreading plants have 2–3-inch flat clusters of small flowers: white, pink, red, purple, blue, bicolors.

ZINNIA (*Zinnia elegans*). Showy, double daisy flowers in wide range of bright colors. Broadly oval, rough leaves on dwarf (6-inch) through tall (3-foot) plants.

PERENNIALS

ASTILBE (*Astilbe*). Mounding clumps of handsome, fernlike foliage. Wiry stems hold tiny flowers in plumelike clusters, to 3 feet; white, pink shades, red, in late spring to summer.

CANDYTUFT (*Iberis sempervirens*). Several varieties, 4–18 inches high, all spreading. Dark, shiny, narrow leaves, white flowers in clusters at stem ends; major bloom in spring.

COLUMBINE (*Aquilegia* hybrids). Lacy, fernlike foliage clumps; dis-

tinctive spring flowers in many colors and combinations. Many strains, from low (12 inches) to tall (3 feet).

CORAL BELLS (*Heuchera sanguinea*). Clumps of roundish, scallop-edged leaves. Wiry stems 12–24 inches tall carry loose spikes of bell-like spring–summer flowers: white, pink shades, red.

COTTAGE PINK (*Dianthus plumarius*). Spreading clumps of narrow, gray green leaves. Thin stems to 1½ feet with fragrant 1-inch summer and autumn flowers: white, pink, red, combinations.

DAYLILY (*Hemerocallis* hybrids). Foliage clumps like young corn plants. Large funnel-shaped blooms in cream, yellow, orange, red, rust, maroon, pink, lavender, purple in late spring, summer.

DELPHINIUM (*Delphinium* hybrids). Summer blooming spires, 2–6 feet high, of rosettelike flowers: white, blue shades, pink. Clumps of fan-shaped, lobed, or cut leaves.

FIBROUS BEGONIA (*Begonia semperflorens-cultorum*). Succulent stems, rounded leaves in green, bronzy green, red bronze on 6–18 inch bushy plant. White, pink, red summer bloom.

GAZANIA (*Gazania* hybrids). Clumping or trailing plants with narrow gray and green leaves. Late spring, summer daisies white, cream, yellow, orange, red, rust, pink on 6–10-inch stems.

GLORIOSA DAISY (*Rudbeckia hirta*). Rough, hairy leaves and 3–4-foot stems. Dark-centered daisies to 7 inches are yellow, orange, rust, mahogany in summer, autumn.

IRIS (*Iris* hybrids). Tall bearded types most widely grown. Distinctive spring blooms, on branched 2–4-foot stems, in all but true red. Swordlike gray green leaves in clumps.

LILY-OF-THE-NILE (*Agapanthus*). Fountainlike clumps of strap-shaped leaves. Heads of tubular flowers, blue or white, on long stems, in summer. Dwarf (1 foot) to tall (5 feet).

ORIENTAL POPPY (*Papaver orientale*). Large spring blooms are bowl-shaped, white, pink shades, red, purple, orange, on 2–4-foot stems above clumps of hairy, divided leaves.

PEONY (*Paeonia* hybrids). Shrubby clumps 2–4 feet high of handsome, divided, fanlike leaves. Spring flowers are fluffy spheres to 10 inches, in white, cream, pink, red.

PHLOX (*Phlox paniculata*). Narrow, pointed leaves; clumps of upright stems 3–5 feet tall. Dome-shaped flower clusters at stem tips; colors are white, pink and lavender shades, red.

PLANTAIN LILY (*Hosta*). Handsome foliage plants of wide variety of size, leaf shape, and color. Leaves form mounded clumps. Thin spikes of white or lilac, tubular flowers in summer.

SHASTA DAISY (*Chrysanthemum maximum*). Clumps of narrow, dark green foliage. Single or double yellow-centered white daisies to 4 inches across on 2–4-foot stems. Summer bloom.

YARROW (*Achillea*). Clumps of gray or green, finely divided leaves; stems 1½–5 feet (depending on variety). Flat-topped clusters of tiny summer flowers: white, yellow, pink, red.

Ground covers for space definition

The term "ground cover" is accurate but unromantic, suggesting something purely utilitarian that is rolled out in carpet fashion to obscure the floor beneath. Actually, a ground cover can be the homogenizing or linking element in a landscape, joining related parts of the design by providing a uniform base. Your choice of particular plants then determines the character of that linkage — whether flat and ruglike or taller, shaggier, more informal. A ground cover can also be a design element in itself, offering an expanse of low vegetation.

AARON'S BEARD. See Hypericum calycinum.

ACHILLEA. Yarrow. Evergreen perennial. Zones 4–10 (West) and 4–9 (East). Sun-loving, drought-tolerant yarrows offer a choice of foliage and flower colors, but all have the same configuration: spreading mats of lobed or finely cut foliage and 4–10-inch stems. Flat clusters of tiny blossoms appear in summer and early autumn. Greek yarrow (A. ageratifolia) has slightly lobed silvery leaves and white flowers in 1-inch clusters. Silvery yarrow (A. clavennae) has more deeply lobed silvery gray leaves and ¾-inch clusters of ivory white flowers. Woolly yarrow (A. tomentosa) has hairy leaves, deep green and finely divided. Flowers are golden yellow; named varieties have cream and light yellow flowers.

AEGOPODIUM podagraria. Bishop's weed, Gout-weed. Deciduous perennial. Zones 4–8. For shady locations in cold-winter climates, this nearly foolproof ground cover spreads by underground rootstocks and can be invasive. Stems grow 6–12 inches high and bear lobed, 3-inch leaflets. 'Variegatum' is the most common variety; it has light green leaflets edged in white. Plant dies to ground each winter and sprouts from rootstocks in spring.

AFRICAN DAISY. See Osteospermum.

AJUGA reptans. Carpet bugle. Evergreen perennial. Zones 4–10. Handsome foliage and showy flower display make this a favorite ground cover for sun or part shade. Dark, lustrous green leaves are broad ovals to 3 inches long in sun, larger in shade. Upright 6–9-inch spikes bear whorls of small violet blue blosoms in spring and summer. Plants spread vigorously by runners, forming low mats of foliage. Several named varieties are sold, varying in foliage size or color.

ARCTOSTAPHYLOS uva-ursi. Bearberry, Kinnikinnick. Evergreen shrub. Zones 3–10 (West) and 3–7 (East). Versatility and year-round good looks are outstanding traits. One plant will spread to about 15 feet, rooting along branches. Dark green inch–long oval leaves are glossy, leathery, and dense. Where winters are cold, foliage turns reddish with cold weather. Clusters of ¼-inch urn-shaped pendent blossoms are white to light pink, coming in late winter (in milder zones) to mid-spring; pink to red berrylike fruit follow. Grows on flat ground and on steep slopes, in sun or part shade.

ARCTOTHECA calendula. Cape weed. Evergreen perennial. Zones 9–10. Rampant growth can earn it weed status, but it's easy to pull up. Plant is a rosette of gray green, long and deeply divided leaves. It spreads by runners; foliage masses to no more than a foot high. Two-inch yellow daisylike blossoms are most abundant in spring, but can appear year-round. Grow in full sun with much or little water.

BACCHARIS pilularis. Coyote brush, Dwarf chaparral broom. Evergreen shrub. Zones 8–10 (West Coast only). Coyote brush thrives in full sun, in high desert or along cool coast. Established plants grow well with either much or little water. Small, slightly toothed oval leaves cover mounding plants that may reach 2 feet high and spread more than 6 feet. Use on steep banks or level ground. Because female plants bear many cottony seeds, look for selected named varieties 'Twin Peaks' or 'Pigeon Point'.

BEARBERRY. See Arctostaphylos uva-ursi.

BISHOP'S WEED. See Aegopodium podagraria.

CANDYTUFT. See Iberis.

CAPE WEED. See Arctotheca calendula.

Carissa grandiflora

CARISSA grandiflora. Natal plum. Evergreen shrub. Zone 10. The basic plant is a tall, dense, thorny shrub valued for glossy, leathery leaves, star-shaped white flowers with powerful fragrance, and conspicuous (and edible) red, plumlike fruits. Several low, spreading forms that make handsome ground covers have been developed from it. Leaves are broadly oval, to 3 inches long; 2-inch blossoms may appear year-round. Varieties 'Horizontalis', 'Bonzai', and 'Prostrata' spread widely but reach no more than 2 feet high. Lower growing 'Green Carpet' has smaller foliage.

CARMEL CREEPER. See Ceanothus griseus horizontalis.

CARPET BUGLE. See Ajuga reptans.

CEANOTHUS. Wild lilac. Evergreen shrub. Zones 8–10. Along the Pacific Coast, two Ceanothus species and their varieties are popular for their polished green foliage and puffy clusters of tiny blue flowers. Carmel creeper (C. griseus horizontalis) builds to 1½–2½ feet high and 15 feet wide; leaves are glossy 2-inch ovals and flowers are light blue. Point Reyes ceanothus (C. gloriosus) spreads to 16 feet and its variety 'Anchor Bay' to 8 feet; both reach 1–1½ feet high. Dark green leaves are spiny-edged 1-inch ovals. In coastal climates, Ceanothus can take regular watering; but where summers are warmer and drier they require little or no watering to avoid death from root rot.

CERATOSTIGMA plumbaginoides. Dwarf plumbago. Deciduous perennial. Zones 6–10 (West) and 6–8 (East). Wiry stems reaching 6–12 inches high bear 3-inch oval leaves that emerge bronzy and turn dark green. The ½-inch-wide, round-faced, intense blue blossoms start in early summer and continue until autumn frosts when plant dies to the ground. The plant spreads by underground stems, and spread is rapid in good soil with regular watering. Use in full sun in small to medium-size areas.

CHAMAEMELUM nobile (formerly Anthemis nobilis). Chamomile. Evergreen perennial. Zones 3–10 (West) and 3–8 (East). Finely cut, light green leaves give soft-textured appearance. Left alone, plant forms somewhat mounding and spreading mats of fragrant foliage bearing small, yellow, but-tonlike (sometimes white, daisylike) flowers in summer. With occasional mowing, chamomile can be used as a lawn substitute. Use in full sun or lightest shade, and give moderate watering.

CHAMOMILE. See Chamaemelum nobile.

CINQUEFOIL. See Potentilla.

CISTUS salviifolius. Sageleaf rockrose. Evergreen shrub. Zones 8–10 (West) and 8–9 (East). Full sun and poor soil encourage rockroses. Don't water regularly during summer unless soil drains rapidly. This shrub grows 2 feet high and 6 feet wide, with rough-textured, wavy-edged oval leaves to an inch long. Late-spring blossoms — round, slightly cupped, and 1½-inches wide — are white with a yellow spot at petal's base. Each blossom lasts for just a day, but the bud supply seems endless. This is a first-rate plant for slopes or for areas receiving little water.

CONFEDERATE JASMINE. See Trachelospermum jasminoides.

COTONEASTER. Evergreen and deciduous shrub. Zones vary. *Cotoneasters* provide two seasons of interest: small, wild-rose-like blooms (white or pinkish) in flattened clusters in spring and summer, and pea-size or larger fruit that become bright red in autumn and may last into winter. All but one have ½–1-inch oval leaves, bright to dark green on top and paler or gray to white beneath.

One slow-growing deciduous species, *C. adpressus,* Zones 4–10, stays below 12 inches; autumn foliage color is red. Variety 'Herbstfeuer' of Willowleaf cotoneaster (*C. salicifolius*), Zones 6–10, is also ground-hugging and of limited spread but is evergreen with narrow 3-inch leaves. Another evergreen, with mounding growth and restricted spread, is tiny-leafed *C. congestus,* Zones 7–10. For rapid growth to cover larger areas, look for evergreen Bearberry cotoneaster (*C. dammeri*), Zones 5–10, which reaches 6 inches high, and *C.* 'Lowfast', Zones 7–10, which grows twice as high. Evergreen Necklace cotoneaster (*C. conspicuus decorus*), Zones 7–10, and Rockspray cotoneaster (*C. microphyllus*), Zones 6–10, produce upright branches from main horizontal stems; the first is quite close to the ground while the latter may send up 2–3-foot stems. Briefly deciduous (with red autumn color) Rock cotoneaster (*C. horizontalis*), Zones 4–10, may build to 3 feet high, spreading to 15 feet; stiff branches are in a flat, herringbone pattern. Depending on the variety, use to cover banks, large flat areas, or small areas beneath trees.

COYOTE BRUSH. See Baccharis pilularis.

CREEPING LILY TURF. See Liriope spicata.

CREEPING ST. JOHNSWORT. See Hypericum calycinum.

DUCHESNEA indica. Indian mock strawberry. Evergreen perennial. Zones 3–10 (West) and 3–8 (East). Nearly everything about this plant suggests strawberry except the blah taste of its red fruit. Tooth-edged leaves consist of three leaflets at the ends of long leaf stalks. ½-inch yellow blossoms are followed by half-inch red berries that stand above the foliage. This ground-hugging plant spreads by runners, and can become invasive with routine watering. Grow in sun or shade; plant does very well beneath shrubs and trees.

DWARF CHAPARRAL BROOM. See Baccharis pilularis.

DWARF PLUMBAGO. See Ceratostigma plumbaginoides.

ERIGERON karvinskianus. Evergreen perennial. Zones 9–10. Threadlike stems form an intricately branched, fine-textured plant 10–20 inches high. Narrow inch-long leaves are lance-shaped or slightly lobed. Spring blossoms are narrow-petaled, ¾-inch daisies, white with pink tints. Plant spreads by rooting from stems touching the ground. Give full sun and moderate watering; use in small areas, such as along pathways.

EUONYMUS fortunei. Winter creeper. Evergreen. Zones 5–10. This is one of the best ground covers for cold-winter regions. There are many varieties in the nursery trade (sometimes incorrectly listed as varieties of *E. radicans*), selected for different leaf sizes (from ¼-inch-long 'Kewensis' to 2½-inch-long 'Vegata') and leaf colors or markings (variegated, light veins on dark leaves, purple winter color). The plant roots along its stems as it grows; coverage is dense and neat. At maturity, it sends out short, nonvining stems. Plant in sun or shade, and on hillsides for erosion control. With support, this evergreen performs well as a vine; rootlets cling tenaciously to any support—even tree trunks.

FIRETHORN. See Pyracantha.

FRAGARIA chiloensis. Wild strawberry, Sand strawberry. Evergreen perennial. Zones 5–10. This ancestor of the edible varieties of strawberry is strictly an ornamental. Spreading by runners, it forms dense mats 6–12 inches high of typical strawberry foliage: 3 dark green shiny leaflets at the end of a leaf stalk. Winter foliage is tinted red. Inch-wide white flowers in spring may set small, bright red, seedy fruit, but this is not common. Fast-growing wild strawberry will grow in full sun where climate is cool and moist; elsewhere it needs part shade.

GALIUM odoratum. Sweet woodruff. Evergreen perennial. Zones 5–10 (West) and 5–8 (East). This woodland plant has 6–12-inch upright stems encircled, at about 1-inch intervals, by whorls of light green, narrow, shiny leaves. In late spring and summer, clusters of tiny, 4-petaled, white flowers appear on threadlike stalks above leaves. Plant sweet woodruff in part shade to shade, along pathways and under shrubs and trees.

Gazania hybrid

GAZANIA. Evergreen perennial. Zones 9–10, primarily West Coast. Sun-loving gazanias produce spectacular flowers: bright daisies, up to 4 inches across, in all shades from cream through yellow, orange, red, bronze, plus pink tones and white. Heaviest bloom is in late spring and early summer, but where summers and winters are mild the bloom can occur year-round. Leaves are usually long and narrow but may be smooth-edged, lobed, or in some cases deeply cut; color may be green, gray green, or even silvery. Trailing gazanias cover large areas easily, both level and sloping ground. Clumping kinds are best used in small, level areas. Both grow 6–12 inches high.

GERMANDER. See Teucrium chamaedrys.

HEAVENLY BAMBOO. See Nandina domestica.

HEDERA. Ivy. Evergreen. Zones vary. Ivy is a highly successful ground cover, needing only periodic mowing down to prevent a buildup of stems beneath the foliage. English ivy (*H. helix*), Zones 5–10, is the more familiar type; dark, dull, green leaves with lighter veins are 2–4 inches wide and long, and are shaped like lobed triangles or diamonds. Specialists offer variegated and fancy-leafed varieties. Much larger is Algerian ivy (*H. canariensis*), Zones 8–10, with lobed 5–8-inch leaves. One variety has variegated foliage.

Ivy also serves well as a vine. Stems attach by rootlets to any surface—even chain link fences. Leaves tend to grow in shinglelike pattern so appearance is usually neat. After some years, vining stems will send out short, shrubby stems with different foliage and clusters of inconspicuous flowers that produce black berries.

HYPERICUM calycinum. Creeping St. Johnswort, Aaron's beard, Evergreen to semievergreen shrub. Zones 6–10. Underground runners send up arching stems to about 1 foot; on either side of stems come paired leaves, each an elongated oval up to 4 inches. In full sun, foliage is rich green, but color is paler in shade. Showy, bright yellow 3-inch flowers appear at stem ends in summer. Roots and underground stems knit soil together for good erosion control. Plant tolerates some drought and grows well in poor soil, but with ample water and good soil, it can be an invasive menace unless controlled.

IBERIS sempervirens. Evergreen candytuft. Perennial. Zones 4–10. Plant reaches 8–18 inches tall and spreads to about 18 inches. Stems are well foliaged in narrow, shiny, dark green leaves. Round clusters of tiny white flowers bloom at stem tips throughout spring; in mild climates, bloom may begin in winter. Plant in full sun or light shade and water moderately. Use this heavy-blooming, noninvasive perennial in small areas.

INDIAN MOCK STRAWBERRY. See Duchesnea indica.

IVY. See Hedera.

IVY GERANIUM. See Pelargonium peltatum.

JAPANESE SPURGE. See Pachysandra terminalis.

JUNIPER. See Juniperus.

JUNIPERUS. Juniper. Evergreen shrub. Zones vary. Junipers are among the most serviceable, adaptable, and widely planted ground cover shrubs. They grow in both the coldest and the warmest zones, are easy to grow, and are relatively drought-tolerant once established. They can blanket level ground or hillsides, producing a uniform, neat appearance. Best growth is in full sun or lightest shade. Variations among juniper varieties include height (ground-hugging to around 3 feet), spread, foliage color (gray green through green to blue green, silvery blue, and variegated with creamy white), and texture (feathery, plumy, spiky).

Not all selected varieties are generally available; visit a nursery to acquaint yourself with choices and the obvious differences in color, texture, and habit. The following species provide most of the ground cover selections: *J. chinensis* (Zones 4–10), *J. communis* (Zones 2–10), *J. conferta* (Zones 5–10), *J. horizontalis* (Zones 2–10), *J. sabina* (Zones 4–10), *J. scopulorum* (Zones 4–10), *J. virginiana* (Zones 2–10).

KINNIKINNICK. See Arcotostaphylos uva-ursi.

LANTANA montevidensis. Evergreen shrub. Zones 9–10. Rough-surfaced oval leaves with a distinctive odor clothe trailing, rough-textured stems, which may spread up to 6 feet, branching to blanket the ground. This is the best lantana for covering large areas. Small flowers (usually lilac) are clustered in dense, round heads 1–1½ inches across; each cluster is borne on a long stem above foliage. Year-round bloom is common in frost-free areas. A white-flowered form is called 'Velutina White'.

LAVENDER COTTON. See Santolina chamaecyparissus.

LIRIOPE spicata. Creeping lily turf. Evergreen perennial. Zones 4–10. When not in bloom, this plant gives the appearance of a coarse-leafed grass. Individual deep green leaves are about ¼-inch wide and over a foot long; each plant is a small clump of arching foliage 8–9 inches tall. Plants spread by underground runners to form a solid foliage cover. Small lilac to white flowers come in spikelike clusters in summer, but are partly hidden by leaves. Plant in light shade (full sun where summer is cool) and give regular watering.

MAHONIA aquifolium. Oregon grape. Evergreen shrub. Zones 5–10 (West) and 5–8 (East). The basic shrub is a dense 6-footer; low-growing forms spread by underground stems in sunny to partly shady areas. Each

leaf consists of 5–9 glossy, oval, spine-edged leaflets to 3 inches long. New growth is bronze to red, darkening to rich green; winter turns leaves red bronze. Spring blossoms are bright yellow in lilaclike clusters at branch tips; blue, pea-size fruit may follow. Variety 'Compacta' is sold, but it seems to vary: one form is shrubby to about 1½ feet tall and the other seldom exceeds 8–10 inches and grows more slowly.

Mahonia aquifolium

MONDO GRASS. See Ophiopogon japonicus.

MYRTLE. See Vinca.

NANDINA domestica. Heavenly bamboo. Evergreen shrub. Zones 8–10. The low, spreading, ground cover varieties do not greatly resemble bamboo. Each leaf is quite large, but is divided into narrow, oval 1–2-inch leaflets. New growth is pinkish to bronzy red, turning light green; in winter it often colors bright red. At least two forms make good ground covers, spreading by underground stems to form colonies. 'Harbour Dwarf' reaches 1½–2 feet high and spreads at a moderate rate. Under the variety name 'Nana' are two (perhaps more) distinct plants. The better has narrow, bright green leaflets and spreads at a moderate to rapid rate, reaching about 1 foot tall. Use *Nandina* in sun to light shade for small to medium-size areas.

NATAL PLUM. See Carissa grandiflora.

OPHIOPOGON japonicus. Mondo grass. Evergreen perennial. Zones 8–10. In all respects this is similar to Creeping lily turf (*Liriope spicata*): plants spread by underground stems and form a grasslike turf. Foliage of Mondo grass is narrower (about ⅛ inch wide), somewhat shorter, and quite dark green. Small, pale lilac flowers on short spikes are almost completely hidden by foliage. Use for dense cover in part shade (full sun where summer is cool) on level or gently sloping ground.

OREGON GRAPE. See Mahonia aquifolium.

OSTEOSPERMUM fruticosum. Trailing African daisy. Evergreen perennial. Zones 9–10 (West Coast only). This daisy provides eye-popping color during peak bloom from

November to March when garden color is at low ebb. Scattering of bloom, however, may come year-round. Rapid-growing plant reaches 6–12 inches high and roots along branches as it spreads. Gray green leaves vary in size and shape—narrowly oval, 2–4 inches long, sometimes with irregular teeth. The most usual form has 2-inch blossoms that open pale lilac and fade to nearly white, the petal undersides remaining lilac purple; in striking contrast is each flower's dark purple center. Nurseries also sell varieties having pure white and deep purple blossoms. Given well-drained soil, full sun, and at least moderate water, trailing African daisy serves admirably in large areas and on hillsides.

PACHYSANDRA terminalis. Japanese spurge. Evergreen shrubby perennial. Zones 4–9. In Eastern North America this is often proclaimed the best ground cover for shaded and semi-shaded position. Polished, rich green, toothed leaves are oval to teardrop in shape, 2–4 inches long, and clustered in whorl fashion toward ends of branches. There is a form with white-variegated leaves. Foliage reaches uniform height in a mass planting. In deep shade, stems may reach 10 inches high, but in light or dappled shade 6 inches is normal. In good, moist soil, plants spread at moderate rate by underground stems. Inconspicuous small white flowers in fluffy spikes appear in mid-spring to early summer; white berries may follow in autumn.

PELARGONIUM peltatum. Ivy geranium. Evergreen shrubby perennial. Zone 10 and warmest parts of Zone 9. The common name describes the plant well: clusters of colorful flowers are just like those of the shrubby "geraniums" (technically *Pelargonium*), but this trailing plant has thick, glossy, bright green 2–3-inch leaves with pointed lobes. Individual plant spreads to at least 3 feet and can reach a foot high. Give it full sun on level or sloping ground. Single or double flowers come in lavender, white, shades of pink and red, and combinations of white and pink or red. Heaviest bloom is in warmer months.

PERIWINKLE. See Vinca.

POLYGONUM. Knotweed. Evergreen and deciduous. Zones vary. Both commonly grown knotweeds are tough, fast-growing, attractive, and invasive. The smaller of the two is evergreen *P. capitatum*, Zones 7–10 (primarily West Coast). Its fairly fine texture of roundish leaves to 1½ inches long and tiny pink flowers (during most of the year) packed in ½-inch spherical heads disguises its toughness. New leaves are dark green but take on pink tinge as they age; stems are also pink. Trailing stems hug the ground, building up to no more than 6 inches high. Use in sun or shade and water regularly. Of quite different appearance is *P. cuspidatum compactum*, Zones 4–10. Its stiff, wiry, red stems grow 10–24 inches high and bear red-veined light green, heart-shaped leaves to 6 inches long. Tiny pink flowers in late summer are showy in spikelike clusters. Plant spreads quickly by rooting stems, and dies back to the ground in winter. Use it on hillsides for erosion control.

POTENTILLA tabernaemontanii. Spring cinquefoil. Evergreen perennial. Zones 4–9 (West) and 4–8 (East). Strawberrylike plants spread quickly by runners. Shiny, toothed leaves consist of 5 leaflets; small clusters of ¼-inch flowers are bright yellow. Give regular watering and, where summers are hot and dry, light shade. When established, spring cinquefoil prevents weed growth and functions well as a lawn substitute (with no foot traffic). Also use under trees, shrubs, and as a cover for early spring bulbs.

PYRACANTHA. Firethorn. Evergreen shrub. Zones 7–10. Low, spreading forms — with the thorns and red to orange winter berries of the familiar large and irregular shrub—make suitable ground covers. Use these less widely known named selections for small to medium-size plantings in full sun on level or sloping ground.

Lowest and least spreading is *P. angustifolia* 'Gnome'. Spread may be up to 6 feet; berries are orange. More wide-spreading—to about 10 feet — and to 18 inches high is red-fruited *P.* 'Walderi'. *P.* 'Santa Cruz' also has red berries and spreads to about 10 feet; plant reaches about 3 feet tall unless pruned lower. Remove vertical shoots as they appear.

ROCKROSE. See Cistus.

ROSA. Rose. Deciduous to nearly evergreen shrub. Zones vary. Among the climbing roses are several with canes so lax that they sprawl on the ground naturally or can be encouraged to do so. All have attractive, nearly evergreen foliage.

Memorial rose *(R. wichuraiana)*, Zones 5–10, is the only natural ground cover in this group. Its 12-foot, ground-hugging canes root as it grows and can cover a sizable area in time. Foliage is profuse: 7–9 highly polished, dark green leaflets constitute each leaf. In mid-summer come 2-inch single white blossoms. Its hybrid 'Max Graf' has similar habit and glossy leaves but bears larger single pink flowers in late spring.

To make a handsome, formidably armed ground cover, pin the canes of the Macartney rose *(R. bracteata)* to the ground. Small oval leaflets are highly glossy, bronze-tinted; leaf shape, texture, and density suggest boxwood. This rose also roots along canes touching moist soil. Its foliage mass is higher than Memorial rose's, and single blossoms are white.

ROSE. See Rosa.

ROSEMARY. See Rosmarinus.

ROSMARINUS officinalis 'Prostratus'. Dwarf rosemary. Evergreen shrub. Zones 7–10 (West) and 7–8 (East). Aromatic foliage

consists of needlelike leaves, glossy bright to dark green up to an inch long. Initially, plants send out stems along the ground; secondary stems arch upward and curve back to the ground. In time the plant may build to 2 feet high in full sun; spread can be almost limitless since stems root easily. Use drought-tolerant dwarf rosemary for garden fringe areas, hillsides, and to cascade down walls.

SAND STRAWBERRY. See Fragaria chiloensis.

SANTOLINA. Evergreen shrubby perennial. Zones 7–10 (West) and 7–8 (East). Two species are generally available. Lavender cotton *(S. chamaecyparissus)* has fringelike gray white leaves about 1 inch long and ⅛-inch wide. In summer, it's decorated with ¼–½-inch daisylike flowers with no petals. Except for its narrower, deep green foliage and creamy chartreuse flowers, *S. virens* is nearly a carbon copy.

Well-foliaged stems arch upward and root as they touch soil; one plant becomes many and will spread widely in time. Grow lavender cotton in full sun and well-drained soil; water only moderately. *S. virens* grows faster and tolerates more water.

STAR JASMINE. See Trachelospermum jasminoides.

SWEET WOODRUFF. See Galium odoratum.

TAXUS baccata 'Repandens'. Spreading English yew. Evergreen shrub. Zones 6–10 (West); best in Zones 6–7 (East). English yew has many growth forms ranging from vertical to horizontal. Of the latter type, variety 'Repandens' is most widely sold. Typical yew foliage — dark green, inch-long flattened needles — densely clothes horizontally spreading branches; small, red, berrylike fruit appear in autumn. Each neat yet graceful plant is a dense, flattened mound no more than 2 feet high. It grows equally well in full sun (but not reflected from a hot wall) and full shade; established plants are fairly drought-tolerant.

TEUCRIUM chamaedrys. Germander. Evergreen shrubby perennial. Zones 6–10 (West) and 6–7 (East). Growth consists of many stems that spread along the ground and arch or branch upward. In time a plant becomes a wide-spreading, low (to 1 foot) mat of glossy, toothed, dark green leaves about ¾ inch long. In summer, small blossoms appear in short spikes at stem tips; one form has red purple flowers, the other has white. Variety 'Prostratum' grows only 4–6 inches high. All grow well in shade, but are most compact and attractive in full sun. Tolerant of drought and poor soil, germander is a good choice for garden fringe or dry areas.

TRACHELOSPERMUM jasminoides. Star jasmine, Confederate jasmine. Evergreen. Zones 9–10. During its early-summer bloom

period, you may smell star jasmine before you see it; the fragrance of many small clusters of 1-inch starlike blossoms floats in the air. Stems are well clothed in lustrous, leathery, pointed-oval dark green leaves. Foliage, flowers, and fragrance make this a fine choice for planting in patios, entryways, and small gardens where it can be enjoyed often. With support, star jasmine stems can climb to 20 feet; although stems twine, they need to be tied to a support to climb. Use on fence, wall, trellis, post, or arbor.

Vinca minor

VINCA. Periwinkle, Myrtle. Evergreen perennial. Zones vary. The larger of the two species, *V. major* (Zones 8–10), should be sold with a "Caution!" sign attached. Slender stems root at tips and at leaf nodes, so it can hopscotch over vast areas if not contained. This vinca will mound 6–12 inches and possibly to 2 feet high. Broad-based medium green leaves are pointed ovals 1–3 inches long, somewhat leathery. A slightly less aggressive form has leaves variegated with creamy white. Both produce flatfaced lavender blue flowers, 1–2 inches wide, in spring. Where summers are hot, it looks best with regular watering and some shade — but with just shade it will get through a summer, looking parched and scruffy, with no apparent loss of vigor. It makes a good bank cover because of its rooting habit. If used as a ground cover, shear close to the ground occasionally to bring on fresh new growth.

Dwarf periwinkle *(V. minor)*, Zones 4–10, is in all ways a scaled-down version of the larger species: leaves are smaller, narrower, and more closely spaced on stems; blooms are half the size; growth is less rampant and lower. Plant looks best if watered regularly. It, too, has a variegated leaf form. In addition, varieties have flowers of white, deeper blue, and double blue. Because it's easier to contain, this is the better of the two for the average garden but it requires more water and feeding several times a year.

WILD LILAC. See Ceanothus.

WILD STRAWBERRY. See Fragaria chiloensis.

WINTER CREEPER. See Euonymus fortunei.

YARROW. See Achillea.

YEW. See Taxus.

THE BASICS OF INSTALLATION

Once you've completed your final plans, it's time to install your new landscape. Depending on your skills, available time, and financial resources, you may want to do all or part of the work yourself, perhaps with a few helpers. This chapter will serve as a guide as you decide what lies within your reach, and what's best left to professionals.

Installing your landscape begins with site preparation and ends with final cleanup. On the facing page, you'll find an outline of the landscape installation sequence, from first step to last. Use this sequence to prepare an outline for your own project, then turn to the how-to discussions that follow.

On the next 45 pages you'll find instructions for the major steps of the landscaping sequence. From the ground up, here is what you'll need to know: how to prepare your site, how to build structural elements from simple edgings to elegant garden pools, and how to install plant materials.

This chapter describes the payoff in any landscaping project: the stage where dream becomes reality. Whether you're remodeling or starting from scratch, looking for step-by-step guidance or just an overview of the building process, this chapter will show you how it's done.

Steps for installing a landscape

Like any building project, installing a landscape is a step-by-step process. Listed below is a typical sequence of steps that's meant to serve only as a basic guide. Whether your plan calls for a major operation or a simple remodel, use it to organize your own work into a logical sequence.

Before you begin, make sure you have all the necessary excavating and building permits. Also, try to have all the materials you need stored in a convenient location on your site.

Sequence of steps

1. Do rough grading (page 130) to bring the soil to the approximate level (or levels) you want for the various areas and structural elements in your new landscape.

2. Have a swimming pool constructed, if you're adding one to your yard.

3. Install a drainage system (page 132), if necessary, to dispose of excess surface or subsurface water.

4. Install underground utilities, such as 120-volt electricity for outdoor lighting, natural gas for a barbecue, or water for a fountain or pond.

5. Prepare the soil (page 134) by adding amendments and digging.

6. Re-establish the rough grade of the soil after digging (page 130).

7. Put in edgings around pavings, planting beds, and lawns (page 136).

8. Build structural elements:
• retaining walls (page 138) or terraces
• patio pavings (page 140)
• raised beds (page 146)
• garden walkways (page 148) and steps (page 150)
• walls (page 151)

• decks (page 157) and overheads (page 160)
• fences (page 162) and gates (page 166)
• garden pools (page 168)

9. Re-establish the rough grade (page 130), if it's been disturbed by construction work.

10. Install a watering system (page 170) for your lawn or for specific plants.

11. Do finish grading (page 130) to prepare the soil for planting.

12. Plant lawns, trees, shrubs, and ground covers (pages 172 and 174).

13. Install low-voltage lighting (page 167) to illuminate paths and highlight plants.

14. Do a final cleanup to dispose of debris.

If you're tearing out an old landscape...

Before you can install a new landscape, you may have to tear out an existing one. You can probably remove many of the unwanted plants and some of the structures yourself, but for the big jobs — large trees and shrubs, heavy structures, or concrete pavings — you may need to hire a tree service, laborers, or a demolition crew to do the work.

Tearing out almost any landscape will result in lots of debris. If you expect to have more than a few loads to haul away, consider renting a dump bin from a local refuse company. Be sure to tell the company what you're planning to get rid of, though. Often there's a limit on the amount of concrete, soil, and rocks you can put in a bin.

Removing plants. To make the desired changes in your landscape, you may have to dig up shrubs, trees, lawns, ground covers, or flower beds that are unhealthy or poorly placed, or that simply don't fit into your plans.

You can cut down most shrubs and small trees with lopping shears, a saw, and an ax. Then dig out the roots with a mattock or grub hoe, and a shovel.

If you're cutting down large trees or trees located near utility lines or other hazards, it's a good idea to get professional help. If you have a stump to remove, a professional can get rid of it using a power stump remover.

In a small area, you can remove a lawn by digging up the sod with a sharp spade. To dig up a large lawn, you'll save yourself hours of work if you rent a power sod cutter.

You can remove ground covers either by mowing them to the ground with a rotary mower or cutting off the tops with a hedge shear, weed trimmer, or sickle. Then dig up the roots with a spade.

To clean out a flower bed, pull the plants up by hand, or dig them up with a shovel. And don't forget the weeds: pull or dig up the larger ones; spray smaller weeds with a short-term contact herbicide.

Removing structural elements. A garden remodel may require removing pavings, decks, or other structures that don't fit into your plans or that aren't in good condition.

Before you begin demolition, have on hand the proper safety equipment, such as gloves, heavy shoes, and safety goggles, and be sure you know how to use the necessary tools safely. You can usually take wood structures down yourself, using a nail puller and crowbar. To break up unit masonry, you'll need a hand sledge and crowbar. If you're removing a concrete slab, it's best to call in a professional. You can haul the broken concrete away, or use the pieces to make a walkway or retaining wall.

Grading your yard

Grading—moving soil so it's at the proper height and slope—ensures adequate drainage, adds contours to a flat landscape, and provides the necessary foundation for walks and patios.

Before you begin, be sure you've determined the grading requirements of your landscape, taking into account drainage and any pavings you're adding. (See the planning information beginning on page 32.) Also, check with your building department for any permits you may need. When you're digging, it's essential to know the location of any underground lines for gas, water, sewer, electricity, telephone, and other utilities. If your home is not connected to a sewer, locate the septic tank and drainage field.

Before you start digging, decide how you'll measure the grade while you're working. Several techniques are described on the facing page.

THREE STAGES IN GRADING

The work of grading progresses hand-in-hand with the other aspects of installing your landscape (see the steps on page 129). Generally, you'll need to begin with rough grading, bringing the areas of your yard to the desired finished level. Then, after you've installed underground systems and completed any construction projects, you'll need to re-establish the rough grade. The final stage is the finish grading. Once that work is completed, you're ready to plant.

Rough grading

The goal of rough grading, usually the first step in installing a landscape, is to remove or add enough soil in each area of your yard to bring the soil surface to the height and slope you want. Rough grading can also include reshaping the soil and making mounds and berms (see opposite page), as well as digging foundations for patios and walks. Remember, though, that it's better to install paving on undisturbed soil, rather than on soil that's been dug up or filled in. Even very careful tamping will not make disturbed soil as firm as undisturbed soil.

Eliminating high spots. Excavate any high places so the level of the soil will be at the desired height and slope. When you dig, put the topsoil (usually the top 2 to 6 inches of soil) and subsoil in separate piles. You'll use them later for filling.

Filling low spots. Fill low spots in your yard by adding soil to bring the level up to the desired height and slope. Partially fill any deep holes with subsoil, leaving room for a final layer of topsoil so plants can grow. Use just topsoil to fill shallow areas.

Digging foundations. Excavate areas for the bases of patios, walks, and other pavings (see pages 140, 142, 144, 150, and 160). You may be able to use the dirt from these excavations as fill in other areas. (You can also use soil from a pool excavation as fill.)

Tamping soil. Use a tamper to compact soil that needs to be firm, such as fill under paving or soil disturbed by digging. Also, tamp each time you add a layer of fill soil to a deeply filled area in your yard.

Re-establishing the rough grade

Re-establishing the grade means moving or removing enough soil to get the working surface back to the height and slope you established when you did the rough grading. You'll probably need to do this several times while you're installing your landscape, such as after you've prepared the soil for planting and after you've completed any major construction.

Often after construction and soil preparation, you have piles of soil scattered around. Use the soil to fill ditches or holes that were dug around the bases of structures.

You may also have to fill in trenches dug for underground systems, or low spots caused by the movement of heavy equipment across your yard. Use a tamper to compact the fill soil over any trenches so it won't settle more than the surrounding soil. Mound the soil over the trench and tamp it very firmly until it's at the same level as the soil around it.

Finish grading

Finish grading is the last step after you've completed all construction,

THREE STAGES IN GRADING

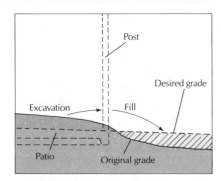

Rough grading for patio includes excavating high spots and patio base, filling low areas to bring grade to desired finished level.

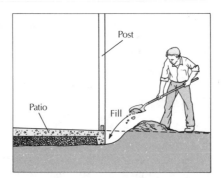

Re-establishing the rough grade involves putting soil back in place when construction is finished.

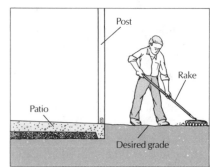

Finish grading gets soil smooth and even in preparation for planting. Usually, visually estimating grade is sufficient.

Contouring with mounds & berms

Mounds and berms are two landscape features that let you make changes in the grade for privacy, wind control, or simply for the sake of beauty. The chief difference between them is their size. Mounds are small—perhaps just a few feet long and a foot or so tall. Berms, on the other hand, can be several yards long and many feet tall.

Constructing a mound is a job that even an amateur gardener can do. But generally, a berm requires heavy machinery and professional skill. Because mounds and berms require lots of soil, it's most economical if you can get the soil for them from an excavation in your own yard.

Building a mound. Choose the site carefully, taking care that the mound won't interfere with good drainage chan-

nels in the yard, and that it's back far enough from a patio, deck, or walk so water running off the mound won't flow onto the paving.

Remove any sod that's covering the soil where you want to place the mound. Dig the soil up lightly to break the surface crust before you bring in any soil for the mound. Then spread out a layer of soil for the mound and, using a shovel or tiller, mix it with the underlying soil to ensure good drainage. Continue this process as you shape the mound.

Tamp the soil down lightly, and smooth the sides with the back of a rake. To prevent erosion, make sure the sides of the mound aren't too steep. Plant the mound as you would any other hillside.

---

installed all underground systems, and re-established the rough grade. The goal is to make the surface smooth enough for planting.

Leveling soil. After rough grading, the soil may be uneven, with shallow mounds and ruts in places. Use a leveler to smooth out the surface and make it even.

Raking soil. Use a steel rake to remove stones, lumps of soil, and other debris turned up in the soil preparation process. Rake the surface until it's smooth enough to make a good planting bed.

GETTING THE GRADE YOU WANT

As you go through the grading process, you'll need a reliable method to ensure that you get the grade you want. During rough grading, you can simply estimate the grade visually, or for greater accuracy use a carpenter's level. For paved areas, use batterboards or a grid. Visually estimating the grade may be all you'll need to do once the rough grade has been established.

Visually estimating. Establishing the grade by "eye-balling" is often all that's required. Inspect the grade closely to be sure any slope goes in the proper direction — away from structures and

toward areas where water can drain away without causing problems. Also, look for high and low spots on lawns and other areas where you want an even surface.

Estimating with a level. Using a level is more accurate than visually estimating. Set the level on an 8-foot-long 2 by 4 placed on the ground. With a tape measure, determine how far you have to raise one end of the board to center the bubble in the level. That will give you a rough idea of how much the ground slopes. (A slope of 2 inches in 8 feet is usually adequate for drainage.)

Grading with batterboards. To make batterboards, nail 1 by 4 boards horizontally to 2 by 4 stakes. Set the batterboards at the corners of the area you're going to pave, placing them at least a foot, but not more than 4 feet back from the edge. Set the tops of all boards at a uniform height above the desired final grade of the paving.

Tie mason's string between the batterboards to outline the area for digging. To establish the grade, keep the distance between the line and the bottom of the excavation constant.

Grading with a grid. To accurately grade a large area for paving, you need to set up a grid of·stakes and strings. First, stake off the perimeter of the area

every 5 or 10 feet (use 5-foot intervals for more accuracy). On one stake, mark the level where you want the final grade of the finished paving surface. (This should be at or above the existing grade.) Attach a chalk line at this point and stretch it along a row of stakes. Level the line and snap it to mark the stakes. Repeat the process for all the stakes.

Adjust your marks to allow for a slope of at least ¼ inch per foot toward the direction you want water to drain. (Be sure the lowest side of the paving ends at or above the natural ground level, not below it.) Snap the chalk line again. To form a grid, stretch mason's lines between opposite stakes.

Improving drainage

Good drainage is vital for growing most plants and for preventing pools of water from forming in low areas of your garden. Methods for solving drainage problems range from the relatively easy one of working with the soil to more complex solutions that include digging trenches or installing a drainage chimney, dry well, or catch basin. Unless your garden has obvious topographical problems, consider the simple solutions first.

Working with the soil

Grading the soil for the proper slope (see pages 130–131) is a basic way to improve drainage. Sometimes, this will eliminate all drainage problems.

Another way to ensure good drainage is to improve the texture of the soil itself. If you're planting a new lawn or garden, follow the instructions for soil preparation on pages 134–135. If you have compacted soil or a shallow hardpan layer (a layer of impervious soil), use a tiller to break up the soil as deeply as possible. In an established lawn, try aerating the soil (see the *Sunset* book *Lawns & Ground Covers*).

Channeling excess water

Often you can improve the drainage in one area by channeling excess water to another place for disposal. To channel water below the surface, use drainage trenches containing gravel, flexible drainpipe, or clay tiles.

Digging trenches. Before you begin digging, be sure to ask your utility companies for the location of underground lines for gas, water, sewer, electricity, telephone, and other services. If your home isn't connected to a sewer, locate the septic tank and drainage field.

You'll probably be able to dig a trench up to about 2 feet deep yourself. Anything deeper may have to be excavated by a pipeline contractor or other landscaping professional.

Use a spade and pick for digging; unlike a shovel, a spade will keep the sides of the trench straight and square. To keep the trench itself straight, tie a string between two stakes and follow it as you dig.

Gravel-filled trenches. You can use gravel-filled trenches to catch and deflect water running off hillsides, roofs, and concrete paving around swimming pools. Dig the trench a foot deep and 6 to 12 inches wide, depending on the volume of water to be handled. Fill the trench with gravel or small stones. Usually, you don't cover the trench with soil.

Flexible drainpipes. Flexible plastic drainpipes, easy even for amateurs to install, carry runoff water away from structures, downspouts, and low spots, and channel water to and from collectors (see below and at bottom of facing page).

Dig a trench about 4 inches wider than the drainpipe's diameter and at least a foot deep; slant it at least 1 inch for every 8 feet of trench.

Put coarse gravel or small stones 2 inches deep in the trench and lay flexible pipe on top. If you use perforated pipe, lay it with the drain holes downward so soil won't seep in and clog the pipe. Fill the trench with gravel. If desired, cover it with a layer of soil.

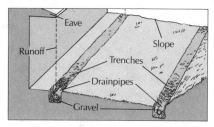

Drainage trenches hold perforated flexible drainpipes in gravel.

Clay drain tiles. You can install clay drain tiles to carry excess water to or from collectors and to disposal areas. You'll need to dig a trench deep enough for the tiles plus a layer of gravel above and below them. Slant the trench at least 1 inch for every 8 feet of length.

Fill the trench with gravel 2 inches deep; then set in tiles end to end. Cover the tops of the joints between tiles with tarpaper to prevent soil from seeping in. Then cover the tiles with gravel 4 to 6 inches deep. If you want, you can put a layer of soil over the gravel.

Collecting excess water

Water collectors—drainage chimneys, dry wells, and catch basins — aid drainage by gathering excess water and providing for its disposal. Drainage chimneys let water pass through impervious soil layers to fast-draining soil below. Dry wells allow water from drainpipes to settle slowly into the ground. The pipes from catch

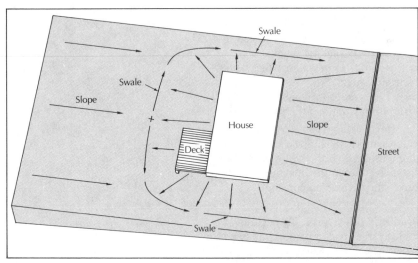

Diagram shows how yard should drain away from house, deck.

Controlling hillside erosion

Preventing soil erosion on a steep slope is a problem many hillside homeowners face. Methods of eliminating or slowing the water runoff that causes erosion include constructing baffles, terraces, and riprap slopes, and growing erosion-control plants.

Before you do any work, make sure the underlying soil is stable. If it's not, consult a landscape architect or soils engineer.

Baffles. Railroad ties or timbers partially buried in a hillside (see the illustration below) deflect water; this slows its rate of flow so the water has more time to soak into the ground.

Terraces. Terraces slow or stop the flow of water, allowing it to soak into the soil. You can make walls for terraces from wood, railroad ties, large timbers, stones, or concrete (see the illustration below and on pages 138–139). Terraces are similar to low retaining walls and are relatively simple for amateur gardeners to construct.

Riprap slopes. Covering a hillside with broken stones or concrete rubble slows the flow of water and helps stop erosion. Dig spaces for the rocks and pack soil and plants tightly around them.

Erosion-control plants. Plants whose roots hold the soil and whose leaves and stems cushion the shock of falling water can help control hillside erosion. A partial list of these plants appears in the chart on page 93. For more information on growing erosion-control plants in your area, contact your county farm advisor.

THREE WAYS TO CONTROL EROSION

Baffles, partly buried in hillside, divert water. Use as many railroad ties or timbers as you need for control.

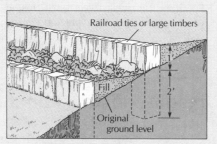

Terraces across slope slow or stop flow of water. Build from bottom of slope upwards, using fill behind each wall.

Riprap (broken stones) half-buried in soil help stop erosion. Stones should be at least 6 inches in diameter.

basins carry excess water to a disposal area such as a storm drain.

Drainage chimneys. Use a posthole shovel or power posthole digger to dig 8 to 12-inch-wide holes spaced 2 to 4 feet apart down through poorly draining soil to gravel or sandy soil. Dig as many chimneys as you need. Fill each with small rocks or coarse gravel to let water pass through quickly.

Dry wells. Dig a 2 to 4-foot-wide hole 3 or more feet deep. (Keep the bottom of the hole above the water table.) Then dig trenches for drainpipes that will carry water into the dry well from other areas. Fill the dry well with coarse gravel or small rocks, and cover with an impervious material, such as

heavy roofing paper; conceal with topsoil.

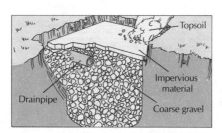

Dry well lets runoff water soak into fast-draining soil above water table.

Catch basins. To drain water from a low-lying area, dig a hole for a catch basin at the lowest point. Then, dig a trench from the hole for a drainpipe that will carry the water to a disposal

place, such as a storm drain. Either set a ready-made concrete catch basin (available at a building supply store) into the hole, and fill in soil around the sides. Or form and pour the concrete base and sides yourself. Set a grate on top.

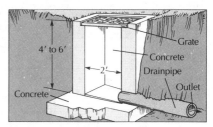

Catch basin drains water away from low area through pipe to street.or storm drain.

Preparing the soil for planting

Although planting is one of the final steps in the landscaping process (see pages 172-174), preparing the soil for planting is usually one of the first. It's done early so edgings and other structural elements aren't disturbed in the process.

Before you prepare the soil, you should first analyze it for both nutrients and moisture content. Then, if the soil is neither too wet nor too dry, you can add any necessary amendments, work the soil with a spade or power tiller, and finally, rake the soil to achieve a smooth surface.

Removing sod

If you're remodeling your landscape, you may first have to remove sod in the area you're preparing. Whether you plan to plant a new lawn or put in other plants, removing the sod is better than tilling it into the soil where it will break down only very slowly.

If the area of sod you need to remove is small, dig up the sod with a sharp spade; for a large area, rent a power sod cutter. Dispose of the old sod.

Analyzing the soil

Soil preparation begins with testing for nutrients in the soil so you'll know what to add as you get it ready for planting. One way to test is to use a soil testing kit. For a more detailed analysis, have samples of your soil tested professionally by a private soil testing company. (In some areas of the country, you may be able to have your soil tested by a state soil testing service.) Refer to the chart below for descriptions of the various soil amendments available.

Before you begin spreading amendments or working the soil, you'll also need to check the moisture content of the soil. Do this by picking up a handful of soil and compressing it. If the soil crumbles to powder, it's too dry to work; if it sticks together in a solid lump, it's too wet. If it breaks apart into small clumps, it has the right moisture content and can be prepared.

If the soil's too dry to work, soak it deeply, wait a few days for it to dry out, and test again. If it's too wet, wait for it to dry out and test it again.

Organic soil amendments

AMENDMENTS	PROS & CONS	MUST YOU ADD NITROGEN?	ASH CONTENT	NUTRIENT-HOLDING ABILITY
Compost	Variable material, depending on what you put in. Must be well rotted, screened. May contain disease organisms.	No.	Variable 40%	Very good
Mushroom compost	May be free from a mushroom grower. Must be well rotted. Moderately saline.	No.	To 40%	Poor
Dairy manure	In some areas, may be free for the hauling. Moderately saline. Must be thoroughly decomposed. Has strong odor.	No. Is a low-grade fertilizer.	50%	Good
Steer manure	Sold in trade-name packages. May be highly saline. Sometimes has strong odor.	No. Is a low-grade fertilizer.	To 60%	Good
Stable bedding	May be free from a commercial stable, but must be well composted. Mixture of straw, chips, sawdust, and animal waste.	No.	Low, but variable	Fair
Sphagnum peat moss	Fibrous or powdery. Hard to wet; do not use dry. Low salinity. Once wet, retains water better than any other amendment.	No.	3%	Very good
Hypnum peat moss	Fibrous; texture more variable than sphagnum, but contains more nitrogen and costs less.	No.	To 30%	Very good
Sedge peat	Fibrous; texture variable. May be saline. May be less expensive than sphagnum.	No.	30–50%	Good
Bark	Must be very fine. Work in well. Low salinity. Long lasting in soil.	To fresh bark add 1 pound actual nitrogen per 10 cubic feet.	3–5%	Poor
Sawdust	Granular. Work in well. Low salinity. Long lasting in soil. Raw sawdust may contain chips, shavings.	To fresh sawdust add ½ pound actual nitrogen per 10 cubic feet.	2%	Poor

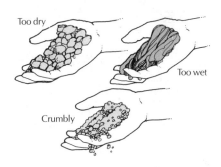

When compressed soil is powdery, it's too dry to dig; too wet soil sticks in a ball. If soil crumbles into pieces, it's ready to work.

Adding amendments

If you need to add bulk amendments to your soil, use a shovel and wheelbarrow to make piles of the amendments throughout the yard. Then rake them over the entire surface in an even layer 2 to 4 inches deep.

Finally, evenly scatter fertilizers and, if necessary, a soil modifier such as limestone or gypsum over the bulk amendments.

STEPS IN DOUBLE-DIGGING

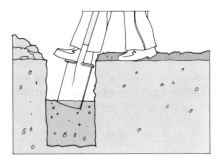

1. Dig a trench 12 to 18 inches wide, 8 to 9 inches deep, running the length of planting bed.

3. Dig an adjoining trench, filling in first one you dug with a mix of soil and amendments.

Working the soil

Turning up the soil is the next step in soil preparation. The method you use — spading, double-digging, or tilling —depends on the size of the area you are cultivating and on how deep you want to dig.

Spading. Spading is a good way to cultivate the soil in a small area. It's also the way to prepare the soil if you're planting annuals, perennials, or vegetables.

To turn the soil over, use a sharp, square-edged spade, digging down about the depth of the spade. Each time you dig, turn the soil half over, not completely upside down. Break up any clumps of soil into smaller pieces. If you have added amendments, be sure they are well combined with the soil.

Double-digging. Digging down two spades deep into the soil is twice the work of single-spading, but it makes a deep, fertile soil for flowers and vege-

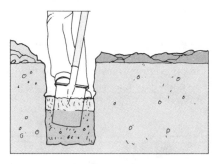

2. Mix soil amendments into next level of soil in trench until they're well combined. Deep roots will grow here.

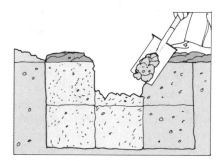

4. Continue digging and mixing until entire area has been worked; use soil from first hole in last trench.

tables. The goal is twofold: to mix soil amendments thoroughly into the upper layer of the soil to enrich it and to break up the lower soil layer so that roots can grow deep into it. To double-dig, follow the instructions in the drawings below at left.

Tilling. When you have a large area to cultivate, using a power tiller will save you aching muscles and lots of effort. Start by tilling in one direction; when you've tilled the entire area, till the soil again at right angles to the first direction.

If you've added amendments, dig up a spadeful of soil to see if the amendments are well combined with the soil. If necessary, till the soil two or three times to make certain the amendments and soil are thoroughly mixed.

Raking the soil

Raking is the final step in preparing the soil. As you rake, you'll turn up stones and large lumps of soil that were not broken up before. (If you find too many large lumps, you may want to go back and spade or till the soil once again.)

Use the rake to remove debris, stones, and large lumps of soil. If possible, break up the soil lumps and return the soil to your garden. Dispose of the stones and debris.

Finally, use the back side of the rake to smooth the surface of the soil and to level it out.

Putting in edgings

Garden edgings hold pavings in place and neatly define lawns and planting areas. To help you decide where to put edgings and what material to use, see the planning information on pages 56–57.

When you use edgings to curb paving, install them after you grade the base and before you lay the setting bed and the paving (see pages 140–145). Install lawn and garden edgings after you've prepared the soil and re-established the rough grade. (For information on grading, see pages 130–131.)

In the following section, you'll find instructions for building and installing wood, brick, and "invisible" concrete edgings.

Wood edgings

Wood edgings are fairly easy to install and work well to define both straight edges and gentle curves. For straight edgings, use dimension lumber; if you need curved edgings, you'll want to use benderboard.

Dimension-lumber edgings (also called headers). Drive stakes into the ground at the end points of your edging. (If it's an edging for paving, see pages 140–145 for details on marking and digging out the area.) Stretch mason's line tightly between the end stakes several inches above ground level, so the shovel will have clearance when you dig.

Dig a narrow trench deep enough so the top of the edging will be flush with the ground or the finished paving's surface. The trench should be wide enough to give you room to work comfortably.

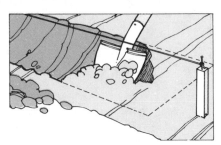

Dig trench as deep as edging board is wide. Mason's line keeps trench straight.

You'll probably have to join boards for a long edge. Either splice them with 2-foot lengths of 1 by 4s or 2 by 4s or butt the boards at a stake and nail them when you set them in the trench. Try to offset the splicing boards slightly so that they won't be visible on the part of the edging that shows aboveground.

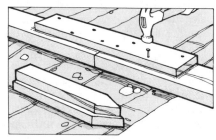

Splice boards with 1 by 4s or 2 by 4s, nailing them so they won't show aboveground.

Next, set the board on edge in the trench and drive 12-inch-long stakes (1 by 2s, 2 by 2s, or 1 by 3s) into the soil alongside the board, no more than 4 feet apart. The stakes should be slightly higher than the edging.

If the edging borders a lawn, place all the stakes on the side away from the lawn so they won't interfere with the use of a lawn edging tool later on. If the edging is a form for poured concrete, place all stakes along the outside edge. On an edging that divides two planting beds, you can alternate the stakes along both sides of the edging board.

Drive stakes so they project slightly above top of edging.

Nail the stakes to the edging board, bracing the board from behind with a heavy hammer head or crowbar (this will also clinch the nails). To keep boards and stakes from splitting when you nail them, blunt the nails or drill pilot holes.

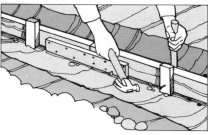

Use hammer head to brace board as you nail it.

Saw off the stakes at a 45° angle so the tip of each stake is level with the top of the edging board as shown below. (Note: Don't saw off stakes that hold temporary forms for pouring concrete.)

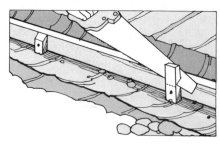

Saw off stakes at 45° angle so tips are level with top of edging.

Replace the soil along the edging as illustrated below. Fill along both sides for a lawn or planting bed edging; for a paved area, fill along the outer edge only. Tamp the soil firmly, using the end of a 4 by 4 or a metal tamper. Make sure the soil is level with the top of the edging board.

Replace soil so it's level with top of edging; tamp soil lightly to settle it.

Benderboard edgings. If your garden design calls for a layout with gentle curves, you can use benderboard. Benderboard is thin and flexible — usually ⅜ inch thick by 4 inches wide.

To determine the arc of your curve, use a homemade string compass (see the inset in the drawing below). For a guideline that won't scuff away, sprinkle a line of agricultural lime along the curve.

Dig a trench as for dimension-lumber edging and drive in stakes every 3 feet or so to mark the inside of the curve. Soak the benderboard in water to make it more flexible; then bend it around the stakes and nail it in place. If you're edging a lawn with benderboard, see the special instructions that follow.

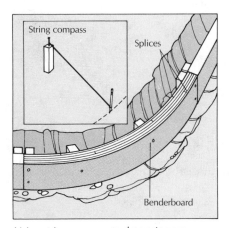

Using string compass to determine arc, layer benderboard to form curve.

Bend and nail additional boards around the outside of the first board, staggering any splices until you have built up the curved edging to the same thickness as your straight edging. Drive and nail stakes along the outside board. Nail all layers of the boards together between stakes to keep them from warping or separating.

When you're edging a lawn with benderboard, remember that you don't want the stakes on the lawn side of the boards to stay in place permanently. If the stakes on the inside of the curve are on the lawn side of the edging, clamp the benderboard to them instead of nailing them in place. Once the layers of benderboard have been built up to the proper thickness, drive in stakes on the outside of the curve and nail the benderboard to these stakes only. Then pull out the temporary stakes on the inside of the curve.

If the inside stakes are on the side of the edging away from the lawn, nail

the benderboard layers directly to the stakes and don't use any stakes on the outside of the curve.

Masonry edgings

Masonry makes a strong, permanent edging. You can install either a simple brick-in-soil edging or an "invisible" concrete edging that acts as an underground footing for brick.

Brick-in-soil edgings. These are easy to construct, but require very firm earth to hold them in place. To install, mark off and dig a narrow trench. Then, simply place the bricks side by side, on end, in the trench. Use a bubble level to get the tops even.

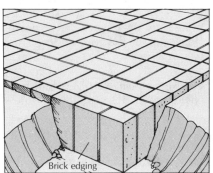

Set bricks on end in very firm soil.

You can bury the bricks completely so their ends will be flush with your finished paving. Or you can tilt the bricks at a 45° angle to give a sawtooth effect.

After you've set the edging, pack soil tightly against the outside of the bricks, tamping it firmly.

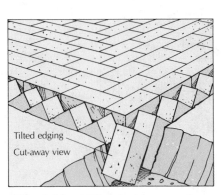

Tilting bricks at 45° angle gives sawtooth effect to edging.

"Invisible" concrete edgings. Effective for retaining unit paving and its base, these edgings are made of bricks set into a poured concrete footing. The bricks conceal the underground footing.

To install, dig a trench where the edging will go; then line the bottom with gravel. Around it, construct a temporary wood form that is one brick-length wide and as high as your finished pavement will be.

Pour concrete into the form and use a bladed screed to level it to the thickness of one brick below the top of the form. As you move the screed along, set bricks in the concrete one by one, tapping them down with a rubber mallet.

Invisible edgings can also be used to make a mowing strip one brick wide between a lawn and a planting area. Follow the directions given above. If you need to build in a curve for the mowing strip, you can make a temporary form for the concrete from benderboard. Follow the directions for making benderboard edgings (see at left).

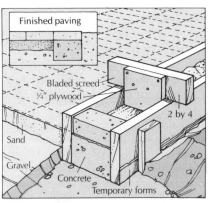

Use screed to make concrete footing for brick edging.

Building retaining walls

Building most kinds of retaining walls is demanding work. High walls especially have to be sturdy and well designed because of the enormous weight of soil they have to hold back.

Most localities require a building permit for any retaining wall. Many require that a licensed engineer design and supervise the construction of any retaining wall over 3 feet high or one on an unstable or steep slope. Always check with your building department before you begin any project more ambitious than a low garden terrace or raised bed.

For information on the kinds of materials you can use for retaining walls and how to design them, turn to pages 60–61.

Before you begin

Before you start building, you may need to do some grading and terracing. Also you'll need to provide for drainage.

Preparing the site. The safest way to build a retaining wall if you're not a professional is to build it at the bottom of a gentle slope and fill in behind it with soil. That way you won't disturb the stability of the soil.

If extensive grading is required to prepare a site for a retaining wall, it's best to hire a professional.

Drainage. All retaining walls must have adequate drainage to dispose of water that could otherwise build up in the soil behind the wall. Various methods can be used. Decide before you begin construction what method you'll use, since it may affect the way you build the wall.

A shallow ditch dug along the top of the wall can collect surface water. A gravel backfill can collect subsurface water, which is then channeled away through a 4 or 6-inch perforated drainpipe buried behind the wall (see the illustration on the facing page, far right). Another way to dispose of subsurface water is to add evenly spaced weep holes at ground level along the wall. A retaining wall with weep holes may require a ditch along the base of

the wall to prevent water from spilling onto your lawn or patio.

Make sure all drainpipes and ditches are properly sloped so they direct the excess water onto the street, toward storm sewers, or to other appropriate disposal areas.

Wood walls

You can make wood retaining walls in various sizes from boards or railroad ties set vertically or horizontally. Use decay-resistant heart redwood, cedar, or cypress, or pressure-treated lumber.

Staked boards. You can make very low retaining walls by nailing boards horizontally to stakes. For instance, you can use 2 by 4s, 2 by 6s, 2 by 8s, or 2 by 10s set on edge. Drive wood stakes firmly into the ground on the downslope side of the wall and nail the boards to them.

Built-up board wall. A 2-foot-high board wall like the one shown below is a good project for a weekend builder.

Set the posts in concrete, spacing them closely and sinking up to half their length into the ground as required by your building department. Nail the boards in behind them on the upslope side of the wall, and line the boards with moisture-proof tarpaper. In the gravel behind the wall, install a 4-inch drainpipe at the base of the wall to carry off subsurface water. Add a cap of 2 by 6s to strengthen the wall and act as a garden seat.

Railroad ties. Railroad ties are popular for bold, rugged-looking walls. However, they are hard to lift, drill, and cut. You'll need heavy-duty power tools and a helper.

To set ties horizontally for a low wall, set the bottom ties in a shallow trench of hard-tamped earth. Then stack two or three ties, staggering the joints and toenailing the ties to one another with long galvanized spikes. You can use pipes or reinforcing rods as shown below to reinforce the walls; or bolt ties to 4 by 4 posts.

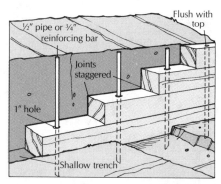

Railroad ties stacked in shallow trench are reinforced with pipes or rods.

To set ties vertically for a straight or curved wall, soak the cut ends of ties with wood preservative. Set the ties in the ground so half their length is aboveground. To stabilize the wall, you can set the ends of the ties in concrete. You can also connect the ties along the back with a continuous strip of sheet metal, such as flashing. Use wide-headed nails to fasten it.

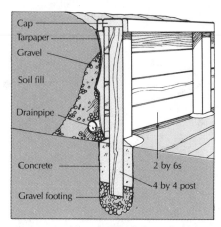

Low, capped board wall of 2 by 6s holds back gentle slope and makes garden seat.

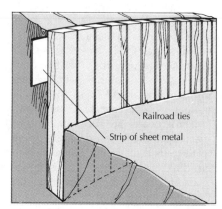

Strip of sheet metal nailed to back of ties strengthens fence laterally.

Cribbing may be an alternative on less stable slopes, but be sure to consult a professional first. Fasten ties to 4 by 8-inch notched stringers buried in the slope. Stagger the ties and nail them to the stringers with 12-inch spikes. (In the drawing below, the stringers are buried in the slope under the overlapping ends of the ties.)

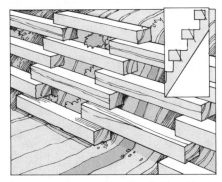

Spikes fasten staggered railroad ties to 4 by 8-inch stringers buried in hillside.

Dry walls

A stone or broken concrete retaining wall laid without mortar is a good choice for a low, fairly stable slope. The spaces between the rocks or concrete are ideal for planting.

Uncut stone. Uncut stone is rough and heavy to handle, but if you have patience, laying it up can be satisfying work. Fit the stones carefully: their uneven surfaces will help hold them in place. Lay the stones so they tip back into the slope. Set soil and plants in pockets between the rocks as you build.

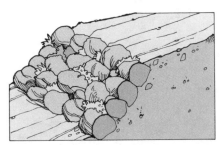

Stones half-buried in soil cover small slope. Set plants in spaces.

Broken concrete. Use a sledge hammer to break up the concrete into pieces small enough to handle. Lay the concrete rubble, smooth side down, in courses, setting the pieces carefully so that joints are staggered. You can put plants in the pockets of soil.

Unit masonry walls

Walls built of masonry units mortared together are good for holding steep or unstable hillsides. Always check building code requirements and seek professional help for such walls.

Brick, adobe, or stone. These materials are suitable for low mortared retaining walls. Check with your building department about requirements for reinforcing. For information on building with these materials, see pages 151–156 and the *Sunset* book *Basic Masonry Illustrated.*

Concrete blocks. For a high wall, concrete blocks reinforced with steel and grout are best. The concrete wall shown below rests on a footing reinforced with steel rods. The wall is built using bond-beam blocks and horizontal reinforcing as often as required. Grouting—filling up the spaces in the blocks with a runny mortar—is done in stages as each bond-beam course is completed.

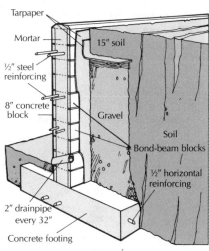

Weight of earth on wide footing anchors cantilevered block wall.

Every other block in the lowest bond-beam course is notched to receive plastic drainpipes, which form weep holes for drainage. Capping the wall with mortar and applying a veneer of brick or stone can make the wall look more attractive.

Poured concrete walls

A poured concrete wall reinforced with steel is the strongest wall that can be built to hold a steep hillside or unstable soil. However, you'll have to call in a professional for help in building such a wall. Both the formwork and labor make it a very costly project.

Poured concrete walls can either be mass walls or cantilevered. They need not be plain: lining the forms or using an exposed-aggregate finish can add surface interest.

Mass wall. A mass wall, such as the one illustrated below, relies on its own weight to prevent it from tipping or sliding. The wedge shape helps hold it in place. The width of the base must be one-half to three-quarters of the wall height. On low walls, steel reinforcing isn't usually required, but a horizontal $\frac{3}{8}$-inch reinforcing rod near the top of the wall gives extra strength.

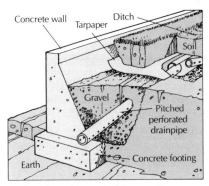

Wedge-shaped mass concrete wall uses its own weight to stay in place.

Cantilevered concrete walls. Cantilevered poured concrete walls, like the concrete block wall at left, rely on the weight of the earth pressing down on a large footing to hold them in place. To construct this type of cantilevered wall, concrete is poured into a form in a process similar to that for the mass wall shown above.

Laying patio pavings

The material you use to pave your patio can set the tone for your whole outdoor living area. For advice on choosing the material, turn to the planning information on pages 50–51. Before you begin any work, check with your building department for any code and permit requirements.

Regardless of the material you're using, you'll follow much the same method for preparing the base. Directions for laying brick, tile, flagstone, and poured concrete paving follow. Concrete pavers and adobe are laid in nearly the same way as brick-in-sand paving; your supplier can provide specific installation instructions.

PREPARING A BASE

To make them stable, all pavings require a base of firm, well-drained soil, and a setting bed of sand or gravel. Concrete paving is poured over a gravel bed. In this case, the concrete can become the base for unit pavings such as brick, stone, or tile. Or you can set unit pavings on a bed of sand.

All bases begin with a properly graded site. Then you'll need to excavate the patio area, build edgings to hold the paving, and prepare the setting bed.

Grading and excavating the site. Unless the area to be paved already slopes away from adjacent structures, you must grade it before paving to prevent water from collecting where it can cause problems.

Stake off the area to be paved, using the 3-4-5 rule (see page 157) to make sure the corners are square. To grade the area, follow the directions on pages 130–131.

Dig out and level the base, allowing for a slope of about ¼ inch per foot; the depth should be equal to the thickness of the paving plus the thickness of the sand or gravel bed. (See the recommendation given for the specific paving you're laying.)

Installing edgings. Build permanent wood or masonry edgings around the perimeter of the base to hold unit pav-

ings firmly in place. Or use temporary wood forms to hold a poured concrete paving until it hardens. For instructions on building edgings and forms, see pages 136–137.

Laying a setting bed. Specific instructions for laying a sand or gravel setting bed for the paving of your choice appear on the following pages.

PAVING WITH BRICK

Once you've decided on the type of brick you'll use and the pattern in which you'll lay it, install your patio using one of the three basic methods described here — setting bricks in sand, setting them in sand with dry mortar, or setting them in wet mortar. Be sure you've adequately prepared the base and installed the edgings.

Cutting bricks

No matter what method you use to lay bricks, you'll have to cut some to make them fit.

Cut soft common bricks with a special wide chisel called a brickset. Place the brick on sand or soil, and score it on all sides by setting the brickset blade on the brick and tapping the handle with a soft-headed steel hammer. Then cut the brick along the scoring with a sharp blow to the brickset.

If you're using hard bricks or want very precise cuts, you'll need to rent a masonry saw. Be sure to wear safety glasses when you're cutting brick.

Setting bricks in sand

To lay bricks in sand, the easiest method for beginners, you'll need to prepare a sand bed, set the bricks, and fill the joints with more sand.

Laying a sand bed. Lay a 2-inch bed of sand on the prepared base. To level the bed, you'll need a screed that rides on the edgings and extends down one brick-thickness below them. For a

wide patio where the screed won't reach from edging to edging, use a movable guide (a 2 by 6 set on edge) on which you can rest one end of the screed. Work in 3-foot-wide sections, laying both sand and bricks in one section before moving on to the next.

Spread dampened sand in the first section, and screed it smooth and level. Tamp the sand or roll it with a roller, and spray with water. Add more sand, if needed, to make a 2-inch base; then screed again. If you're using a movable guide, leave it in place until you've set the bricks in this section.

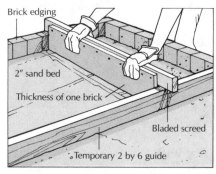

Use bladed screed to level sand bed.

Setting bricks. Stretch a mason's line between edgings to aid in alignment, and use a level often as you lay the bricks. Working outward from one corner, set the bricks into position, making sure they're tight against each other. (Don't slide them — you'll displace sand from the bed and trap it between the bricks.) Tap each brick into place with the handle of a rubber mallet or hammer.

Repeat the sanding, screeding, and bricklaying process section by section.

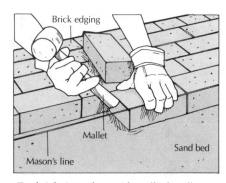

Tap bricks into place with mallet handle.

Sanding joints. When you've paved the entire area, spread fine sand over the surface. Let it dry thoroughly, then sweep it into the joints, adding sand as necessary to fill them. Finally, wet the finished paving with a fine spray from a garden hose to settle the sand between the joints.

Setting bricks with dry mortar

If you want to set your bricks in sand but prefer a wide joint, plan to mortar the joints to keep the bricks from shifting. First you'll need to prepare a sand bed as described on the facing page. Then you set the bricks in the sand bed and dry-mortar the joints to keep the bricks in place.

Placing bricks and mortar. Set all the bricks on the sand bed, leaving ½-inch open joints (use a piece of ½-inch plywood for a spacer and a mason's line for alignment). Check the bricks frequently with a level. Occasionally stand back to check the pattern.

Prepare a dry mortar mix of 1 part cement and 4 parts sand. Use a brush to spread the mix over the surface, brushing it into the open joints and keeping it swept off brick surfaces. Kneel on a board to avoid disturbing the bricks.

Tamping the mortar. Use a tamper (a piece of ½-inch plywood) to pack the dry mix firmly into the joints, as shown below. Add more mix, if needed. Carefully sweep clean the tops of the bricks before going on to the next step, because any mix that remains can leave stains.

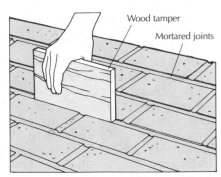
Use wood tamper on dry-mortared joints. Pack down dry mortar until firm.

Wetting the surface. Using an extremely fine spray, wet down the paving. Don't let pools of water form, and don't splash the mortar out of the joints. During the next 2 to 3 hours, frequently wet the paving. When the mortar is firm enough (pressing with your thumb leaves a slight indentation), tool (finish) the joints. Run a convex jointer or a piece of steel pipe (see below at right) along the mortar joints so they are neat and well compacted. To remove mortar tags forced out of the joints, wait a few hours and then scrub the finished paving clean with damp burlap.

Setting bricks with wet mortar

Bricks wet-mortared over a concrete slab make a firm, durable paving. The bricks can be laid on a new concrete base or on existing concrete that's in good condition (see pages 142–143 for information on pouring concrete). Ask your brick supplier if you need to prepare the concrete before laying the bricks.

Preparing a mortar bed. Build temporary wood edgings around the concrete slab. They should rise above the concrete one brick-thickness plus ½ inch (the thickness of the mortar bed).

Wet the bricks several hours before you start work so they won't absorb too much moisture from the mortar. To make the mortar, mix 1 part cement and 4 parts sand, gradually adding enough water so the mortar spreads easily but doesn't run. Mix only as much mortar as you can use in an hour.

Then lay and screed a ½-inch wet-mortar bed between the edgings. Use a bladed screed that rides on the edgings and extends one brick-thickness below them. If your area is large, use a movable guide (see facing page). Screed only about 10 square feet at a time, an area that's reasonably easy to work.

Placing bricks. Place the bricks in your chosen pattern, leaving ½-inch open joints between them (use a piece of ½-inch plywood for a spacer and a

mason's line for alignment). Gently tap each brick with a rubber mallet to set, checking with a level as you go. Wait 24 hours before finishing the joints with wet mortar.

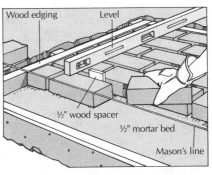
Level, wood spacer, and mason's line aid in setting bricks in wet mortar.

Finishing joints. Using a small mason's trowel, pack mortar (1 part cement to 4 parts sand, plus an optional ½ part fire clay to improve workability) into the joints. Work carefully to keep mortar off brick faces. Tool (finish) the joints with a jointer or a steel pipe.

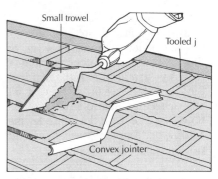
Pack mortar into joints with trowel; then tool with jointer.

Several hours later, scrub the paving with damp burlap to remove mortar tags and any stains. If any further cleaning is necessary, wash the surface with a solution of trisodium phosphate and laundry detergent (use ½ cup of each in a gallon of water); rinse well with clean water.

Keep the mortar damp for about 24 hours by covering the bricks with a plastic sheet; stay off the bricks for 3 days so they can set.

(Continued on next page)

...Laying patio pavings

PAVING WITH POURED CONCRETE

You can pour a concrete patio in almost any shape you want and finish it in whatever texture suits your needs — plain or patterned, smooth or pebbled.

To make a poured concrete patio, you first need to prepare the base. Then you mix the concrete (or arrange for its delivery), and pour, finish, and cure it. Below are instructions for building a basic concrete patio. If you want to add a special textured surface, see the *Sunset* book *Basic Masonry Illustrated*.

Preparing a base

A well-built concrete patio begins with a firm soil base, sturdy wood forms, and a setting bed of sand or gravel. The base may also include steel reinforcement for a large patio, and an expansion joint for a patio next to a house foundation. Check with your building department to find out if either is required for your project.

When you grade (see pages 130–131), be sure to build in a slope of at least ¼ inch per foot for drainage. Dig out and level the area, allowing for the thickness of the concrete slab (4 inches is standard) plus the depth of the setting bed (see the drawing at left on page 130). Then follow the directions below to build the forms, lay the setting bed, and, if necessary, add reinforcing.

Building forms. Construct strong temporary or permanent wood forms as you would build edgings (see page 136). If they'll be permanent edgings, make the forms of rot-resistant heart redwood or cedar, or pressure-treated wood. Wet concrete exerts considerable pressure, so make sure your forms are strong and securely anchored to the ground.

For a 4-inch-thick paving, use 2 by 4s on edge for forms and 12-inch 1 by 2s or 2 by 2s for stakes. Use double-headed nails for construction so that you can remove them easily when you

strip the forms. Check the corners of the forms with a steel square.

Use a straight 2 by 4 with a spacer and level (as shown below) to make sure the forms follow the proper slope for drainage. To prevent concrete from oozing under the boards, pack soil against the outside of the forms.

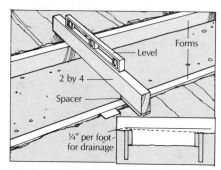

Check slope of forms using straight 2 by 4 with spacer and level.

If you're paving a large area, you may want to divide it into sections to give it a more attractive appearance and to help prevent the concrete from cracking. (Smaller sections are also more convenient to pour.) Build a permanent grid of 2 by 4 redwood dividers, and leave them in place after the concrete is poured.

If you don't want to use permanent dividers in paving a large area, set temporary divider forms inside the outer forms so you can screed each batch of concrete as you pour it.

Laying the setting bed. In areas where frost is not a problem, add at least a 2-inch sand or gravel bed; where the ground freezes, use a 4 to 6-inch gravel bed. Lay the bed after the forms and any dividers are in place. Use a bladed screed (see page 140) to level the bed.

Adding reinforcing. Installing dividers as described above is one way to prevent concrete from cracking. Other methods include using welded steel mesh, installing expansion strips, and cutting grooved control joints (see facing page).

If the area being paved is larger than 8 square feet, reinforce it with 6-inch-square welded steel mesh, sold at building supply stores. Cut the mesh to size with bolt cutters, and support it

on bricks, stones, or broken concrete so it will be held midway in the slab.

You can also install expansion strips (available at building supply centers) every 10 feet or less. Always use an expansion strip when pouring concrete up to an existing structure, such as a house foundation.

Pouring concrete

Pouring concrete involves several steps: you mix the concrete and pour it, finish the surface, and then cure it. Once the pour begins, however, it should proceed right through to the final curing step without interruption. (If your patio is divided into sections, you can pour any number at a time.)

Make sure you have enough helpers and tools on hand, and wear gloves and rubber boots while you work.

Mixing concrete. You can purchase bulk dry materials or dry ready-mix concrete to mix yourself. Or you can have ready-to-pour concrete delivered by a truck. Bulk dry materials are cheapest, but require the most labor. Dry ready-mix is expensive, but more convenient. Transit-mix, though expensive, is best for a large project because you can finish in a single pour. (For more on concrete, see the *Sunset* book *Basic Masonry Illustrated*.)

If you're making concrete from bulk dry materials, use the following basic formula (all measured by volume): 2½ parts sand, 1 part cement, 2¾ parts gravel, and ½ part water. If you live in a cold-winter area, use a mix containing an air-entraining agent to minimize cracking as the concrete expands and contracts.

When working with small quantities, use a shovel or hoe to mix concrete on a wood platform or in a wheelbarrow. Measure the sand, spread it evenly, and spread the cement on top. Turn and mix the dry ingredients until no streaks of color appear. Add the gravel and mix until evenly distributed. Then make a depression in the mixture and slowly add the water, turning until the ingredients are thoroughly combined. Use a rolling motion with a shovel to speed up the job.

For large quantities, it's best to rent a power mixer. Air-entrained concrete must be power mixed.

Spreading and tamping. If you plan to remove the forms after the pour, oil them with motor oil. Start pouring the concrete at one end of the form while a helper uses a shovel or hoe to spread it. Work the concrete up against the form and tamp it into all corners, without overworking it or spreading it too far: overworking will cause the elements to separate. Space out the pours along the form, working each batch just enough to completely fill the form.

Striking the concrete. With a helper, move a screed across the form to level the concrete. On a long pour, do this batch-by-batch, rather than after all the concrete is poured. Move the board slowly along the form, using a rapid zigzag, sawing motion. A third person can fill hollows with concrete.

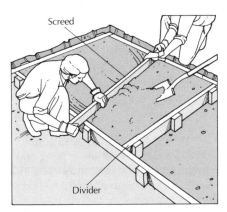

Screed concrete level while third person shovels concrete into hollows.

Edging and jointing. Before and after floating (see at right), you must edge the concrete. First run the point of a trowel between the concrete and the form. Follow up with an edger; run the tool back and forth to smooth and compact the concrete, creating a smooth, curved edge that will resist chipping. Then cut a grooved control joint every 10 feet, using the edger or a special jointer with a straight board as a guide. (A control joint is a deliberate weak point in the concrete where cracking can occur beneath the joint and not be seen.)

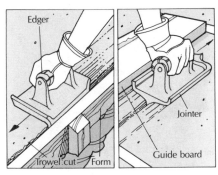

Edger creates smooth edge; jointer cuts grooved control joints.

Initial floating. After screeding and edging, use a bull float, darby, or wood float (depending on the size of your project) for the initial finishing. Floating smooths down high spots and fills small hollows left in the surface after screeding.

Use a bull float (shown below) on large areas. Push it away from you with its leading edge raised slightly, and pull it back nearly flat, overlapping your passes.

On smaller areas, use a darby, a wide, hand-held float. Move it in overlapping arcs; then repeat with overlapping straight, side-to-side strokes. Keep the tool flat, but don't let it dig in. On very small projects, a wood float (shown below) can be used in a similar manner. Redo edges and joints after floating.

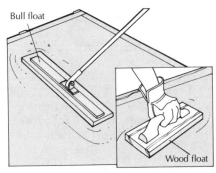

Finish concrete with bull float for large areas, wood float for small ones.

Final floating and troweling. After the water sheen has disappeared from the concrete but before the surface has become really stiff, either give it a final floating with a wood float or broom the surface (see drawing at right).

For a slick, smooth surface, follow with a steel trowel. Make your initial passes with the trowel flat on the surface; use some pressure, but don't let the blade dig in. For a smoother surface, wait a few minutes and repeat the operation, this time with more pressure and with the leading edge raised. Kneel on boards to reach the center of a large slab.

Brooming the surface. If you want a nonskid surface, substitute brooming for final floating and troweling. The texture you produce will depend on the stiffness of the bristles and whether you use the broom wet or dry. The pattern you make can be straight or wavy, depending on how you move the broom.

Drag the broom over the concrete immediately after floating, always pulling it toward you. Avoid overlapping passes; this tends to knock down the grain texture and produces too many "crumbs." Finish by redoing the edges with the edging tool.

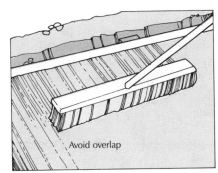

Brooming finished concrete makes nonskid surface; avoid overlapping passes.

Curing the concrete. A slab needs to be moist-cured to keep its surface from drying too fast and becoming powdery or flaking away. Cure concrete by keeping it wet. You can do this by covering it with straw or burlap and wetting it down. Or you can cover the slab with a plastic sheet or a commercial curing compound so water evaporating from the concrete will be trapped, eliminating the need for wetting. If no covering material is available, keep the surface damp by hand sprinkling. Cure for at least 3 days—longer in cold weather. To be on the safe side, allow about a week for curing.

(Continued on next page)

...Laying patio pavings

PAVING WITH FLAGSTONE

Flagstones, one of the toughest outdoor surfaces available, can be laid in a sand bed or set with wet or dry mortar. The size and weight of the stones help keep them stable whatever the method used to set them. Note that it takes more effort to cut and fit flagstones together than other kinds of paving materials.

The sand-bed and wet-mortar methods are described below. To dry-mortar flagstones, lay the sand bed and set the stones as for flagstones in sand; then follow the directions for setting bricks in dry mortar given on page 141.

Fitting & cutting flagstones

Most flagstones are irregularly shaped; you'll need to fit and cut each stone before setting it. First, lay out the stones approximately where you want them. Overlap stones that don't fit exactly into the space available. To cut or trim a stone, set the part of the stone to be cut under the adjoining one. Leave room for a joint and mark the cutting line with a pencil.

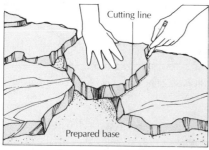

Set stone to be cut under edge of adjoining one; mark cutting line with a pencil. Allow space for joint between stones.

Then cut the stone by scoring a ⅛-inch groove along the line with a brickset and soft-headed steel hammer. Place a length of wood under the stone so the waste portion and a slight portion behind the scored line overhang it. Strike sharply along the line with a brickset and a mallet or soft-headed steel hammer. (Be sure to wear safety glasses.) Trim the stone and cut curves by chipping off pieces.

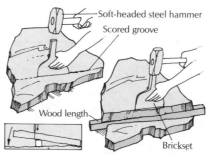

Score stone along marked cutting line; set stone over a length of wood and using a brickset, cut off excess piece.

Setting flagstones in sand

This is the easiest method for setting flagstones. To prepare a graded base (see the drawing at left on page 130), dig out and level an area deep enough for a 2-inch sand bed plus the thickness of the flagstones. Spread and level the sand bed, following the directions for the brick-in-sand paving given on page 140.

Lay out the flagstones as desired, and cut and trim them. Set and level the stones, scooping out sand or filling it in as necessary. Tap the stones firmly into the sand bed with a rubber mallet. When all stones are laid, fill the joints with more sand as for brick-in-sand paving, or add soil to the open joints, and plant with grass or a low-growing ground cover.

Setting flagstones with wet mortar

For the most permanent flagstone surface, set stones in a mortar bed on top of a 3-inch or thicker concrete slab. You can use an existing slab in good condition or one built for this purpose (see pages 142–143). A new slab should cure for at least 24 hours before you lay the stones. (Ask your stone dealer whether you need to use a bonding agent on the concrete surface.) Once the concrete slab is ready, you set the stones in mortar and grout the joints with mortar. If the stones are porous, wet them a few hours before you set them.

Laying stones. Before laying the mortar bed, arrange the stones in a pleasing pattern. Where necessary, cut and trim the flagstones for fit so there's minimum space between them for mortar joints.

Then mix a batch of mortar (3 parts sand to 1 part cement) to cover 10 to 12 square feet. Add water slowly — the mortar should be stiff enough to support the weight of the stones, but not so stiff that you can't work with it.

Starting at one corner, remove a section of stones and set them to one side in the same relative positions. With a trowel, spread enough mortar (at least 1 inch deep for the thickest stones) to make a full bed for one or two stones. Furrow the mortar bed with your trowel to make a good surface for the stone to adhere. Set each stone firmly in place and bed it by tapping with a rubber mallet.

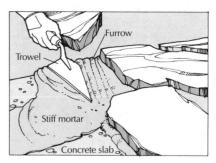

Furrow mortar with trowel to bed stone solidly and evenly.

To maintain an even surface, use a level. If a stone is not level, lift it and scoop out or add mortar as needed. Again, furrow the mortar, and bed and level the stone.

Align the edges of the outer stones with the perimeter of the slab, or let them overhang it slightly. Remove any excess mortar from the perimeter after bedding the stones.

Grouting joints. After the mortar has set for 24 hours, grout the joints with the same mix of mortar used for the bed, plus ½ part fire clay to improve workability. Pack the joints with mortar; then smooth them with a trowel. Clean the flagstones with a sponge and water as you work.

Keep the grout damp for the first day by sprinkling repeatedly or by covering with plastic sheeting, and keep off the paved area for 3 days to let the mortar harden.

PAVING WITH TILE

Outdoor tiles are available in a variety of colors and sizes; for help in choosing one that will be compatible with your patio design, see the planning information on pages 50–51.

You can set tile in sand, dry mortar, or wet mortar. Directions follow for all three methods. To minimize tile cutting, try to plan your area to accommodate full-size tiles. If you need to cut tiles, use a wet-saw.

Setting tiles in sand

Heavy tile — tile that's at least ¾ inch thick — can be laid in a sand bed. After grading the site, level the soil to allow for a ½-inch sand bed plus the thickness of the tile. (A thicker base may allow the tiles to tilt out of position.) Build permanent wood edgings to hold the paving in place; set them so their tops will be flush with the finished paving's surface.

Lay the sand bed and tiles as for bricks in sand (see page 140), using a bladed screed to level the ½-inch sand bed. Set tiles with butted joints (edges touching). Finish by sweeping sand into the joints as for brick paving.

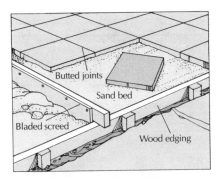
Use bladed screed to level sand bed; set tiles with butted joints.

Setting tiles with dry mortar

You'll need a specially prepared base for extra stability when setting tiles in dry mortar. Level the soil 3 inches plus one tile-thickness below the desired grade of the paved surface, and build temporary wood edgings (see page 136) around the area to be paved. Set the tops of the edgings so they'll be flush with the surface of the tiles. Pack soil around the outside of the edgings.

Fill the leveled area with a 3-inch bed of sand. Using a bladed screed (with the blade set for the thickness of one tile), screed the sand level between the edgings. Over every 100 square feet of surface, evenly distribute 2 bags of dry cement. Mix the sand and cement together with a rake, being careful not to mix in the soil below; then tamp and rescreed the mix to a smooth surface.

Evenly sprinkle the screeded sand-cement mixture with half a bag of dry cement for every 100 square feet. Place the tiles on the surface, aligning them with ⅜-inch open joints (use a length of ⅜-inch plywood as a spacer). Make sure tiles are level, and bed them by tapping with a rubber mallet.

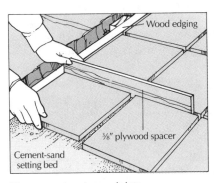
Use spacer to set open joints.

Wet the entire area with a fine spray until sand, cement, and tiles are moistened, but don't let the water puddle or splash mortar out of the joints. Let the tiles set for 24 hours; then grout the joints with a mixture of 1 part cement and 3 parts sand, and tool them with a jointer. After the grout has cured, remove the temporary edgings and fill the recesses with soil.

Setting tiles with wet mortar

This is a particularly stable method for laying tile as thin as ⅜ inch. Use an existing or newly poured concrete slab as a base. (Check with your tile dealer to find out whether any preparation of the concrete surface is necessary.) Add permanent or temporary wood edgings (see page 136). The edgings should rise above the concrete base one tile-thickness plus an inch for the mortar bed.

Lay down a 1-inch wet-mortar bed using the same method as for brick wet-mortared paving (see page 141). Using a screed that extends one tile-thickness below the edgings, level the mortar. Then set and level the tiles with ½-inch open joints (use a length of ½-inch plywood for a spacer).

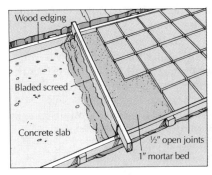
Lay tiles on screeded mortar bed.

Let the tiles set for 24 hours. Prepare a mortar mixture of 1 part cement, 3 parts sand, and enough water to make the mortar thin enough to pour. To grout the joints, pour the mortar from a coffee can bent to form a spout. Clean spills immediately with a damp sponge.

Tool the joints as for brick, using a jointer or a piece of steel pipe. Keep the grout damp for about 24 hours by covering with a plastic sheet, and stay off the area for 3 days.

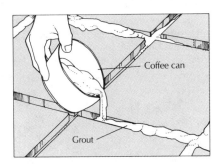
Pour grout into joints between tiles.

Constructing raised beds

You can use raised beds in your garden to show off special plants, to grow vegetables, or to make the transition from one level of your yard to another. Ideas for making use of raised beds, as well as information about design and materials, appear on pages 58–59.

Raised planting beds can be constructed of wood, brick, stone, or concrete—any material that's suitable for a wall. In fact, a raised bed is like a low-level retaining wall; many of the methods used for building a retaining wall (see page 138) apply also to building raised beds.

Under some conditions, the restrictions that apply to retaining walls may apply to raised beds, too. If your raised bed will be higher than 3 feet or if you're planning to build it on sloping or unstable ground, check with your building department before going ahead.

Drainage is important in any kind of bed. If the bed is open to the ground at the bottom, most excess water will drain out. If it's closed, make weep

holes 2 to 3 inches up from the ground, spacing them 2 to 3 feet apart. It's also a good idea to place at least a 4-inch layer of crushed rock in the bed before you fill it with soil.

Following are detailed instructions for building beds of 2 by 12 planks, railroad ties, and brick. The illustrations below show a variety of methods for constructing other types of raised beds.

Low plank bed

This sturdy box—a good one for planting vegetables — is easy to build. A good width for the bed is 4 to 5 feet; the length can vary. (The bed shown at upper right measures 4 by 10 feet.) Two-by-twelves set on edge make the sides and ends. Be sure to buy straight lumber that's naturally resistant to insects and rot, or that's been treated with preservative. Supporting stakes along the insides are pointed 2 by 4s; the corner posts are 36-inch sections of 4 by 4 timbers set on end.

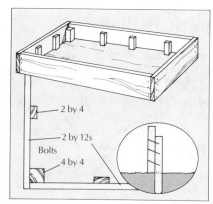

Use carriage bolts to fasten planks to posts at corners; nail planks to stakes (see inset).

Level the ground and locate the corner posts. Make sure the corners are square. Use a posthole digger to make holes about 24 inches deep; then sink the posts so they protrude about 12 inches aboveground.

At the corner posts, join the planks with simple butt joints, and fasten them to the posts with carriage bolts. Drive stakes into the ground

SIMPLE-TO-BUILD RAISED BEDS

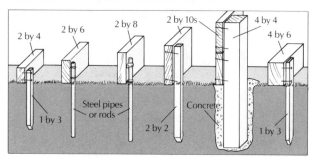

Rough-finish redwood or cedar planks make durable raised beds; stake at corners according to plank size. (For details on building a plank bed, see above.)

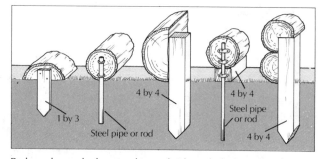

Redwood or cedar logs can be used either whole or cut in half to make rustic-looking beds. Brace logs with stakes or steel pipes.

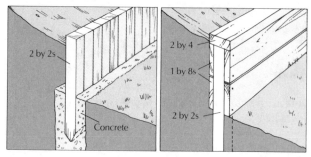

Wood stakes can be driven into ground in a row, or embedded in a small concrete footing (see page 151). Add facing and cap of lumber to stakes spaced 2 feet apart as shown at right.

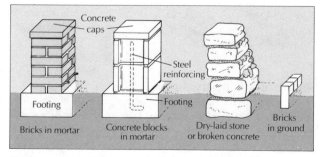

Brick, concrete, and stone make lasting raised beds (follow directions on pages 151–156 for building walls). Add weep holes for drainage in closed-bottom beds.

along the inside edge of the planks, and nail the planks to them. Tamp the soil firmly around the corner posts using a tamper or a 4 by 4.

Railroad-tie bed

You can stack railroad ties to make a raised bed that's compatible with many garden designs. The planter shown at right is stacked three ties high, and is firmly anchored by steel pipes or rods driven through the ties into the ground.

Use railroad ties that have been treated with creosote or another preservative. The hardest job will be to cut and drill the dense, heavy ties. Use a power saw or crosscut saw to cut them the length you need.

Prepare a solid base of well-tamped soil, and stack ties in place with ends overlapping as shown in the drawing. With a heavy-duty drill, bore a 1 inch wide hole through each tie where the ends overlap. To secure the ties, use a sledge hammer or club hammer to drive steel pipes or reinforcing rods through the holes and at least a foot into solid ground. Also

nail the unsecured ends of ties to adjacent ties with long spikes.

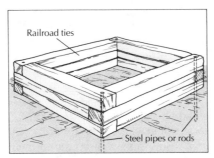

Drive steel pipes or reinforcing rods at least a foot into solid ground through holes drilled in ties.

Simple brick bed

You can construct a simple raised bed of brick like the one shown at right using the basic techniques on page 154 for building brick walls. The bed's dimensions should be a multiple of standard brick and paver sizes.

This 4 by 4-foot brick planting bed sits on top of a footing of six 12 by 24 by 2¼-inch concrete pavers. To make it, dig a 4 by 4-foot trench deep enough for a 2-inch bed of sand plus the thickness of the concrete pavers.

Add the sand bed and level it; arrange the pavers as shown in the inset so their tops are level with the ground.

Lay out a dry course of bricks, marking mortar joints on the concrete with a pencil. Lay up the bricks with ½-inch mortar joints. Leave some vertical joints in the base row of bricks open as weep holes for drainage. Tool the mortared joints according to directions on page 155.

Apply a parge coat of mortar ¾ inch thick to the inside of the planter just up to the top course of bricks; this helps waterproof the sides.

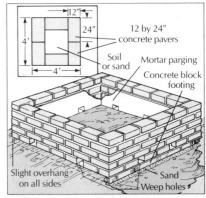

To help waterproof brick bed, add parge coat of mortar just up to top course.

A raised bed that preserves a tree

A raised bed may be the perfect solution when you need to change the soil level around a mature tree. If grading removes only a few inches of soil, you can simply add a thick organic mulch of peat moss or ground bark around the tree. But when you lower the grade more drastically, you should build a raised bed to retain the soil around the tree at its original level. Otherwise, you risk damaging the tree's roots.

Build the bed's walls of a material you would use for other walls or raised beds — stone, concrete, brick, or wood. Locate the walls at the drip line under the tree's outermost branches. (The branches mirror the underground root structure, enabling you to determine where the roots lie.) The walls may surround the tree, or they may be constructed only on the sides where the grade has been changed.

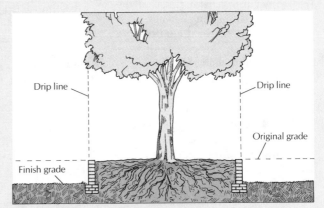

Raised bed protects tree roots in graded area by retaining soil at original level around tree.

Creating a garden walk

Depending on the look you want to achieve in your garden, you can use almost any kind of building material to make a garden walk. For help in choosing the material and location of your walk, see pages 52–53.

If you're building your walk of fieldstone, wood, gravel, or concrete block, the instructions that follow will explain how to do the work. If your choice is poured concrete, flagstone, brick, or tile, construct the walk as you would a patio made of the same material (see pages 140–145). Remember that before you build you'll need to grade the site properly (see pages 130–131).

A natural fieldstone path

For durability and rustic appeal, fieldstone is hard to beat. Though the stones are heavy and sometimes awkward to handle, with just a shovel and a little muscle you can create a path of steppingstones that looks like a natural element of the landscape.

The first step is to do a dry run, laying the stones down in an arrangement that's both pleasing to the eye and comfortable underfoot. Then you can set the stones permanently into the ground.

Arranging stones. Choose random-size fieldstones that are flat-topped and large enough to stand on. Try different arrangements for the path. Set larger stones in place aboveground first to get the general shape of the path; then fill in any spaces with smaller ones. Leave a comfortable stepping distance between stones — usually no more than 18 inches.

If your path has a turn in it, set a large stone there as a stopping place. Vary the size of the stones, and try to relate shapes of adjoining stones harmoniously. In most cases, lay stones broadside across the path rather than lengthwise.

Setting stones. To set large, widely spaced stones in the ground, dig a hole for each one, add a little sand, and position the stone, adjusting sand and earth around it until it's firmly set. For stones that will lie close together, dig a trench in firm soil and lay a ½-inch bed of sand or gravel. Bury at least two-thirds of each stone so the stones won't tilt or wobble. When the stones are set in the trench, fill the spaces between them with soil; then wet the soil with a fine spray of water. If the first layer of soil settles, add more soil.

Ideally, the surface of the stones should be slightly higher than ground level. Plant grass or a ground cover around the stones, or surround them with a bed of fine gravel. If you use gravel, you may want to add a wood edging (see pages 136–137) along each side of the path to prevent the gravel from spreading.

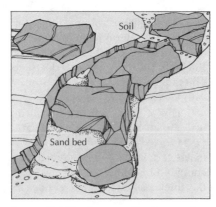

Arrange fieldstones on sand bed in trench to create natural-looking path.

Easy wood paths

Wood makes an attractive, informal garden walk. You begin with a sand bed; then either lay down wood rounds as steppingstones, or set end-grain wood blocks in a regular pattern much as you would set bricks in sand. Make sure the wood you use is decay-resistant or has been treated with a preservative to protect it.

Wood rounds. Constructing a simple path using 3-inch-thick wood rounds is an easy job. Dig a trench about 5 inches deep, and spread a 2-inch bed of sand on the bottom. Then set in the rounds, making sure the tops are flush with the surface of the ground. You can fill the spaces between the rounds with loose gravel, bark, or sand as shown in the illustration above at right, or add soil and plant grass or ground cover between them.

Lay wood rounds on sand bed in trench, and surround with gravel, bark, sand, or soil.

End-grain blocks. Cut the blocks to any thickness from pressure-treated railroad ties or other large timbers, or from heart redwood.

To install the blocks, dig a trench 1 inch deeper than the thickness of the blocks. Build a wood edging of 2 by 4s, placing the stakes on the outside of the edging (see page 136). Tamp the ground in the trench; then add a 1-inch bed of sand, using a straight 2 by 4 to screed it level. Set the blocks as for the brick-in-sand paving shown on page 140, with 1-inch open joints.

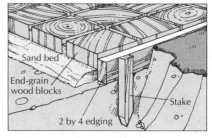

Lay end-grain wood blocks in sand; wood edgings hold them in place.

A gravel walk

A walk made of base rock (sharp-edged crushed rock) covered with a layer of pea gravel is economical and fairly easy to install. However, you'll need to rent a piece of special equipment — a heavy roller — to finish the walk's surface.

Preparing the base. Dig a trench deep enough to accommodate a 2½ to 4-inch-thick layer of base rock plus a ¾-

inch top layer of pea gravel. Construct wood edgings of 2 by 4s or benderboard (see pages 136–137), setting them in the ground so the tops of the edgings will be level with the finished path's surface.

Laying gravel. Spread a 1-inch layer of base rock over the bottom of the trench, using a rake to distribute it evenly; then wet the base rock down. Roll the surface with a heavy roller to pack it firmly. Repeat the process until you've built up the base to the desired level. While the base is still wet, add a ¾-inch layer of pea gravel and roll it into the base. Make the center of the walk higher than the edges for good drainage.

As time goes by, walking on the path will pack it down further. You may have to add more gravel from time to time to maintain the path.

Use heavy roller to set layers of base rock and gravel in wood-edged path.

A concrete block walk

You can use either ready-mix concrete or concrete mixed from bulk dry materials to pour a concrete block walk. Two techniques are described here. With one method, you cast blocks one at a time directly in the ground; with the other you cast several at a time in a multiple-grid mold.

Casting blocks in a ground mold. The easiest way to make blocks is to cast them right in the ground. The finished blocks have the uneven look of natural steppingstones.

To plan your path, tear newspaper into irregular shapes and arrange the pieces on the ground. Blocks should

be no more than 18 inches apart for easy walking.

For each block, dig a hole 4 inches deep in the shape you want. Fill each hole with ready-mix concrete, or make your own concrete from a mixture of 1 part cement, 2 parts sand, 3 parts gravel, and ½ part water (you can throw in a few small rocks as filler).

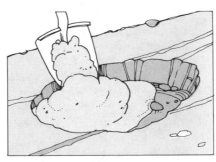

Shovel concrete mixture into hole dug in ground.

Tamp the wet concrete and smooth the surface with a wood float as shown below (a trowel makes it too slick). If the blocks are set in a lawn, keep the tops below ground level so you can mow over them. To cure the concrete, cover each block with burlap, wet it down, and wet it periodically for at least 3 days.

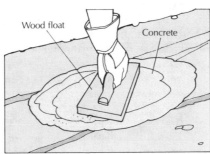

Use wood float to smooth surface of wet concrete.

Casting blocks in a multiple-grid mold. To speed up the process of laying a long walk, use a mold to cast several blocks at one time. Build a grid of 2 by 4s, attaching cleats to either side as handles. (Though you can make the grid in a size and design of your choosing, the dimensions shown above at right will yield an easy-to-handle mold.) Make certain to sand

the inside surfaces smooth so concrete doesn't stick to them.

To make the blocks, dig a shallow trench in firmly compacted soil. Oil the inner surfaces of the mold with light motor oil and set the mold in the trench. Then shovel in the same concrete mixture as for blocks cast in the ground (at left). Screed the surface level with the top of the form, and finish the surface with a wood float.

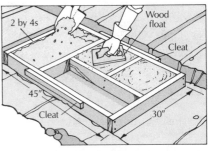

Shovel concrete into grid mold, smoothing surface with wood float.

When the blocks are partly hardened, carefully lift off the form. Use two trowels as shown below to clean up the edges. Clean and re-oil the form, move it along the path, and repeat the process. Allow all blocks to cure completely by covering them with burlap, wetting it down, and dampening it periodically for at least 3 days. Then you may fill the joints with soil and plant them with grass or ground cover.

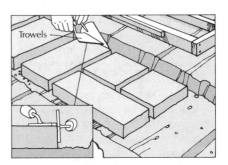

Use trowels in tandem to clean up edges of concrete blocks.

Constructing garden steps

Changes of level in your garden may call for just a few steps or perhaps an entire flight. Well-designed steps begin with an understanding of proper step proportions and the steps' relation to the slope they'll cover. For information on design, materials, and any cautions affecting your project, see pages 54–55.

On this page are instructions for building concrete steps and railroad-tie steps with tread variations. To build wood steps, see page 159; for information on steps built of other materials, consult *Sunset's Garden & Patio Building Book*.

Concrete steps

You may build steps entirely of concrete, or use concrete as a base for mortared brick or other unit paving. The basic method, which requires some masonry skills, is the same. You excavate a base, build wood forms, and pour the concrete. Then you finish the surface, adding brick or other paving if you wish.

Preparing a base. Following your design, dig out your slope to form rough steps in the earth, keeping treads as level as possible and risers as perpendicular as possible. Allow space for at least a 6-inch gravel setting bed and at least a 4-inch thickness of concrete on both treads and risers.

Building forms. Build forms of 2-inch-thick lumber in the same way as for wood edgings (see page 136). Position the forms so the concrete will be the required thickness. Level and nail the forms to stakes driven into the ground on the outside of the forms so you can remove both forms and stakes after the concrete has cured.

Spread and level the gravel, keeping it at least 4 inches back from the riser forms to leave room for the thickness of the risers. To reinforce, add 6-inch-square welded mesh as for concrete paving (see page 142).

Pouring and finishing. Mix, pour, and screed the concrete as for a poured concrete paving (see pages 142–143).

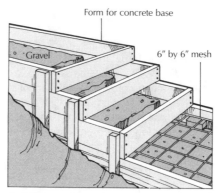

Build stepped forms for concrete. Reinforce with steel mesh.

To make the treads less slippery, roughen them by brooming the surface or scoring tread edges. Cure the concrete as for paving.

An alternative treatment is to lay a mortar bed over the concrete and install bricks, tiles, or other paving units. Follow the steps for patio pavings of these materials (see pages 140–145).

Railroad-tie steps

Building railroad-tie steps isn't difficult, and you can combine the ties with a variety of materials to complement different garden settings. Railroad ties are usually 6 inches by 8 inches by 8 feet. Since each tie weighs about 150 pounds, you'll probably need a helper to handle them. You can cut them into the lengths required for your steps with a power saw or crosscut saw.

Setting ties. Prepare the slope by excavating, then tamping the soil in the tread area very firmly. Set the ties in place so they don't rock or wobble.

On firm soil, secure them with ½-inch steel pipes or ¾-inch reinforcing rods. Drill a 1-inch hole about a foot from both ends of each tie. Position the ties; then drive pipes or rods through the ties and directly into the ground with a sledge hammer (wear safety goggles). Be sure to drive in the pipes so the ends are flush with the tops of the ties.

If the soil is not firm and the ties need extra support, you may want to

use anchor bolts set in concrete footings. For information on constructing footings, see the facing page.

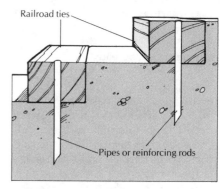

Secure railroad-tie risers by driving pipes or rods into ground through holes drilled in ties.

Installing treads. Once you've set the risers, you can add any one of several treads. One simple option is to plant the soil portion of the treads with grass or dichondra.

You can also choose masonry treads — poured concrete, tile, stone, or brick (see pages 140–145 for installation methods). Brick-in-sand treads look especially handsome with railroad-tie risers. Install these in the same basic way you would a brick-in-sand patio paving. Excavate the tread area enough to accommodate the bricks plus a 2-inch bed of sand. Add sand, and tamp and level it. Then set the bricks, tapping them into place with the handle of a mallet. Brush sand into the joints, and wet down the joints with a fine spray from a garden hose to settle the sand.

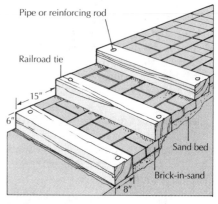

Brick-in-sand treads complement railroad-tie risers.

Constructing masonry walls

When you want to build a wall that will last a lifetime, build it out of masonry — concrete block, brick, or stone. Your options in material, design, and location are extensive; for help in making your decisions, see pages 62–63.

In this section you'll find instructions on how to build masonry walls. The instructions apply equally well to such projects as planters, borders, and barbecues.

Many localities require permits for building freestanding masonry walls more than 3 feet high. You may even have to have your project designed by an engineer. The following discussion applies only to walls up to 3 feet high; if you're planning a higher wall, check with your building department. They'll give you information on footings and the kinds of reinforcement to install. They can also tell you if you need an engineer's help.

For more information on working with masonry, refer to the *Sunset* book *Basic Masonry Illustrated*.

BUILDING A FOOTING

Most masonry walls rest on an underground foundation, or footing, that supports and stabilizes the wall. Typically, footings are twice the width of the wall and at least as deep as the wall is wide; there are exceptions, so consult your local building code.

Use poured concrete for the footing of any concrete or mortared wall. The footing rests on a 6-inch gravel bed in a trench dug deep enough so the bottom of the footing will be below the frost line in your area. You may need to add reinforcing rods to the footing, so decide on the type of reinforcement you'll use (see pages 152–153) before you pour the concrete.

Digging the trench. Lay out the entire course of the wall, marking the corners with stakes. Outline a trench that's the same as the desired dimensions of the footing by building batterboards of equal height at each corner and stretching mason's lines between opposite batterboards. As you dig, the mason's lines will be a reference for checking trench's width and depth.

For firm soil, dig a straight-sided trench, level the bottom, and tamp it firmly. Shovel in the gravel base, making sure the top of the gravel layer lies below the frost line. To guide the screed, build a simple wood form (see below); if the soil is too soft to allow vertical sides in the trench, let the form extend down to the top of the gravel. You can use the technique for wood edgings to make a form, too.

Pouring concrete. Pour the concrete directly into the trench, tamping it with a shovel as you pour. Screed the surface with a piece of wood to make it flat and level. Before the concrete hardens, insert any vertical reinforcing rods you need.

Let the concrete cure by covering it with a plastic sheet for 3 days; then you can remove any forms and begin working on the wall. For more information on pouring concrete, see pages 142–143.

(Continued on next page)

POURING A CONCRETE FOOTING

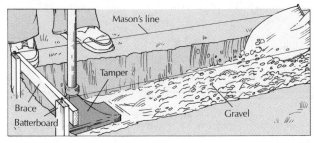

Prepare base for footing by leveling and tamping bottom of trench, and adding 6-inch layer of gravel. Mason's lines tied to batterboards at both ends of trench mark outline for digging and also act as guides to measure depth of trench.

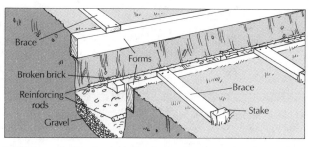

Build forms for footing by lining both sides of trench with 2-inch-thick lumber, using stakes and braces to hold forms in position. Make sure forms are level. Set any reinforcing rods on broken bricks or other rubble.

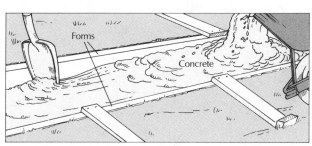

Pour concrete into forms oiled with motor oil; tamp firmly with a shovel, running it up and down along forms to eliminate voids. Work from one end. To allow for screeding, be sure not to overfill form.

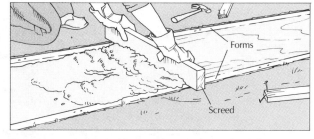

Screed concrete level with top of forms, using a piece of wood. Zigzag screed from one end to the other, striking off high spots and filling hollows. Insert any required vertical reinforcing rods into concrete.

...Constructing masonry walls

BUILDING A BLOCK WALL

The large size of concrete blocks makes wall-building a rapid process. Blocks are available in many shapes and sizes, though usually you can make a freestanding wall of just one kind. Your block work has to be precise, so base the overall dimensions of your project on the size of the block you'll use.

You use the same mortar for concrete blocks that's used for bricks. For extra strength, you can fill the blocks' hollow cores with steel reinforcing rods and grout. Check with local building authorities about required reinforcing.

Below are the steps you'll need to follow for building and reinforcing a concrete block wall.

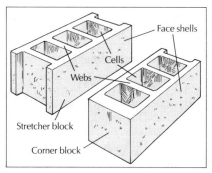

Standard concrete blocks—8 by 8 by 16—make for rapid wall construction.

Building tips

To build the concrete footing for the wall, follow the directions on page 151. Be sure to put in any required steel reinforcing rods for the footing or wall as you build.

When the footing has cured, fit a dry course of blocks on the footing; allow ⅜-inch joints between blocks for mortar. Mark the position of each block and set it aside. Then mix the mortar (see page 154).

The building process, shown below, involves building up leads at either end and filling in each course with the remaining blocks. If you're adding reinforcement, you'll do that work at the same time.

Three ways to reinforce walls

It's a good idea to reinforce concrete block walls, especially if they'll be exposed to strong winds or the danger of impact from a car. You can use vertical or horizontal reinforcing rods, or pilasters.

STEPS IN BUILDING A BLOCK WALL

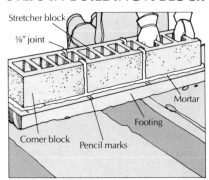

Set blocks into mortar spread 2 inches thick and long enough for 3 blocks. Allow ⅜-inch joints. Tap blocks firmly and check for level.

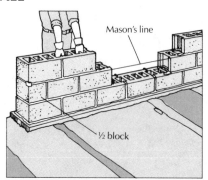

Build up leads at ends with corner blocks first. Use ½ block to start each even-numbered course; mason's line keeps blocks straight.

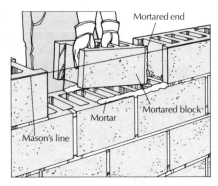

Fill in between leads, mortaring one end of each block. Apply ribbons of mortar to blocks below. Place mortared end against last block set.

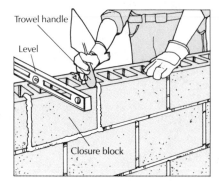

Mortar ends of closure block and all edges of opening; set block in place. To embed block, tap firmly with handle of trowel as you check with level.

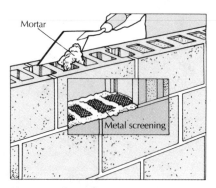

Place ¼-inch metal screening before mortaring and laying if extra reinforcing is required. Fill cells with mortar; smooth with trowel.

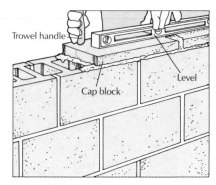

Set cap blocks on ribbons of mortar spread along web surfaces of top course of blocks to make decorative finish. Tap into place and level.

Vertical reinforcing rods. Handy for strengthening a block wall, vertical rods are tied with wire to short rods set in the concrete footing before any blocks are mortared. When you're fitting the dry course, check to make sure the vertical rods will pass through the cells in the blocks. After the blocks are mortared in place, pour grout (a runny mortar made with extra water) into the cells with the rods for extra strength.

Horizontal reinforcing rods. Horizontal rods are laid in bond-beam blocks (blocks with cutaway webs). Use rows of bond-beam blocks with steel reinforcing at various levels in the wall and at the top of the wall. Wherever horizontal rods cross vertical rods, tie them together with wire for extra strength.

At the top of a wall, bond-beam blocks, reinforcing rods, and grout

poured into the blocks substantially increase the strength of the wall. Together they form a unit which acts as a large reinforcing beam.

Pilasters. Square columns partly offset in block walls help keep long walls from tipping. Make pilasters of full and half-width blocks, overlapping successive courses for greatest bonding strength (see below).

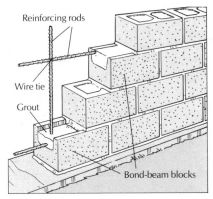

Vertical and horizontal steel reinforcing rods strengthen block wall. Tie rods at joints with wire.

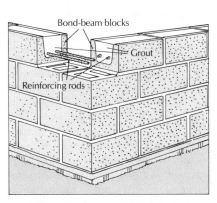

Bond-beam blocks cap wall. Steel reinforcing rods and grout act like solid beam to strengthen wall.

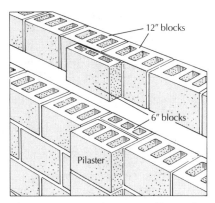

Pilasters—square columns in wall—made of 6 and 12-inch blocks offset in wall keep long wall from tipping.

(Continued on next page)

Stone veneer on a block wall

Applying stone veneer to an ordinary concrete block wall is a good way to dress it up. The resulting wall looks like a stone wall, but it's accomplished with much less labor and expense. You can veneer either a new block wall or an existing one.

Placing the wall ties. If you're constructing a new wall, first pour the footing (see page 151); then build the wall according to the instructions. As you build, place noncorrosive metal wall ties in the mortar joints in every other row of blocks and space them 2 to 3 feet apart.

For an existing block wall, you'll need to insert wall ties in the wall. Use masonry nails, screws in fiber plugs, or a stud gun, spacing the ties every 2 to 3 square feet.

Attaching stones. Attach the stones to the core wall using mortar. Bend as many of the wall ties as possible into joints between the stones. As you build, slush fill the spaces between the wall and stones with soupy, but not runny mortar, filling the spaces completely.

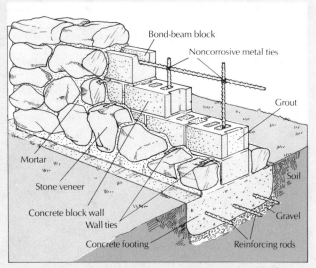

Stone veneer on concrete block gives rugged appearance to wall. Mortar and metal wall ties hold stones in place.

...Constructing masonry walls

BUILDING A BRICK WALL

Though you can build brick walls in many shapes and sizes, the easiest to build is a straight, freestanding one. The instructions that follow are for a wall up to 3 feet high. Since walls more than a foot high must usually be two bricks thick, the wall is built in two tiers. In effect, it's two 4-inch-thick walls built side by side and connected by bricks laid crosswise to give support to the two half-walls.

This wall is built on the common bond pattern. Headers (bricks running perpendicular to the wall's length) and stretchers (bricks running parallel to the wall's length) are combined in a particular pattern in each course, or layer, of bricks. In this wall, header courses act as reinforcement. Usually, you don't need steel reinforcing for low walls, but it's a good idea to check with your building department for any exceptions.

If your wall will turn corners, be sure to read the instructions for building corners on the facing page before you start.

Getting ready to work. Before you begin, distribute the bricks in several stacks along the job site. This will save you time later and will help you develop a rhythm to your bricklaying. Unless the bricks are already damp, hose them down several hours before beginning work. Dampening prevents the bricks from absorbing too much moisture from the mortar.

Working with mortar. Mortar is the bonding agent that holds masonry units together and seals out water. You can mix mortar from bulk materials or purchase it dry by the bag. Though recipes vary with the job, the most common formula is 1 part Portland cement, ½ to 1¼ parts hydrated lime, 6 parts clean sand, and water as required. Basically, mortar should be stiff enough not to drip, yet wet enough to stick; since lime weakens mortar, use only enough to ensure workability. Mix only the amount you can use in an hour. Keep a hose or bucket of water handy for rinsing your tools occasionally as you work.

Applying mortar correctly takes some practice. To apply a mortar bed along a course of bricks, scoop up some mortar with a mason's trowel. Starting with your arm extended, bring the trowel back toward you, rotating it as you go and depositing a bed of mortar about an inch thick, one brick wide, and 3 or 4 bricks long. Masons call this "throwing a line."

Once the line is thrown, furrow it down the middle with the trowel tip, using a stippling motion. Take care to just divide the mortar; don't scrape it toward you. This furrow ensures that the bricks will be evenly bedded and that excess mortar will be squeezed out to either side, where it's easy to

LAYING A BRICK WALL

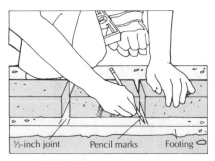

Lay a dry course of bricks along chalk line outlining edge of wall. Allow ½ inch for joints, marking spaces on footing with a pencil.

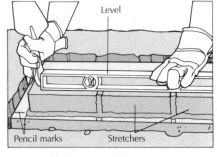

Lay first 3 bricks on mortar bed spread on footing. Level; then tap bricks into place with trowel handle. Check joint thickness.

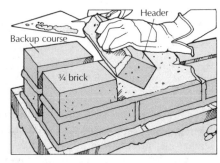

Begin header course by cutting two ¾ bricks and mortaring them in place. Apply mortar and lay 4 headers across width of wall.

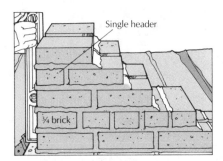

Finish lead using stretchers (note 1 header at start of fourth row) until lead is 5 courses high. Then build lead up at other end.

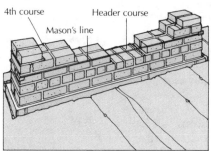

Fill in between leads, keeping mason's line stretched between leads flush with top of brick course being laid. Lay bricks from both ends to center.

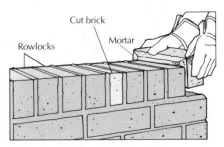

Cap top of wall with headers laid on edge (rowlocks). Spread mortar on top course and on each brick; set cut brick in from end.

trim. After you've laid the first brick of each course, be sure to apply mortar to one end of all subsequent bricks before you place them.

Laying a dry course. To begin building, snap a chalk line to mark the location of the wall's outer edge on the footing. Be sure the wall is centered on the footing. Lay a single dry (unmortared) course of stretcher bricks along the chalk line the full length of the wall, allowing ½-inch spaces for mortar joints. With a pencil, mark the joints directly on the footing as shown on the facing page. Remove the bricks. (Note: If the wall has corners, lay these first as shown below.)

Laying the first bricks. Spread mortar along the footing and lay the first brick. Mortar one end of the second and third bricks and set them in place, using the pencil marks as guides. Check that the bricks are level and tap them gently into place with the handle of the trowel.

Beginning the backup course. Lay a course of three backup bricks alongside the three bricks already in place. (There's no need to mortar the joint between the courses.) Make sure that the courses are at the same height and that the wall's overall width equals the length of one brick laid across it.

Beginning the header course. You'll need to cut two ¾ bricks. Using a brickset, score the bricks on all sides by tapping on the handle of the brickset with a soft-headed steel hammer. Cut the bricks along the scoring with a sharp blow to the brickset.

Use the ¾ bricks to begin the first header course. Mortar them in place. Applying mortar as shown on the facing page, lay four header bricks across the width of the wall. Finish the joints as you lay the bricks (see the instructions at right).

Completing the lead. Continue laying bricks until the lead is five courses high and looks like steps. Note that the fourth course begins with a single header rather than two ¾ bricks. Check to see that all surfaces are straight, level, and plumb. Build

another lead at the other end of the footing, following the same procedure.

Filling in between leads. Stretch a mason's line between the leads, and begin laying bricks from both ends toward the middle, course by course. Keep the line ¹⁄₁₆ inch away from the bricks and flush with the top edges of the course being laid. Double check the bricks with a straightedge since the line will sag if the wall is very long.

Closing the top course. Mortar both ends of the closure, or last, brick, and insert it straight down. To build the wall higher, build new five-course leads and fill in between them. Check often with a straightedge and level.

Planning and setting the cap. Lay a dry course of headers on edge (called rowlocks), allowing space for mortar joints. If the last brick overhangs the end of the wall, mark it and cut off the excess. Place it three or four bricks from the end where it will be less noticeable. Remove the bricks, spread mortar along the top of the wall, and begin laying the bricks. Thoroughly mortar the face of each brick and keep a careful check on joint thickness as you go.

Finishing joints. The mortar in the joints is ready to finish when pressing on it with your thumb leaves a slight indentation. Tool (finish) the joints as you go before the mortar hardens. Run a jointer or a steel pipe along the horizontal joints first. Then draw the tool along the vertical ones. Slide a trowel along the wall to remove excess mortar. When the mortar is well set, clean the entire wall with a stiff brush.

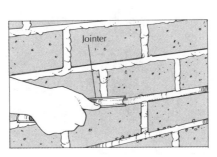

Run jointer along thumbprint-hard mortar to compact and smooth it. Do horizontal, then vertical joints.

Building corners

To build a brick wall with corners, you'll use the same techniques as for a straight wall. After laying out square corners, you begin by building up the corner leads. You'll fill in between the leads as described at left.

Snap chalk lines on the footing for the wall's outer edges. To make sure the corners are square, use the 3-4-5 rule (see page 157).

After making a dry run for the entire wall, spread mortar and lay the first brick exactly in the corner, lining it up with the chalk lines. Then lay two bricks on each arm of the wall, making sure they're straight and level. Spread mortar and lay the backup course in the same way (see below). Don't disrupt the outer course and don't mortar the joints between the courses.

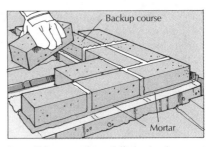

Spread mortar and carefully lay backup course of bricks alongside outer ones.

Check for level; then start the header course. Cut two bricks into ¾ and ¼ closure pieces. Lay them as shown below and finish the lead header course. Complete the lead with three stretcher courses, alternating the position of the corner bricks. Then you're ready to finish the wall between the leads.

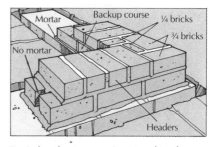

Begin header course using ¼ and ¾ closure bricks at corner; complete lead course.

(Continued on next page)

...Constructing masonry walls

BUILDING A DRY STONE WALL

Building a dry stone wall is laborious and demanding, but if you work carefully, you can build a good-looking wall that will grace your garden. If you're considering a stone wall higher than 3 feet, or if you're faced with unstable soil conditions, be sure to consult a landscape architect and your building department.

Bonding in stone walls

In a dry stone wall, the stones hold each other in place by weight and friction. Though construction is simple, you must build with care to ensure a long-standing wall.

To help secure the wall, batter (slope) both faces inward. The amount of slope required depends on the size and purpose of the wall and the shape of the stones. A good rule is 1 inch of batter for every 2 feet of rise, but this can vary with the shape of the stones. Check with your landscape architect, building department, or stone supplier to be sure. Unless your stones are very flat and rectangular, plan on a battered wall no higher than it is thick at the base.

Make a tapered batter gauge from lumber or plywood cut so that the taper matches the desired batter of the wall (see the illustration below). Use it to check your work as you go. Use a level to keep the outer edge of the gauge vertical while you're checking.

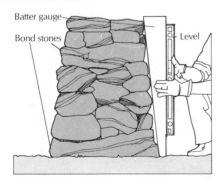

Use batter gauge to give wall proper inward slope as you build. Level keeps outer edge of gauge vertical.

Building the wall

Place your stones near the site for convenience while you're building the wall. Use the largest stones for the foundation course. Reserve longer ones for bond stones—long stones that run the entire width of the wall. Set aside broad, flat stones to use for the top of the wall.

Foundation course. Begin by laying the foundation stones in a trench about 6 inches deep. First, place a bond stone at the end; then start the two face courses at either edge of the trench. Choose whole, well-shaped stones for the face courses. Fill in the space between the face courses with tightly packed rubble (broken pieces of stone) as shown below.

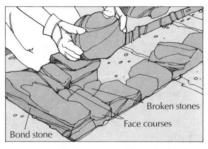

Place bond stones at ends of trench; lay face courses and fill in with rubble.

Second course. To build the second course, lay stones on top of the first course, being sure not to line up vertical joints. Select stones that will fit together solidly. Tilt the stones of each face inward toward each other. Use the batter gauge and level on the faces and ends of the wall to maintain proper slope.

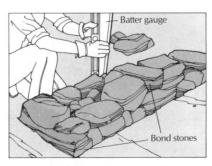

Lay courses, adding bond stones. Check inward slope with batter gauge as you build up courses.

Place bond stones every 5 to 10 square feet to tie the faces of the wall together. Again, pack the center with rubble and small stones.

Upper courses. Continue in the same manner, staggering the vertical joints from course to course and maintaining the inward slope so gravity will help hold the wall together. Use small stones to fill any gaps, tapping them in with a soft-headed steel hammer (see illustration below). Don't overdo it — driving them in too far will weaken the structure and may dislodge stones you've already set.

Using soft-headed hammer, tap small stones into gaps in wall. Don't drive them in too far or larger stones may be dislodged.

Top course. Finish the top, using as many flat, broad stones as possible. If you live in an area with severe freezing, you may want to mortar the cap (see inset in drawing below). This will allow water to drain off the wall and help prevent ice from forming between the stones and pushing them apart.

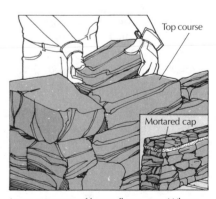

Lay top course of large, flat stones. Where winters are severe, mortar top stones to prevent ice damage.

Building a deck

A wood deck makes a good-looking and versatile floor for your garden. Described on the following pages are the three steps in building a simple, low-level deck attached to a house wall — installing the foundation, building the substructure, and attaching the decking. For instructions on building a deck with more complex features, see the *Sunset* book *How to Plan & Build Decks*. If you want to build a hillside or high-level deck, or if your site has unstable soil, you should probably consult a professional.

Plan your deck carefully before you begin building, and make sure the site is properly graded and has good drainage (see pages 130-133).

The basic parts of a deck are the foundation, the substructure, and the surface decking. The foundation, consisting of concrete footings and piers, supports a substructure of posts, beams, and joists. The substructure can be freestanding or, like the one shown on these pages, attached to a wall of your house. Decking is nailed over the substructure to form the finished floor. For help in designing your deck, see pages 66–67.

Installing the foundation

The foundation of a deck consists of footings and piers. Concrete footings must be poured on the spot. Piers can be poured along with their footings or purchased at a building supply center and set into place.

Laying out footings. From your plans, you'll know how many footings you need and how far apart you must place them. Now you're ready to lay out the deck perimeter and footing locations on the ground. Following the instructions below, locate the corners first, then the deck outline, and finally the footings, being sure to get lines straight and corners square.

First, attach a ledger to the side of the house (see "Attaching the ledger," page 158). Then use the 3-4-5 rule, as follows, to lay out square corners.

Drive one nail into the end of the ledger to mark the corner where the deck will meet the house, and another

nail into the ledger exactly 3 feet away from the first nail. Hook the end of a steel tape measure over each nail. Have a helper pull out both tapes until the 4-foot mark on the tape attached to the corner nail intersects the 5-foot mark on the other tape. Drive a stake into the ground at this point. (This triangulation method works in any multiple of 3-4-5.)

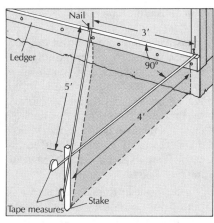

Use 3-4-5 method to lay out square corners.

To locate the outside corner of the deck, extend the staked line to the desired deck width and drive in another stake. Repeat the entire process at the other end of the ledger.

Build batterboards about 18 inches outside each corner stake. Level the tops with each other and with the top of the ledger, using a mason's line and line level.

To mark the deck's sides, run mason's line from the nail at one end of the ledger to the opposite batterboard, making sure the line passes directly over the corner stake. Use the same method to mark the other side. Mark the outside edge of the deck with mason's line attached to opposite batterboards.

Measure the diagonal distance between opposite corners (forming an X) and adjust the two diagonal lines until the distances are equal. Your deck outline now has square corners.

To locate corner footings, use a plumb bob or level to plumb down from the intersections of the mason's lines. Measure along the lines and plumb down to locate any other footings required by your design.

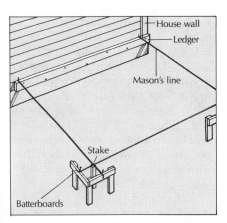

Use batterboards to help locate deck edges and footings.

Constructing footings. Footings should be about twice the width of the piers they'll support. Dig holes for the footings down to solid ground, allowing for the footing to extend below the frost line in your area.

To make the footings, you can use dry-mix or transit-mix concrete, or you can mix your own, using 1 part cement, 2 parts clean sand, and 3 parts gravel. Add water, a little at a time, as you mix until the concrete is plastic, but not runny. Then fill the holes with fresh concrete to within 6 inches of ground level.

Positioning piers. Use ready-made piers with wood nailing blocks as shown below. Soak them well with a hose before placing them; position them on top of the footings 5 to 10 minutes after the footings have been poured. Then check for level and adjust, if necessary.

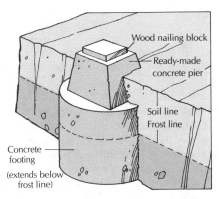

Position ready-made pier with nailing block on concrete footing 5 to 10 minutes after pouring footing.

(Continued on next page)

...Building a deck

Building the substructure

When you're attaching the deck to the wall of your house, you'll need to install a ledger to support the joists on one side of the deck. Then you can build the rest of the substructure — supporting posts, beam, and joists. (For information on an alternate post-and-beam construction method that doesn't require joists, see *Sunset's Garden & Patio Building Book.*)

Attaching the ledger. The most secure way to attach a deck to a house is to use a 2 by 4 or 2 by 6 ledger fastened to the wall studs or the floor framing. Wall studs are usually located on 16 or 24-inch centers. Floor framing members, often 2 by 10s, generally have about 1½ inches of subflooring and flooring on top of them. About 6 inches below the interior floor level you should find the approximate center of a framing header to which you can anchor your ledger. A window sill makes a handy reference point for positioning the ledger (see the illustration below).

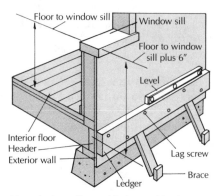

Use window sill as guide for positioning ledger.

To attach the ledger to a wall made of wood (for a masonry wall, see the next paragraph), brace the ledger in position and temporarily nail once at the ledger's approximate center. Level the ledger with a carpenter's level and temporarily nail at both ends. Drill holes for the lag screws through the ledger and into the floor frame header. Screw the ledger in place and remove the braces.

If the house wall is made of masonry, first drill holes in the ledger for lag bolts. Brace and level the led-

ger on the wall and mark the holes' locations. Remove the ledger, drill holes for expansion shields, and insert shields in the holes. Then brace the ledger and screw it into place.

You must cover the ledger with galvanized metal or aluminum flashing to protect it from water damage. Nail the flashing in position with galvanized nails long enough to penetrate at least 1 inch into the wall studs or other structural members.

Measuring and setting posts. Set 4 by 4 wood posts in place temporarily and use a mason's line and line level to mark each post even with the top of the ledger. From this mark, subtract the thickness of the beam that will rest on top of it and make a new mark. Take down the posts and cut them to the correctly marked height (see "Measuring post height," page 160).

Set posts upright on the piers and plumb them carefully. (Tack on temporary braces to steady the posts while you plumb them.) Then toenail the posts to the nailing blocks.

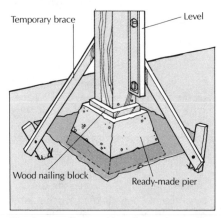

Plumb two adjacent sides of post; then nail post to pier.

Securing the beam. Position the beam across the tops of the posts; use a straight 2 by 4 and a level to make sure it's level with the ledger. Adjust by shimming the posts with wood shingles. (In some cases, you may need to allow a slight outward slope for drainage.)

Next, fasten the beam to the posts. Toenailing, the simplest method, is probably sufficient for a ground-hugging deck. For a stronger deck, use

post caps, beam clips, or framing clips (many building codes require the use of these metal connectors).

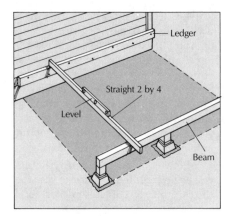

Use 2 by 4 to level beam with ledger; check at several locations.

Attaching joists. To attach joists to the ledger and beam, you can either toenail them, support them with a 1 by 2 cleat, or set them in metal joist hangers (the most secure method).

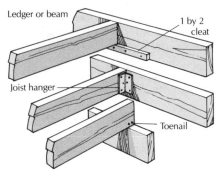

Connect joists by toenailing or using cleats or hangers.

Position a joist at each side of the deck. To make sure the joists are perpendicular to the ledger and the beam, use a carpenter's square or the 3-4-5 method (see page 157). Working from either outside joist, measure, set, and fasten the other joists, using the spacing specified in your local building code. You may have to set the last joist closer than planned to the outside joist so you don't exceed the maximum allowable joist spacing.

To prevent joists from twisting or bowing, brace them with wood spacers. A single row of spacers is usually sufficient for a 6 to 10-foot span; use a double row for 10 to 20-foot spans. Simply cut and fit them; then secure them by nailing to the joists. If joist spans are less than 6 feet, you can brace the joists by nailing solid boards across joist ends.

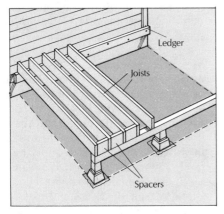

Position joists on ledger and beam; fasten and brace with spacers at ends.

Installing the decking

Placing, spacing, and nailing the decking is the final step in construction. If you plan to add steps, do so *before* nailing the decking (at right).

Arranging boards. To ensure that the pattern you've chosen for the decking will come out even, make a dry run first. Position, square, and nail the first board. Then lay out the rest of the boards, using a 16-penny common nail as a spacer (see inset, right), but don't nail the boards down yet. Depending on the space left at the end, increase or decrease the spacing between boards; use a different size nail or a wood spacer for the new measurement.

If the boards are too short to run the full length or width of the deck, position any joints directly over a joist. Stagger the joints so no two line up consecutively over one joist. To minimize cupping, place boards so the curved end grain faces down.

Nailing boards. To fasten decking, use galvanized ring or spiral shank nails. With 1½-inch decking, use 16-penny nails. To prevent board ends from splitting when you nail them, drill pilot holes slightly smaller than the diameter of the nails.

Nail decking boards at every joist. Use two nails for 2 by 4s and 2 by 6s; use three nails for 2 by 8s or wider. Finally, mark the uneven deck edges with a chalk line and trim the uneven edges with a power saw.

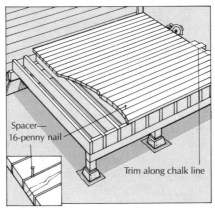

Space boards evenly and nail. Mark edge with chalk line; trim with power saw.

Adding wood steps

You'll need to build steps between the deck and the ground if your deck is more than a foot or so above ground level. Because wood steps must be connected to the deck's substructure, it's easiest to build them before you nail down the decking. Below are instructions for building two of the most common types of steps: open steps and closed steps.

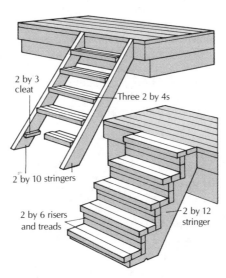

Top drawing shows open steps with cleats; at bottom are closed steps with notched stringers.

Before you can build your steps, you need to plan them carefully. For information on determining both the number of steps and their proper proportions, see page 54.

Make stringers from 2 by 10s or 2 by 12s and mark the tread or riser-tread pattern on them. Steps 4 feet wide or less need a stringer on each side; wider steps need a third stringer in the middle. Attach 2 by 3 cleats to open-step stringers; for notched stringers cut along riser-tread lines carefully.

Fasten the tops of the stringers to the deck's substructure using galvanized bolts or metal joist hangers as shown below. When you use bolts, the first tread is below the decking; with joist hangers, the first tread must be level with the decking (below left).

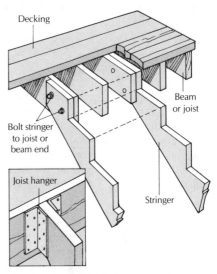

Attach stringers with bolts; or use joist hangers (see inset).

Anchor the lower ends of the stringers to wood nailing blocks embedded in concrete footings. Attach treads and risers.

Putting up an overhead

When you build an overhead structure for your garden, you have several options: it may be freestanding or attached to your house, and have open rafters or a roof of lath, glass or acrylic panels, reed mats, or cloth. Information on pages 68–69 will help you choose the design, materials, and construction method for your overhead. Before beginning any work, be sure you're familiar with any building code requirements that could affect your choices.

Here you'll find instructions for building a basic overhead — either freestanding or attached to the house — using rafters. You'll need to start with a concrete foundation that will support the posts. After you set the posts and, for an overhead attached to a house, affix the ledger, you add the beams, rafters, and, if you wish, roofing material.

Building the foundation

Unless your overhead will be attached to an existing deck, you'll need to construct a foundation of concrete footings poured in the ground. The supporting posts may be anchored either directly to the footings or to piers placed on top.

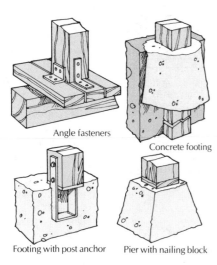

Angle fasteners

Concrete footing

Footing with post anchor   Pier with nailing block

A variety of post foundations are available for different building situations.

First, locate the footings where you want the posts to be. If your overhead spans an existing patio, you can set the posts on footings and piers located outside the edge of the patio. You can use ready-made piers on wet footings (see the instructions on pages 157–158), or pour footings and piers at the same time. Or you may have to break through existing paving, dig a hole, and pour new concrete footings and, if necessary, piers.

If you're installing a new concrete patio, pour footings and paving at the same time, embedding post anchors in the wet concrete (shown at upper left on the facing page).

If you're installing an overhead above a deck, you can use angle fasteners to attach posts directly to the deck. Make sure that a support member, such as a sturdy beam, is located directly underneath.

Installing a ledger

If you want to attach an overhead to your house, you must install a ledger. Usually made of a 2 by 4 or 2 by 6, a ledger is fastened to the house framing through the exterior wall with lag screws. If your eave line is high enough for adequate headroom, you can easily attach a ledger for an overhead to wall studs — or, in a two-story house, to floor framing (to locate floor framing, see "Attaching the ledger," page 158). Measure first to make sure there'll be enough room for rafters between the ledger and eave line.

If your house has wood siding, brace, temporarily nail, and level the ledger as for a deck (see page 158). Drill holes for lag screws, and screw the ledger to the wall, making sure you fasten it to studs. To attach a ledger to a masonry wall, see the instructions for ledgers on page 158.

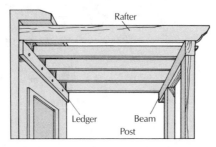

Rafter

Ledger   Beam
Post

Ledger supports rafters on overhead attached to house.

Setting posts

Overheads are usually supported by 4 by 4 posts. Choose posts of either decay-resistant heart redwood or cedar, or pressure-treated wood. You measure the posts for height, then plumb and set them in place on the piers.

Measuring post height. It's essential to measure post height accurately. For an overhead attached to the house, your guide is the top of the ledger. Set a post in place temporarily; plumb and brace it. Run a mason's line from the top of the ledger to the post, level with a line level, and mark the post. From this mark, subtract the thickness of the support beam you'll use and make a new mark as shown below. Repeat with all other posts; then take them down and cut them.

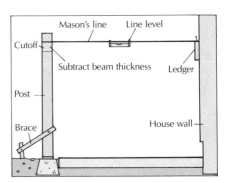

Mason's line   Line level

Cutoff

Subtract beam thickness

Post

Brace

Ledger

House wall

Stretch mason's line from ledger to post to measure post height; subtract thickness of beam.

For a freestanding overhead, mark the desired height on one post, use a mason's line and line level to mark the other posts at the same height, and cut them to size.

Attaching posts. Set each post upright on its footing or pier and position it in the post anchor. Check for plumb using a level on two adjacent sides; then nail the post to the anchor. Making sure the post is still plumb, nail temporary braces to it.

Attaching beams & rafters

To anchor beams securely in place, use post caps, beam clips, or framing

BUILDING A FREESTANDING OVERHEAD

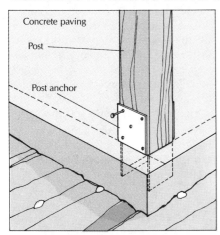

Set post in post anchor embedded in concrete, after cutting post to length and attaching post cap at top; nail post securely through holes in post anchor.

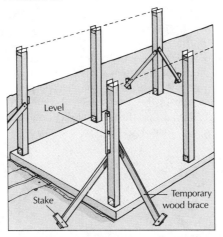

Plumb posts with level on two adjacent sides; secure with temporary 1 by 3 braces nailed to stakes driven into ground. Check post alignment.

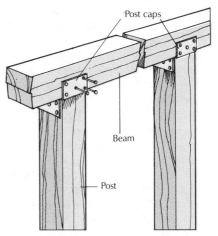

Position beam on top of posts. Check that beam is level and posts are vertical; nail post caps to beam. Shim posts, if necessary, for a tight fit.

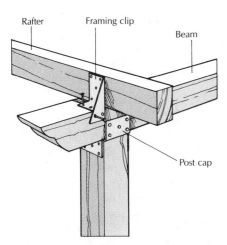

Set rafter on top of beam and secure with framing clip. If span is great, install spacers between rafters as for deck joists (see drawing on page 159).

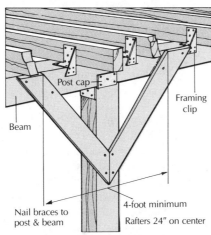

Nail or bolt braces (1 by 4s or 1 by 6s with ends cut at 45°) to beams and posts. Ends of braces should be at least 2 feet from post caps.

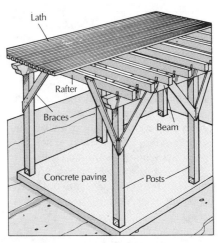

Nail lath 1 by 2s or 2 by 2s to rafters, spacing them to achieve desired amount of shade. Or attach other roofing material of your choice.

clips. Before nailing the beams, check that they're level and that the posts are vertical. If the ends of the posts don't fit tightly against the beam, shim the posts with wood shingles—just wedge the shingles in place between the beam and post cap, check the beam for level, and fasten the beam securely.

To attach rafters to the top of a beam, either toenail them or, for a sturdier connection, use metal framing clips as shown above. Rafters can also be notched to fit over beams. If you're using a ledger, toenail rafters to the top

of the ledger or attach them to the ledger with joist hangers.

For overheads less than 12 feet high, normally only outside posts on unattached sides need braces (see above). Check with your building department for any exceptions.

Adding a roof

You can simply let the rafters act as a roof for your overhead, or, if you prefer, use lath, or panels of shade cloth, woven reed, or some other material.

Wood lath 1 by 2s or 2 by 2s, as shown above, can be spaced to give just the right amount of shade. Or you can nail on lath in a grid pattern for a roof with a lattice effect. If you want to build a roof with another material, see Sunset's *How to Build Patio Roofs* or *Garden & Patio Building Book*.

Putting up a fence

The key to success in building a fence is careful planning. Before you begin construction, you'll need to choose the style, materials, and location for your fence. Since local codes and ordinances can influence those decisions, be sure to check with your building department. For tips on planning, see pages 64–65.

The frame of a basic fence consists of vertical posts supporting horizontal rails (sometimes called stringers) which, in turn, support siding. On the following pages you'll find instructions on the three basic stages in fence building—plotting the fence line, installing the posts, and attaching the rails and siding. Tips on applying the finish are also included.

PLOTTING THE FENCE LINE

The first step in building your fence is to locate the exact course it will take, and mark the line with stakes and a mason's line. For a fence that's on or near a boundary line, it's wise to have a surveyor or civil engineer lay out the corner stakes unless you're absolutely positive where the property line is. Following are directions for plotting both a straight fence and one with right-angle corners.

Plotting a straight fence

Measure the desired length of the fence line and mark each end or corner post location with a solidly driven stake. Then tie a mason's line tightly between the stakes.

To locate the remaining posts, measure along the line and mark post centers on it with chalk. (Usually, posts are set 4 to 8 feet apart, depending on the design of the fence.) Using a level or plumb bob, transfer each mark to the ground and drive in a stake to mark the post location.

Plotting a right angle corner

Use the 3-4-5 measuring method described in this section if your fence

layout calls for a corner that forms an exact 90° angle.

Establish the first fence line (point A to point B), following the directions for plotting a straight fence. Then locate the second fence line (point B to point C) roughly perpendicular to the first, substituting a batterboard for the end stake beyond point C, as shown below.

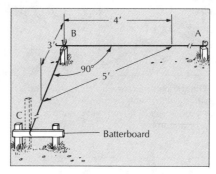
Use 3-4-5 rule to lay out a corner that's exactly 90°.

On the first fence line, measure 4 feet from corner stake B and mark the mason's line with chalk. Then mark the second fence line 3 feet from corner stake B.

Adjust the second fence line on the batterboard until the diagonal measurement between the two marks equals 5 feet—the two lines will then form a 90° angle—and mark a spot on the ground directly beneath the point where the mason's line is tied to the batterboard.

Remove the batterboard and retie the mason's line to a stake driven at the marked spot, being careful not to move the mason's line out of alignment. Finally, locate the remaining posts as described for plotting a straight fence.

INSTALLING FENCE POSTS

Post installation—setting and aligning posts—is the most important part of fence building. Posts must be set firmly in the ground, aligned vertically ("plumb") in their holes, and located exactly on the line, or you'll encounter difficulties when adding rails and siding materials.

The process of installing posts can be divided into three steps: (1) digging postholes; (2) setting posts; and (3) aligning posts. Steps 2 and 3 are in fact done simultaneously. Though it's easier with two people—one to hold and align the post while the other fills the hole with concrete or earth and gravel—you can do the job yourself.

There are a number of ways to install posts; two of the most commonly accepted methods are described and illustrated here.

Digging postholes

The size of the postholes you dig depends on the height and weight of your fence, the stresses it must withstand, and the soil conditions along the fence line. The tools you use to dig the holes will depend on the number of postholes and the type of soil.

Determining posthole size. For fences less than 3 feet high, sink your line posts at least 18 inches into the ground. For most fences between 3 and 6 feet high, set line posts at least 2 feet deep. End posts and gate posts need to be stronger and should be set 12 inches deeper than the line posts.

Fences taller than 6 feet or fences subject to unusual stress (strong winds, unstable soil, or heavy siding) should have one-third of their post length in the ground and set in concrete.

To prevent fence posts from settling, dig each hole deep enough so you can set the bottom of the post on a large, flat-topped stone or on 6 inches of well-tamped gravel. If you're building in an area where the ground freezes, posts should be sunk at least 12 inches below the frost line.

The diameter of a posthole should be 2½ to 3 times the width of a square post or the diameter of round posts (10 to 12 inches for a 4-inch post).

Selecting tools. The two most popular hand tools for digging postholes are the auger and the two-handled clamshell. The auger is best for loose soil, the clamshell for rocky or hard soil. If the soil is too rocky or hard to dig with these tools, use a digging bar or jack-hammer to break it up.

If you have more than six holes to dig and the earth isn't too rocky, a power digger will save you time and effort. Models that can be operated by one or two persons are usually available at tool rental shops; you'll find jackhammers there, too.

Setting posts

For strongest installation, set fence posts in concrete. If the soil is stable (not subject to frost heaving, sliding, or water saturation), you can set posts for lightweight or low fences (less than 3 feet high) in earth-and-gravel fill. The concrete or earth-and-gravel fill should be angled down from the post to ground level to divert water away from the post.

Though you can set posts with their tops at the exact height wanted, you'll find it easier to allow a few extra inches in height and then cut them down to the correct height later.

Setting posts in concrete. If this method is best for you, plan to work carefully to prevent concrete from creeping under the posts where it can retain moisture and speed decay.

To mix your own concrete, use 1 part (by volume) cement, 3 parts sand, and 5 parts gravel, adding water as needed. Keep the mix rather dry so earth from the side of the hole will not mix in and weaken the concrete. To save time and effort, you can make the concrete using bagged ready-mix. You'll need about one bag of mix for a 4-inch post set 2 feet deep.

Place a large and relatively flat-topped stone in the bottom of the hole. Fill in with gravel (about 6 inches) until it's level with the top of the stone. Set the post on the stone and shovel in 4 more inches of gravel, tamping it well with a 2 by 4. Plumb and align the post, using one of the methods described under "Aligning posts" at far right. Finish filling the hole with concrete, 2 to 3 inches at a time, tamping it in. Add another 1 to 2 inches of concrete aboveground, sloping it as shown for water runoff.

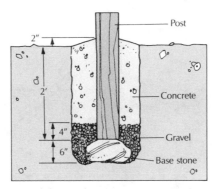
For stability, set fence posts in concrete.

Be sure to double check your post for plumb and for alignment. You can force the post into a new position for about 20 minutes after pouring the concrete. Wait at least 2 days before installing rails and siding.

Setting posts in earth-and-gravel fill. Set the base stone and post in the hole, shovel in about 6 inches of gravel, and plumb and align the post (see at right). Dampen the gravel and tamp it with a length of 2 by 4. Continue filling with a mixture of earth and gravel, dampening and tamping firmly every 2 to 3 inches. After the hole is filled and the top sloped, check the plumb and alignment of the post again.

To minimize side movement of posts set in earth and gravel, you can add rocks to the fill as you near ground level. Fill the voids with earth and tamp it well.

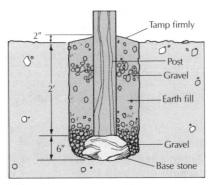
Tamp earth-and-gravel fill firmly around post.

Preventing frost damage. In freezing climates, frost heave can be a major problem. When water in the ground freezes and expands, it can push a fence post right out of its hole. And

water that freezes and expands inside of wood posts can crack the concrete around them.

To minimize damage from frost heave, use 16-penny common nails to stud the sides of the post that will be below the frost line. First make sure the posthole extends 12 inches below the frost line. Then set the post in gravel, and plumb and align it. Fill the hole with concrete up to the frost line, as shown below, and tamp well. (The nails will embed in the concrete, increasing resistance to frost heave.)

Next, add earth fill to within 6 inches of the surface and tamp. Fill the hole with concrete, sloping the top so water will run away from the post.

To prevent concrete from cracking when wet posts freeze, you can cut shingles to the post width, coat them with motor oil, and temporarily nail them around the post before you set the post. When the concrete has set, pull out the shingles and seal the open spaces with caulking or tar (see below).

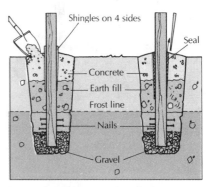
Prevent frost damage with nails driven into posts and tarred or caulked joints.

Aligning posts

The most critical step in post installation is aligning the posts so they're exactly vertical and in a straight line. If you have a helper, the corner post or end post method, described on the next page, is a good one to use for sections of fence less than 100 feet long. If you're working alone, you can use the bracing method, also described on the next page.

(Continued on next page)

...Putting up a fence

Corner or end post method. Begin with two corner or end posts. Position them with their faces in flat alignment, plumb them with a level, and set them permanently.

Nail a 2-inch-long 1 by 2 spacer block to each corner or end post about 1 foot above the ground, as shown below. (The blocks will keep the intermediate posts from touching the line and throwing it out of alignment.) Stretch and tie a mason's line between the posts, making sure the blocks are between the line and the posts.

With a helper, set and align the intermediate posts so their faces are exactly the thickness of a spacer block away from the line. (Measure by holding a block against each post.) Before and after filling the hole, check each post for plumb and alignment, using a level on two adjacent faces. Make any needed adjustments before the concrete hardens.

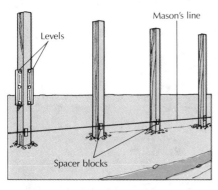

Use spacer blocks and levels to align posts.

Bracing method. You can set fence posts without a helper if you use braces to hold them in position while you fill the holes with concrete or earth-and-gravel fill.

Make the braces from 6-foot lengths of 1 by 4s and stakes. To position them, drive stakes into the ground and attach the braces so they can be lifted and nailed to adjacent sides of the posts, as shown at the top of the next column. Use only one nail to attach each brace to the stake so the brace pivots freely. Plumb and align each post; then nail the braces to it to hold the post in position while you carefully fill the hole.

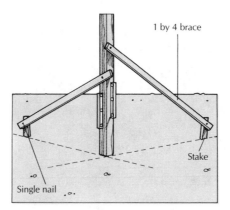

Temporary braces hold post in alignment until hole is filled.

Post height adjustment

If you didn't set the tops of your posts at the finished height, now is the time to cut them. Use a combination square to mark the height you want on all four sides of an end post. Tie a mason's line to the post at your mark and stretch the line to the other end post if it's less than 35 feet away. If it's farther, use an intermediate post.

Hang a line level in the middle of the line. Have a helper pull the line tight and move the end of the line up or down the post until the line is level. Mark this point on the post, tie the line to it, and mark the intervening posts where the line touches them.

Using a combination square, extend the mark around all four sides of each post as a guide for cutting. Continue this process until all posts are marked. Cut the posts at the marks, using a crosscut or power saw.

ATTACHING RAILS & SIDING

Once the fence posts are set and aligned, the hardest part of your fence building is over. The next step is to carefully attach the rails and siding to the posts. If the rails are not attached firmly and squarely to the posts, all of your painstaking work in aligning the posts will be wasted.

Remember that posts set in concrete should be left for at least 2 days before you attach rails and siding. You may also have to treat or prime rails

and siding before attaching them (see "Applying the finish," facing page).

Rails

This part of the framework ties the fence together and must support the weight of the siding. Most fence designs require at least two rails. If the rails are set on edge, siding is less likely to sag. This is particularly important with heavy siding, and if it's especially heavy, you may need to add a third rail or install a wood or masonry support under the center of the bottom rail.

Rails can either be butted between the posts or lapped across the tops or sides of the posts.

Butted rails. In this method, you cut rails to fit snugly between posts. You can attach them to the posts with fence brackets or angle brackets, or by toenailing them. If you toenail the rails, nail 2 by 4 cleats to the post first to help support the rails. Make sure rails are level before fastening them.

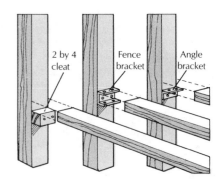

Attach butted rails to fence posts with cleats or brackets.

Lapped rails. These rails are the easiest to install and are most often used with vertical board fences. Simply lap rails across the tops or sides of the posts. Be sure the rails are long enough to span at least three posts, and stagger the joints of top and bottom rails.

Level the rails and nail them to the posts with hot-dipped galvanized common or box nails that are at least three times as long as the thickness of the rails. If rails lapped on tops of posts meet at a corner, miter the ends. If rails meet on an intermediate post, butt the ends at the middle of the post.

Siding

Adding siding is the easiest part of building your fence, but don't be tempted to start nailing before you check to see that the framework is just right. If it isn't, the siding will make any problem all too apparent.

In the following section, you'll find general instructions for attaching boards, pickets, slats, and panels.

Vertical board siding. Though there are several ways to attach board siding to a frame, the simplest method is to nail vertical boards to the top and bottom rails. To be sure boards are aligned vertically, use a level to check each board for plumb before nailing it.

To keep the siding at an even height, first make sure all the boards are exactly the same length. Then stretch mason's line tightly along the fence where you want the boards to end; check the line with a level. Align the bottom of each board with the line, or you can nail a temporary guide to the posts (see "Pickets" below).

Leave a slight gap between boards, since they'll expand and contract with weather changes.

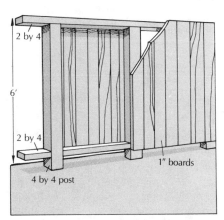

Nail vertical boards to top and bottom rails for a fence that's attractive on both sides.

Pickets. To keep picket bottoms aligned, use a temporary straightedge guide (as shown at top of next column)

or a mason's line and level. To keep spacing between pickets uniform, cut a slat the width of the desired gap and attach a woodblock cleat to the back of it. Use the cleat to hang the wood slat on the top rail of the fence beside the first picket. Move it along as you attach pickets for even spacing.

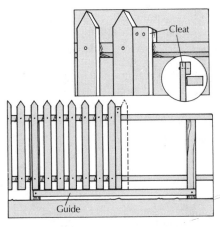

Align pickets using spacing guide between pickets on top rail, temporary straightedge to ensure pickets are even along bottom.

Slats for basketweave siding. Wood slats for a basketweave fence are usually 4 inches wide and from ¼ to ¾ inch thick. Vertical spacers are 1 by 1s or larger; the smaller the spacers are, the closer the weave.

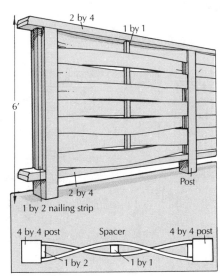

For basketweave siding, thread 1 by 1 spacer through slats, weaving it in from top before top rail is attached.

If your plans call for a horizontal basketweave design, complete the siding before you nail on the top rail. For a simple basketweave, nail 1 by 2 strips to both sides of each post as shown in the drawing at left below. Then nail the slats to the strips, alternating sides. Insert a 1 by 1 spacer strip, weaving it in between the slats from the top. Then you can attach the top rail.

Panels. If you're using wood, plastic, or glass panels for siding, you'll need a helper or two to lift the panels into position and hold them while you level and fasten them in place on the frame.

APPLYING THE FINISH

Unless you're making your fence entirely of decay-resistant heartwood, you'll probably need to treat the wood with water repellent before applying stain, bleach, or primer and paint. (See page 64 for information on finishes.) Rails and siding should be treated and/or primed (especially where they'll be in contact with other fence members) before you attach them to the posts. Paint, stain, or bleach the entire fence after it's completed.

Before applying any finish, make sure the surface is clean and dry. If you've used green (unseasoned) lumber in your fence, allow 3 weeks to a month seasoning (drying) time before painting or staining. If the wood has been pretreated with water repellent, wait 60 days after the treatment before applying a bleach or stain.

Paints and stains can be applied with a brush, roller (on large, flat surfaces), or spray gun. (If you use a spray gun, cover nearby plants and shrubs with plastic sheeting to protect them from overspray.) Because heat may create drying problems and winds can stir up dust, leading to marred or roughened surfaces, try to paint on a cool, windless day. Apply bleach in one or two coats with a thick brush, taking care to avoid drip or lap marks. For all finishes, follow the manufacturer's application directions.

Building a gate

Before you build your gate, take the time to plan it carefully so both the design and materials will fit with your fence. For information on gate design and materials, refer to pages 64–65.

On this page are directions for building a basic wood gate with a rectangular frame of 2 by 4s and a diagonal 2 by 4 brace. Though the illustrations show board siding, you can use whatever siding complements your fence. To build a basic gate, you must set and align the gate posts, build the frame, add siding, hang the gate, and attach the latch. You'll also need to add a gate stop to keep the gate from swinging past its closed position.

Unless you're using existing posts, your first job is to set the gate posts. These must be set deeper into the ground than ordinary fence posts because of the added stress placed on them (see below). The spacing of the posts determines the width of the gate.

Measure the distance between the gate posts at both top and bottom. (If it varies greatly, you'll have to straighten the posts, if possible, or else build a lopsided gate to fit.) The gate frame width should allow at least ½ to ¾ inch between the latch post and the gate frame to give the gate room to swing freely, and a ¼-inch hinge space between the frame and hinge post. The gate's height depends on the height of the fence and the gate's design.

Measure and cut the lumber as precisely as you can. Make sure you cut

perfectly square corners when you saw, and check any ends that have been cut at the lumberyard to make sure they are square, too. As you build, check corners carefully to see that they're square.

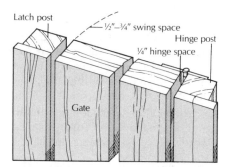

Allow sufficient space for swinging of gate and for hinges.

BUILDING A GATE IN SIX STEPS

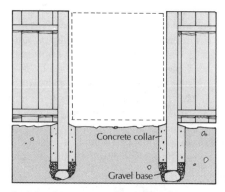

Set 4 by 4 gate posts at least 3 feet deep in concrete and gravel for extra stability. Add sloping concrete collars to direct water away from the wood. (For more information on installing posts, see pages 162–164.) Plumb and align posts carefully.

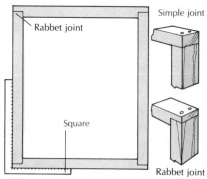

Build the frame of 2 by 4s, working on a table or other flat surface. You can use either simple butt joints or rabbet joints, as shown. Join pieces with galvanized nails and water-resistant glue. Use a square to keep the frame corners at right angles.

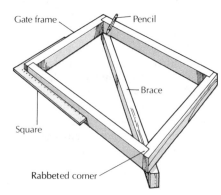

Cut the diagonal brace next. Place the frame on top of the 2 by 4 brace and mark sawing angles with a pencil. For a tight fit, saw just outside the pencil marks. Nail and glue the brace to the frame. Then nail on the siding of your choice.

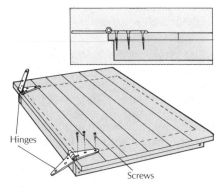

Attach the hinges firmly to the frame. Drill screw holes with a bit slightly smaller than the diameter of the screw. Use long screws for holding power. If the gate is over 5 feet high or 3 feet wide, use three hinges; otherwise, two hinges should be adequate.

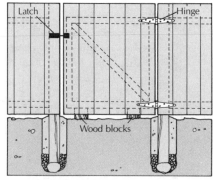

Fit the gate into place. Prop it on wood blocks to hold it in position. If it's too close to the posts to swing freely, trim the latch side until the gate fits. Attach loose ends of the hinges to the hinge post. Finally, attach the latch with long screws or bolts.

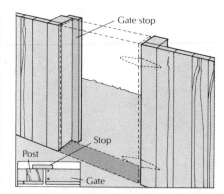

Attach a vertical 1 by 1, 1 by 2, 1 by 4, or 2 by 2 strip of wood to the latch post. This stops the gate when it closes, keeping it from swinging past its closed position and loosening the hinges. (Stop should run from top to bottom of gate.)

Installing low-voltage lights

Installing an outdoor low-voltage lighting system is relatively simple. You can lay the cable on the ground, or bury it a few inches deep. Most fixtures can be connected to the cable without stripping off the wire insulation and splicing the wires, and you don't need to make grounding connections. Furthermore, no permit is required to install an outdoor lighting system that extends from a low-voltage, plug-in transformer (the most common kind).

Careful placement of outdoor lights can result in effective and unexpected lighting effects. Using lighting to achieve these effects is explained on pages 78–79.

Equipment for a 12-volt system

To install a 12-volt system of adequate capacity, you'll need up to four 100-foot runs of two-wire outdoor cable, a transformer, and a set of 12-volt fixtures. To activate the system, the transformer must be connected to an outdoor 120-volt power source.

Wire size. Most low-voltage outdoor fixtures use flexible stranded-wire cable. The size of the wires in the cable will depend on the total wattage rating of the fixtures you plan to connect to the cable. Check the manufacturer's instructions for the correct size.

Transformers. Usually, transformers designed for low-voltage outdoor lighting are encased in weatherproof boxes that are mounted outdoors. They have three-pronged (grounded) plugs that are inserted into outdoor grounded outlets or shockproof outlets protected by ground fault circuit interrupter (GFCI) types of circuit breakers.

Most transformers for home use are rated from 100 to 300 watts. The rating shows the total allowable wattage of the fixtures served. The higher the rating, the more light fixtures you can connect to the transformer. Select a transformer with a built-in timer or ON-OFF switch (some models have both) so you don't have to wire in a separate switch for the system.

Assembling a 12-volt system

To assemble the system, you'll need to connect the cable to the transformer box, the fixtures to the cable, and the transformer box to the power source.

Installing the transformer and cable. To be safe, plan to install the transformer box at least a foot off the ground in a sheltered location. If you don't already have an outlet into which to plug the transformer, you'll need to install a GFCI-protected outlet (for instructions, see the *Sunset* book *Basic Home Wiring Illustrated*).

Before you plug in the transformer, attach the low-voltage cable to the transformer box. Simply wrap the bare ends of the two wires in the cable clockwise around the terminal screws on the box (if the transformer accommodates more than one cable, the terminal screws will be arranged in pairs); then tighten the screws.

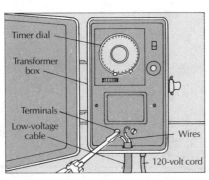
Attach low-voltage wires to terminals on transformer box.

Connecting fixtures to the cable. Once your transformer box is in place and you've decided where to put the fixtures, you'll need to hook them into the cable.

With some fixtures, you simply pierce the cable with a screw-type connector already attached to the back of the fixture. With others, you must connect the short cable from the fixture to the cable from the transformer box, using a clamp connector. (See the drawing at the top of the next column.) Neither connector requires removing insulation from the cable.

Some fixtures require splicing into the cable. Use weatherproof plas-

tic junction boxes to insulate splices that can't be pushed back into the fixtures.

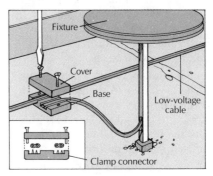
Use clamp connector to hook cable from fixture to cable from transformer.

After each fixture is attached to the cable and set in place, you can bury or hide the cable; then plug in the transformer. Check to see that all fixtures are working properly.

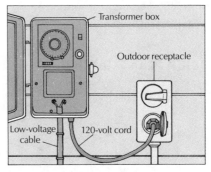
Plug 120-volt cord from transformer box into outdoor receptacle.

Creating a garden pool

Building a sunken pool of brick or concrete—even a small, simple one—is a challenge: you have to be a mason, a plumber, and sometimes an electrician, all rolled into one. But careful planning and a few weekends of work will reward you with an attractive addition to your garden.

All sunken pools, whatever their style, need a raised border — usually an inch or two above the ground. This rim keeps ground water from running into the pool during heavy rains and helps to prevent overflow.

Before you begin work, check with your building department for information on building codes and permit requirements. Also, make sure the site is properly graded (see pages 130–131).

On these pages are general instructions for building two types of garden pools. Working from your plans, you'll need to excavate the site, construct the shell, and install coping around the edge. For more information on masonry construction and plumbing,

consult the Sunset books *Basic Masonry Illustrated* and *Basic Plumbing Illustrated*.

Building a brick planter pool

This two-section pool allows you to grow water plants, such as water lilies, in one section and bog plants, such as giant arrowhead, in the other. You can build the pool any size you wish, but the water should be at least 18 inches deep for water lilies to thrive.

To begin, excavate for the pool, making sure the bottom is level and the soil well tamped. Then do the plumbing for the drain. Use a galvanized steel or plastic overflow pipe to prevent the pool from flooding: overflow water is led away by a channel of 4-inch drain tiles and simply drains into the ground.

To lay the concrete floor, place ³⁄₁₆-inch steel reinforcing rods every 6 inches, bending the rods up to extend

into the walls. Pour, finish, and cure as you would a patio floor (see pages 142–143).

Build the brick walls next. Construct exterior walls with two parallel rows of stretchers (bricks laid lengthwise), leaving a space between rows for the vertical reinforcing rods. Apply mortar very carefully to make sure the bricks are well bonded; then fill the space around the rods with grout.

Build the dividing wall between the pool and the bog with a single row of bricks. Leave some of the vertical joints unmortared to let water enter the bog and keep the soil wet. Then build the coping around the outside edges with bricks laid flat, side by side.

After the mortar has cured, apply two coats of commercial waterproofing compound to seal the walls. After the sealant dries, fill the bog section with good, rich soil, and the pool with water. When the soil is saturated, you're ready to plant. Design: Osmundson-Staley.

BRICK PLANTER POOL

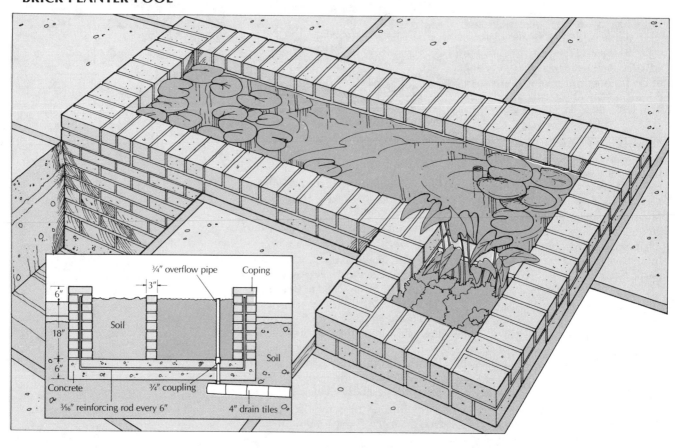

Building a concrete & stone pool

To construct this freeform, natural-looking concrete pool, begin by outlining the shape you want. Then excavate and compact the soil. If you plan to keep fish in the pool, make it at least 18 inches deep to discourage cats. In regions with severe freezing weather, allow an additional 3 to 4 inches for a gravel base. Slope the sides at 45° and allow for a shallow perimeter lip to support the stone coping.

You must reinforce the concrete to prevent cracking. In a pool up to 250 square feet in area, use 6 by 6-inch wire mesh for reinforcing. In a larger pool, bend ¼-inch or ⅜-inch reinforcing rods to follow pool contours, arranging them in a grid pattern. Space them 6 to 12 inches apart and tie the intersections securely with wire. Use pieces of brick or stone to support the mesh or rods 2 inches off the ground.

Drive stakes into the earth every square foot, with the tops extending at least 6 inches above the earth or gravel. Mark the stakes 4 inches above the surface to guide you in packing the concrete to uniform thickness.

To make concrete, mix 1 part cement, 2 parts sand, and 3 parts gravel, with just enough water to wet all ingredients. This mix will be stiff enough to stay in place on the pool's sloping sides. Use a shovel or trowel to pack the mix firmly around the reinforcing up to the marks on the stakes, removing the stakes and filling the holes with concrete as you work.

Finish the surface with a trowel or a float; then cover and cure the shell (see page 143). The final step is to add a stone coping; mortar the stones to each other and to the concrete lip.

If you plan to put in plants or fish, you'll need to remove free lime from the concrete after you've cured the shell. Fill the pool with water and let it sit for 24 hours. Drain, refill, and repeat three or four times. The last time, let the water stand for a week. Then rinse the pool thoroughly and refill it. If you use tap water, wait 24 hours before putting in fish or plants.

A submersible, recirculating pump moves water for the waterfall and can be used to drain the pool. Route the pump's power cord and return line behind the waterfall.

CONCRETE & STONE POOL

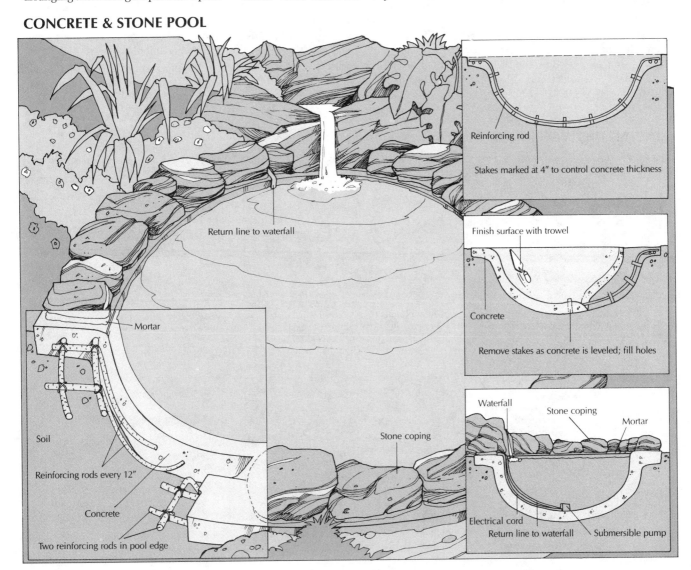

Reinforcing rod

Stakes marked at 4″ to control concrete thickness

Finish surface with trowel

Concrete

Remove stakes as concrete is leveled; fill holes

Mortar

Soil

Reinforcing rods every 12″

Concrete

Two reinforcing rods in pool edge

Return line to waterfall

Stone coping

Waterfall

Stone coping

Mortar

Electrical cord

Return line to waterfall

Submersible pump

Installing a watering system

A permanent irrigation system will save you hours of work and help keep your plants evenly and well watered.

The two kinds of irrigation systems are sprinkler and drip. A sprinkler system uses high water pressure and volume to disperse water over a large area, such as a lawn. A drip system dispenses water at low pressure and volume to specific areas — often to individual plants. Depending on what areas you have to water, you may want to use one or both systems.

Planning. The first step is to make a scale drawing (¼ inch to 1 foot) of your garden, outlining the locations of buildings, walks and driveways, patios and decks, the water meter, hose bibbs, the water supply pipe to the house, and all the plantings you want to water.

The actual design of the system depends not only on your requirements, but also on the type of heads you select. Manufacturers' literature,

available where irrigation equipment is sold, usually contains all the information you'll need to make the selection and design the system. You'll need to mark on your drawing the locations of sprinkler heads or drip emitters, pipes and pipe fittings, an antisiphon control valve for each branch, and the main shutoff valve for the system. Check with your building department for any required permits.

Connecting to the water supply. To ensure adequate water at adequate pressure, connect the irrigation system directly to the water supply pipe (1-inch diameter or larger is best) that serves the house, on the house side of the water meter. Regardless of the size of your home's water supply pipe, don't install a pipe smaller than ¾ inch to supply your system.

Because drip systems require only low water volume and pressure, you may be able to connect a small drip system to a convenient outdoor faucet;

the manufacturer's literature will help you determine what's best for your situation. If you have a water softener, run a by-pass from the unsoftened water supply to the outdoor faucet.

Assembling a sprinkler system

To install a sprinkler system, follow the step-by-step illustrations below. Materials you'll need for assembling your system include the following: a supply of PVC pipe and fittings, PVC pipe-cleaning compound and solvent, a main shutoff valve, an antisiphon control valve for each branch, plastic cutoff pipe for sprinkler head risers, and sprinkler heads.

Several kinds of sprinkler heads are available, including spray heads with quarter, half, three-quarter, and full spray patterns; impulse or cam-driven heads; and bubbler heads.

PVC pipe comes in 10 and 20-foot lengths. If you need shorter ones, mea-

INSTALLING A SPRINKLER SYSTEM

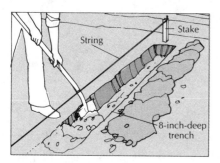

Dig 8-inch-deep trenches for pipes. To keep trench lines straight, run string between two stakes.

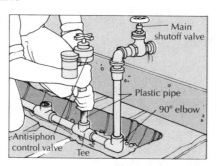

Connect antisiphon control valve to water supply, using thick-walled plastic pipe; set valve at least 6 inches aboveground.

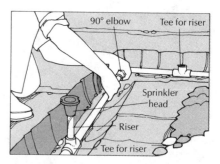

Assemble pipe from control valve outward, fitting risers and heads to tees as you move along.

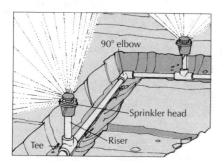

Flush out pipes with heads removed when welds have dried. Replace heads and test for leaks and coverage.

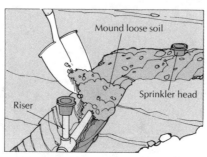

Fill in trenches, mounding loose soil above ground level along center of each trench. Don't bury sprinkler heads.

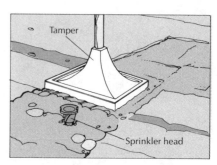

Tamp soil firmly along trenches, using a heavy tamper to minimize settling. Avoid hitting heads.

sure carefully and cut with a hacksaw, making the ends square; remove any burrs with a file.

When you're joining plastic parts, work quickly. PVC solvent cement dries rapidly, and once it dries, joints can't be broken apart. First, apply cleaning compound; then before it dries, daub solvent on both parts, shove the parts tightly together, and give them a half-twist to make a seal.

After installing the control valves, let the welds dry for 6 hours. Then turn on the water and check for leaks. If there are any, apply more solvent to the joints. If there are still leaks, cut out the leaky fitting and replace it.

Installing a drip system

To assemble a drip system (see illustrations below), you'll need the following: a supply of ½-inch black polyethylene hose and fittings (you can buy these in a kit with instruc-tions), a shutoff valve, an antisiphon control valve for each branch, a pres-sure regulator, a filter, end caps, trans-fer barbs, polyethylene microtubing, and emitters.

Choosing emitters. Emitters, devices that dispense water in a drip system, slow the flow of water from the line and dispense it drop by drop. Some types of emitters can be plugged directly into the hose and, if desired, extended with a length of microtub-ing; others can be plugged into the end of a length of microtubing that's con-nected to the hose with a transfer barb. Some emitters have adjustable flow rates, some are self-flushing, and some can be shut off except when they're needed.

Other types of dispensing devices are available for use with drip systems. In-line emitters and perforated or drip tubing in a variety of types can be used to irrigate row crops. Misters, micro-sprayers, and minisprinklers can be connected to a drip system to create a small-scale sprinkler system.

Assembling the system. Polyethylene hose is much easier to unroll if you leave it in the hot sun for an hour to soften. When it's pliable, connect the hose and lay out the main lines, con-necting lateral lines with tee or 90° elbow fittings. You can bury the lines in shallow (2 to 4-inch-deep) trenches, or lay them on the ground, leaving them exposed or covering them with mulch. Locate filters and hose ends so they're easy to flush.

After all lines have been laid and flushed, attach end caps. Then drill holes in the hose as the manufacturer directs, insert emitters or transfer barbs, and cut and fit microtubing.

The system will require regular maintenance because sand and dirt can plug microtubing and emitters. Flush the lines every 4 to 6 months, wash filter elements every month, and clean any plugged emitters.

INSTALLING A DRIP SYSTEM

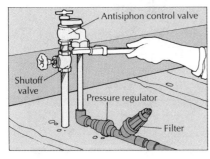

Assemble antisiphon control valve (at least 6 inches aboveground), filter, and pressure regulator.

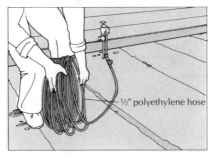

Connect polyethylene hose and lay out main lines on surface or in shallow trenches.

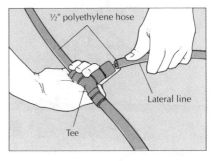

Lay out and attach lateral lines. This kind of tee has barbs that hold tubing without cement.

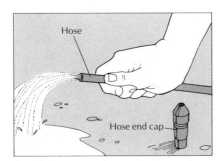

Flush any dirt out of system by running water through lines after all are assembled. Attach end caps.

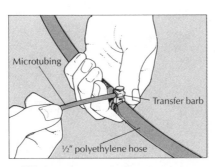

Drill holes in hose; insert transfer barbs (or emitters). Cut and fit microtubing from transfer barbs.

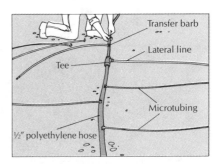

Flush again, making sure all emitters work. Cover lines, if desired, leaving ends of microtubing aboveground.

Planting a lawn

If you're planting a new lawn, you can either start it from seed or lay down strips of sod. The advantages and disadvantages of each method are compared on the facing page.

Decide on your planting method before you begin any preparatory work, since the method determines the finished grade of the lawn area. For a lawn from seed, the finished grade should be about ½ inch above the level of the surrounding ground or paving to allow for settling. For sod, make the grade level with or ½ inch lower than the surrounding area.

Before you plant, be sure you've completed the finish grading, provided for adequate drainage, prepared the soil, and installed edgings (see pages 130–137). If you want to put in a sprinkler system (see pages 170–171), do that work now also.

From seed

To plant a lawn from seed, begin by rolling the prepared soil with a roller one-third full of water. This will compact the seed bed lightly in preparation for sowing.

Then scatter seeds evenly over the soil, either by hand or using a mechanical spreader. If you hand-scatter seeds, sow half of them as you walk one way across the area, and the other half as you walk at right angles to the first direction. Scatter the seeds at the rate that's recommended on the label of the package.

Use a steel rake to lightly scratch the seeds into the soil; don't stir the soil deeply, and don't try to cover every seed with soil.

Cover the soil with about a ¼-inch-deep layer of organic mulch, such as peat moss. (Dampen dry peat moss before you spread it.) The mulch will keep the upper layer of soil from drying out too fast.

Using a mechanical spreader, apply a lawn fertilizer evenly over the surface of the new lawn, following the directions on the fertilizer bag. Don't use a fertilizer that's combined with a weed killer or weed preventer because the grass seed will not grow.

Water the entire lawn with a fine, even spray, or use the sprinklers. Soak the soil to a depth of 4 to 6 inches, being careful not to let water puddle or wash seeds and soil away. For the first week or two (until the seedlings appear), water as often as needed to keep the soil moist—even as often as three times a day. Then water at least once a day until the lawn is well established.

PLANTING A LAWN FROM SEED

Compress seed bed lightly with roller ⅓ full of water.

Sow seeds with mechanical spreader (as shown) or by hand.

Rake soil very lightly to cover seeds for germination.

Spread mulch over soil to prevent top layer from drying out.

Spread fertilizer over mulch to help seedlings grow.

Water lawn with fine spray; keep soil moist until seedlings appear.

Surround the newly planted area with a barrier to keep people and dogs off the lawn for about 2 months. Usually, the grass will be ready to mow for the first time in 4 to 6 weeks.

From sod

Depending on the supplier and your climate, you'll probably be able to choose from several kinds of sod. To find the right one for your lawn, check with your local nursery or garden center, or look in the Yellow Pages under "Sod and Sodding Services." The supplier may also recommend a specific fertilizer to add to the soil before you roll out the sod.

To install a lawn from sod, unroll the sod on the prepared soil, laying the strips parallel and staggering the ends (see below at left). Press each strip snugly against the previous one. Feel the joints after laying each strip. If one side is low, fill it in with loose soil; if it's high, remove some of the excess soil. At corners and edges, trim any excess sod with a sharp knife.

When all the sod is in place, roll the entire lawn with a roller half-filled with water to smooth out any rough spots and to bond the sod to the soil.

Finally, water a little more than usual for a few days until the roots of the sod have grown down into the soil.

INSTALLING SOD

Roll out sod strips in parallel rows; stagger ends and keep seams between strips tight and level.

Trim excess sod at corners and edges with sharp knife. Make sure that cut edges fit snugly.

Roll entire lawn with roller half-filled with water to smooth out rough spots and bond sod to soil.

Seed versus sod

Before you begin the finish grading for your lawn, you'll need to decide whether you want to plant grass seed or roll out a carpet of sod. Each planting method has its own advantages and disadvantages.

The pros and cons of seed. Though lawns from seed require more work to install and much more care to establish, they do have several advantages over sod. First and foremost, seeded lawns are much less expensive to plant. The wide variety of seed that's available is another important advantage: it allows you to choose the grass or mixture of grasses that will do best in your own garden. Finally, because seeded lawns establish deep roots to anchor the turf, they are generally more durable than sod for heavy use.

The pros and cons of sod. Ease of installation is probably the principal advantage of sod, but running a close second is the fact that such lawns don't require a lot of care to establish. You must water them, of course, but you don't need to fight weeds, seedling diseases, washouts, or birds, as you do with seeded lawns.

Another persuasive argument for sod is that it covers the ground immediately. You get an instant reward for your effort, and you don't need to worry about tracking dirt or mud into your house for the next few weeks.

For areas under trees, sod lawns have still another advantage. Because sod already has roots, it doesn't have to compete with established tree roots for nutrients and water. Grass seedlings do compete—often unsuccessfully.

On the other hand, sod is much more expensive than seed and isn't available in as many varieties of grasses. Because it introduces a layer of foreign soil, sod may not bond well to the soil beneath it. Sometimes, in fact, a sod lawn can wear out.

Planting trees, shrubs & ground covers

The trees, shrubs, and ground covers you plant are the living components of your landscape. Planting them carefully and correctly will ensure they'll get a good start. A comprehensive description of all the different kinds of plants you can choose from is in Chapter 4, beginning on page 80.

Four ways to plant

The method used for planting a tree, shrub, or ground cover depends mainly on how it's sold — in a container, balled and burlapped, bare root, or in a flat. The four basic methods are described below.

Plants in containers. To plant a tree or shrub from a container, dig a hole that's twice as wide and half again as deep as the root ball. If the soil is very dry, fill the hole with water and let it drain out. Rough up the bottom and sides of the hole, and add a little organic amendment and superphosphate to the soil in the bottom of the hole.

Mix the soil removed from the hole with more organic material: 2 parts soil to 1 part organic amendment. Use this soil mixture to fill the hole about halfway.

Remove the plant from its container, and loosen roots that encircle the root ball. Set the plant in the hole. If necessary, add more soil to the bottom of the hole so the top of the root ball is about an inch above the ground. Continue adding soil, firming it, until the hole is filled. Make a watering basin and water deeply.

Loosen encircling roots with knife or stick, but don't break root ball.

Balled and burlapped plants. Dig a planting hole twice as wide as the root ball and about 6 inches deeper. Mix the backfill soil with an organic amendment: 3 parts soil to 1 part amendment. Put enough amended soil back in the hole so the root ball is an inch or two higher than the surface of the surrounding soil.

Set the plant in the hole with the burlap still wrapped around the roots. Put enough soil around the root ball to hold the plant stable. Cut the twine holding the burlap, spread the burlap open, and scrape away any crust. (Don't remove the burlap — it will rot away in time.)

Partially unwrap burlap from root ball and gently scrape away any crust.

Add more soil to the hole. When it's half full, tamp the soil firmly. Then fill the hole with soil and tamp again.

Drive a stake into the firm soil beneath the hole. Make sure the stake doesn't damage the root ball. Tie the plant securely to the stake. Make a watering basin around the plant, and water deeply.

Bare-root plants. You can plant some trees and shrubs as bare-root plants in winter or early spring.

Dig a hole large enough to hold the roots easily. Make a cone of soil in the bottom of the hole. Spread the roots evenly over the cone, snipping off any broken roots. Place the plant in the hole so the old soil mark (visible on the stem) will be at the surface level of the surrounding soil.

Add more soil to the hole, firming it around the plant and making sure the plant stays straight. Water slowly; then finish filling the hole to ground level. Cover the plant with loose soil or peat moss until growth begins. Then make a watering basin, and soak the soil deeply.

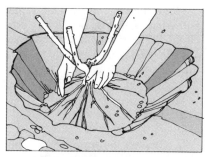

Spread roots evenly over cone of soil in hole; cut off broken roots.

Plants in flats. Some ground covers are sold in flats. To plant them, carefully separate the plants from one another by gently pulling or cutting the root balls apart; then plant them in a grid pattern. Spacing depends on how large the plant will grow and how quickly you want it to fill in.

Special situations

When you're planting a hedge or on a hillside, you'll need to consider the special needs of each situation.

Hedges. Plant as you do other shrubs, but space plants equal distances apart. As a rule, if your hedge is to be 6 feet tall, space plants 3 feet apart. If you're growing a hedge a foot tall, space plants a foot apart. The spacing for heights in between should be 1 to 3 feet apart.

Hillsides. On gentle slopes, plant vining or spreading ground covers and train them up or down the slope. On steep slopes, you can build terraces or retaining walls (see pages 138–139), or make individual terraces for each plant as shown below.

Plant tree on individual terrace, digging watering basin on upslope side of hill.

Index to General Subject Matter

(For Index to Plant Encyclopedia,
　see next page)

Index to Plant Encyclopedia